Al

P

ACADEMIC FREEDOM IN OUR TIME

A STUDY PREPARED FOR THE
AMERICAN ACADEMIC FREEDOM PROJECT
AT COLUMBIA UNIVERSITY
Robert M. MacIver, Director

ACADEMIC FREEDOM

IN OUR TIME

By ROBERT M. MacIVER

GORDIAN PRESS
NEW YORK
1967

Printed in U.S.A. by
EDWARDS BROTHERS, INC.
Ann Arbor, Michigan

AMERICAN ACADEMIC FREEDOM PROJECT

EXECUTIVE COMMITTEE

Louis M. Hacker, Dean of the School of General Studies, Columbia University
Executive Secretary

R. M. MacIver, Lieber Professor Emeritus of Political Philosophy and Sociology, Columbia University
Director of the Project

R. Freeman Butts, Professor of Education, Teachers College, Columbia University

Lawrence H. Chamberlain, Dean of Columbia College

Henry Steele Commager, Professor of American History, Columbia University

Walter Gellhorn, Professor of Law, Columbia University

Richard Hofstadter, Professor of History, Columbia University

Arthur W. Macmahon, Eaton Professor of Public Administration, Columbia University

I. I. Rabi, Higgins Professor of Physics, Columbia University

Louis M. Rabinowitz, Council Member, School of General Studies, Columbia University

PANEL OF ADVISERS

Frederick B. Adams, Jr., Director, The Pierpont Morgan Library
Ralph A. Beals, Director, The New York Public Library
Sarah G. Blanding, President, Vassar College
Alan W. Brown, President, Hobart and William Smith Colleges
William S. Carlson, President, The State University of New York
Harry J. Carman, Dean Emeritus of Columbia College
Charles W. Cole, President, Amherst College

Louis Finkelstein, Chancellor, The Jewish Theological Seminary of America

Frank P. Graham, Ex-President, University of North Carolina

Theodore M. Greene, Professor of Philosophy, Yale University

Rufus C. Harris, President, Tulane University

Edward C. Kirkland, Professor of History, Bowdoin College

Mrs. Eugene Meyer, Trustee, Barnard College

The Rev. J. Courtney Murray, S.J., Woodstock College and Seminary

J. Robert Oppenheimer, Director, The Institute for Advanced Study

Charles Seymour, Ex-President, Yale University

Mrs. Arthur Hays Sulzberger, Trustee, Barnard College

Ralph A. Ulveling, Director, The Detroit Public Library

Sir Llewellyn Woodward, The Institute for Advanced Study

In addition the following gentlemen served on the Panel for part of the time but owing to other demands on their time found it necessary to resign from this activity.

John S. Dickey, President, Dartmouth College

A. Whitney Griswold, President, Yale University

Erwin N. Griswold, Dean of the Law School, Harvard University

Lewis Webster Jones, President, Rutgers University

This project, the first to undertake its particular task of investigation in this country or elsewhere, is an outcome of the initiative and the generosity of Louis M. Rabinowitz. His offer to finance it, made to Columbia University in the spring of 1951, was readily welcomed by the University authorities, and under the leadership of Dr. Grayson Kirk a committee, headed by Dean Louis M. Hacker, was appointed to make the necessary arrangements. Professor R. M. MacIver was made its Director. The study was planned to consist of two parts, one a historical survey of the rise, development, and vicissitudes of academic freedom in this country, the other an analysis of the contemporary situation and a study of the problems it presents, against a background designed to bring out the significance of academic freedom and its relation to the society in which we live. The first part, *The Development of Academic Freedom in the United States,* was entrusted to Professors Richard Hofstadter and Walter P. Metzger, both of the History Department of Columbia University. The second part was undertaken by the Director. The work is now published in two companion volumes. The general theme of these books is the same as that of Columbia University's Bicentennial activities in 1954—"Man's right to knowledge and the free use thereof."

In the furtherance of the work a Panel of Advisers was enlisted, which held several two- or three-day sessions besides giving to the working staff the benefit of their comments and criticisms on the various sections of the study as they were initially drafted. The Executive Committee joined with the Panel in these activities and was also brought together for special discussions. It owes a great debt to this distinguished group of associates; their suggestions have been throughout most helpful. However, it should be clearly understood that neither the Panel of Advisers nor the Executive Committee is in any way to be held responsible for the conclusions expressed by the authors. The same, it need scarcely be said, is true of Columbia University. Thanks are due for the University's very generous hospitality to the Project and for its willingness to manage the grant made by the Louis M. Rabinowitz Foundation.

PREFACE

BEHIND the troubles that beset our institutions of higher learning, behind the weaknesses inherent in their own organization and the inadequate resistance they have, with important exceptions, offered to the attacks upon them, there lies, widespread throughout the land and even infecting the halls of learning themselves, a failure to understand and to appreciate the worth, the service, the mission of the university. We use the term "university" here, as frequently in the text, to include, for want of any adequate word, not only universities but also colleges and other institutions dedicated to the pursuit as well as the purveyance of knowledge, to the open-minded search for the truth about man and society, about the world we live in, and the unfathomable universe itself.

The aggravated assaults on academic freedom and the general disesteem of intellectual enterprise characteristic of our country at this time furnish the occasion for this work. It will serve its purpose so far as it helps to show the need for a stouter defense and the yet greater need for a wider understanding of the intrinsic values of higher education.

ROBERT M. MacIVER

May, 1955

ACKNOWLEDGMENTS

THE AUTHOR expresses in the first place his grateful recognition of the services rendered by his office staff. Leo Koutouzos, as researcher, efficiently undertook a major portion of the investigation and follow-up of cases, prepared and organized the materials used in the section on student affairs, and conducted an on-the-spot study of the so-called "self-investigation" at the University of Colorado, which is presented as Appendix B. Joan Moravek, as research assistant and general secretary of the Project, was unstinting in her devotion to the many tasks that fell to her and showed initiative, ingenuity, and excellent critical judgment in dealing with a variety of problems.

Beyond the services they were invited to render as members of the Panel of Advisers or of the Executive Committee, the following gentlemen gave constant counsel and support to the author, contributing greatly to the quality of the work: Walter Gellhorn, Theodore M. Greene, Edward C. Kirkland, Arthur M. Macmahon, and Sir Llewellyn Woodward.

While we have drawn on the publications of a wide variety of organizations and on the information given us by their officers, we owe a particular debt to the following: the late Dr. Ralph Himstead of the American Association of University Professors; The American Book Publishers Council; Dr. Louis Joughin of the American Civil Liberties Union; the staff of the American Council on Education; Dr. Irvin R. Kuenzli of the American Federation of Teachers; the staff of the American Jewish Committee and of the Anti-Defamation League; Mr. David K. Berninghausen, former chairman, and other members of the Intellectual Freedom Committee of the American Library Association; Mary Alice Baldinger of the National Civil Liberties Clearing House; Drs. Willard Givens, Richard B. Kennan, and Robert A. Skaife and others of the National Education Association; the national and regional officers of the National Student Association; the local and national leaders of Students for Democratic Action; Francis P. Jennings of the Teachers Union in Philadelphia; and Ethelyn M. Hartwich of the Washington Committee for Academic Freedom.

We are also indebted to a number of ladies and gentlemen who were invited to attend one or more meetings of the Project associates and contributed a variety of useful suggestions. For aid thus rendered we are particularly indebted to Dorothy Dunbar Bromley, author and radio commentator; Mrs. Samuel A. Lewisohn, Chairman, Board of Trustees, Public Education Association; Professor Edna Macmahon, Vassar College; and Mr. John D. Conners, Director, Workers Education Bureau of the American Federation of Labor.

We are indebted to the publishers and authors concerned for permission to use quotations as follows: Hubert P. Beck, *Men Who Control Our Universities,* Columbia University Press; Algo D. Henderson and Dorothy Hall, *Antioch College: Its Design and Liberal Education,* Harper & Brothers; Mildred McAfee Horton, "Academic Freedom," in Amos N. Wilder, ed., *Liberal Learning and Religion,* Harper & Brothers; Frank L. McVey and Raymond M. Hughes, *Problems of College and University Administration,* The Iowa State College Press; Harold A. Innis, *Political Economy in the Modern State,* The Ryerson Press; Monroe E. Deutsch, *The College From Within,* University of California Press; R. S. K. Seeley, *The Function of the University,* Oxford University Press; Ordway Tead, *Trustees, Teachers, Students,* University of Utah Press; *Communism and Academic Freedom,* University of Washington Press.

R.M.M.

CONTENTS

ACADEMIC FREEDOM IN OUR TIME

Introduction: WHAT ACADEMIC FREEDOM MEANS

So sure as it is that men live not by bread, but by ideas, so sure is it that the future of the world lies in the hands of those who are able to carry the interpretation of nature a step further than their predecessors; so certain is it that the highest function of a university is to seek out those men, cherish them, and give their ability to serve their kind full play.

THOMAS HENRY HUXLEY

THE BROAD MEANING of academic freedom is plain enough. It is the freedom of the scholar within the institution devoted to scholarship, the "academy." In this reference "academy," named after the garden in Athens where Plato taught, means any institution primarily concerned with the advancement of knowledge, any institution of higher learning, where knowledge is pursued and not merely purveyed. Academic freedom is one aspect of the freedom that redeems man alike from superstition and from brutal servitude, the freedom of the mind, of which Milton said: "Give me the liberty to know, to utter, and to argue freely according to conscience, above all liberties." What occupies us in this book is the range and quality of this freedom, and particularly its impediments, in the colleges and universities of the United States.

The question might perhaps be raised: Does academic freedom mean the freedom of the academy or the freedom of the scholar in the academy? Have we academic freedom when the academy runs its own affairs without outside interference? An academy is a corporate body, directed by a governing board. Is it then the freedom of the governing board? But suppose this board decides how and what the faculty members should teach? Obviously that would be a violation of what is always meant by academic freedom. True, it means the freedom of the academy, but it refers to the intellectual life of the academy. For that is what gives it its

The quotation at the head of the Introduction is from T. H. Huxley, "Founder's Day Address," Johns Hopkins University, 1876.

character, its being. This intellectual life consists in the activities of a faculty, including in the first place their relation to the students. It is an educational freedom that is at issue. The academy is free when the scholars who make it are free, as scholars. And the academy is free when its governing board is free to protect and to advance this freedom.

Colleges and universities are preeminently the institutions in which knowledge is sought, fostered, and imparted. Their distinctive feature among all other institutions of society is their dedication to the all-round communication of knowledge through teachers to students—teachers and students who alike are continuously engaged in the search for knowledge. The genuine teacher is interested in knowledge for its own worthwhileness, no matter what else it brings. The genuine student is interested in learning for its own sake, no matter what utility it may also serve. In seeking *knowledge* he is seeking *truth.*

We must pause here a moment, for the word "truth" has different overtones from "knowledge." A statement is true when it is "in accord with the facts," that is, when the connection it asserts actually exists in the manner and in the place in which it is asserted to exist. The business of the scholar is with the discovered and discoverable relationships between things. He carries on this business by studying the data, the phenomena, and applying the logic of evidence. Men have always held "truth" to be one of the supreme values, like "beauty" and "goodness." But they have spoken of two kinds—or rather two sources—of truth, one revealed truth, God-given or at least delivered by some not-to-be-questioned authority, and the other the truth that men discover by the exercise of their own ingenuity. It should be obvious that when we speak here of the search for truth as the business of the scholar we mean truth in the latter sense alone. In our context the word "truth" is relevant only to knowledge that depends on investigation, that can always be questioned and retested, and that is never accepted on the ground that it is the deliverance of any authority, human or divine.

When the scholar says something is true, he means true *so far as our knowledge goes,* and no further. His truth has no finality, it is never absolute, and in this sense also it differs from what is claimed to be delivered or authoritative truth. It is not the whole truth about anything, for our knowledge never goes far enough. It does not reach to the depths of nature or of life, nor do we even know what that would mean. But this discovered knowledge, this limited and most partial but ever-increasing truth about things, has meant a great deliverance for mankind and could mean far more if we only learned to use it aright. When we say "truth," we think of knowledge as illumination. "Let there be light" has been in one mode of expression or another the motto of many an ancient university. When we say "truth," we think of knowledge as perspective, as comprehension of the interrelatednesses of things and of the systems they thus compose.

It is the search for truth, so understood, and not the mere uncovering of hidden items of knowledge, that raises the problem of academic freedom. There are those who hold that the goal of scholarship is simply to get at "the facts." There are even those who teach as though knowledge were nothing more than an array of separate bits of "information" and who carry on research on the theory that it should have nothing to do with theories but should confine itself to presenting the "evidences" and letting the facts "speak for themselves." If such were indeed the goal of scholarship, there would be little need to defend academic freedom, because there would be no one who had much interest in attacking it.

What constitutes knowledge is not the data as such, not the figures, not the graphs, not the instrument readings, but the conclusions rationally derived from the data. Galileo would never have been brought before the Inquisition if he had merely presented the data of his astronomical observations and not drawn the *inference* concerning the earth's motion in space. The relations of things are never given, they are always inferred. Mere items of information do not add up to knowledge. Those who say the scholar should not go beyond the data, beyond the "facts," do not understand what knowledge is.

But the whole history of science, of the advancement of knowledge, repudiates the immature "positivism" that follows this line. Perhaps it is only in certain areas of social and psychological study that the doctrine is entertained. Anyhow, science has always advanced by taking a braver, a more adventurous course. Eternally seeking for evidences, it is first of all interested in the relationships they suggest, in the questions they raise concerning the order and organization of things. So-called "facts" are opaque by themselves, uncomprehended, intractable, until they are given place and proportion and structural significance within a system.

The system, the field of relationships, is never *given*. It cannot be seen by microscope or telescope. It is the construct of the scientific imagination, controlled and disciplined by the logic of evidence. It is an hypothesis that the scientist keeps on testing, not a sacred doctrine that he keeps on defending. It is inferential. It is always subject to modification. Some seemingly well-established constructs may be rejected altogether in favor of new ones that are more in accord with the behavior of the phenomena of the field.

In every area of knowledge the scholar seeks thus to explain the relationship of things. In so doing he may disturb preconceived opinions. He is most likely to do so when his hypotheses, his inferences, run counter to preconceptions that sustain some currently accepted social valuations or group interests or authoritatively based doctrines of any kind. The mere fact that these preconceptions are regarded by the scholar as a proper subject for investigation subjects him to suspicion. In our times this danger besets particularly the social scientist, but it may be incurred also by the historian, the philosopher, the student of literature, the biologist, or even the physicist. The attack on academic freedom is made on different fronts at different times.

Academic freedom is, from this aspect, a right claimed by the accredited educator, as teacher and as investigator, to interpret his findings and to communicate his conclusions without being subjected to any interference, molestation, or penalization because these conclusions are unacceptable to some constituted authority within or beyond the institution. *Here is the core of the doctrine of academic freedom. It is the freedom of the student within his field of study.* In order, however, that his freedom be safeguarded, the faculty of every institution of learning require certain supplementary protections. There must be no conditions of appointment or controls over promotion of educators designed or in effect so operated as to give preference, irrespective of professional qualifications, to those whose views on any controversial issues, social, economic, political, religious, or other, are more congenial to administrative or other authorities. We shall in due course take up the question whether there is any legitimate limitation of any kind to this principle. We shall also have to take under consideration the question whether some infringement of the principle is not involved in the very existence of denominational colleges or universities.

Various impulses lead men on in the endless search for truth. The true scholar knows that he can never plumb the depths or attain the heights of being. He knows that his task is never accomplished, whether he studies atoms or stars or viruses or men. He knows that the heralded achievements of science and scholarship shrink to almost nothingness compared with the infinite unknown. He knows also the difficulties and uncertainties of knowing. And he resents the petty arrogance of authority that interferes with his task or presumes to dictate his approach or his conclusions.

Essentially the university [1] is a company of scholars and learners, teachers and students. It is a guild serving the community, and while it serves more immediately the region to which most of its students and teachers belong, it serves also the whole of mankind. Knowledge, once attained, is imperishable and universal. Knowledge has no frontiers, and the great gifts it brings are at the service of all mankind, no matter what barriers we raise, no matter how we may abuse the powers it gives us.

The aspects of knowledge that fall within the distinctive function of the university extend beyond any narrow connotation of that word. In old days the major focus of scholarly concentration was what was known as the "humanities." The university has been the main transmitter of the cultural achievements of mankind. In modern times, science has found its kingdom and taken an ever larger role within the whole curriculum of the university. With this advance, knowledge itself tends to be identified with the fields of scientific discovery. But the need for the "humanities" is not lessened, instead it is rather increased by the triumphs of the physical sciences and of the technology that accompanies them. The "learning" for which the university stands is the whole domain of scholarship, whether applied to the biological and physical realms or to the creative expressions of the mind and heart of man.

The point of these remarks is to suggest the incalculable significance of this guardianship and advancement of learning that is entrusted to the university, the paramount need for the assurance of its integrity and, therefore, of the maintenance of the principle of academic freedom.

The mission of the university confers a high responsibility alike on its governing board and on its faculty. It is a primary duty of the governing board to resist the pressures of ideological groups and of special interests

[1] We shall not infrequently throughout this work speak of the university when we intend to include also, at least in degree, liberal arts colleges, noncommercial research institutes, and other institutions of higher learning, unless the context makes it clear that only the university in the stricter sense is under consideration. In the immediate context, however, our characterization of the intrinsic nature of the university cannot be applied, without considerable qualification, to denominational institutions. For these see Appendix A.

that for the promotion of their own ends would narrow its outlook. It is the duty of governing boards, and of all administrative officials, to protect the faculty against the clamors and demands of those who do not appreciate the goals of scholarship. Sometimes these demands come from alumni who have learned too little or forgotten too soon what a university stands for and through what processes it contributes to human advancement. Sometimes they come from donors, sometimes from politicians, sometimes from the press, sometimes directly from an excited portion of the public. But the primary obligation of the governing board is not to any of these. Its first responsibility is to safeguard and foster the institution of higher learning. It should never forget that this institution has grown and flourished only where the minds of men were free to search for truth, only where authority did not dictate the conclusions they must find.

If the governing board has this primary obligation, rooted in the essential mission of the institution over which it presides, the members of the faculty are in turn obligated by the freedom they claim. To abuse a freedom is to betray it, especially when this freedom is rendered precarious by the hostile presence of strong interests and strong prejudices. The educator asks and needs this freedom in order to pursue knowledge within his chosen field and in the process communicate it to his students and share it with any others who also may want to learn. His task is also a status. He is given on account of it a place in the institution, a place in the social structure beyond it.

His competence lies in a particular field—not in all fields. In most areas of knowledge he is little more qualified than any layman. He should not therefore arrogate to himself an authority beyond the range of his competence. He should not regard the rostrum of his class as a platform from which to broadcast his opinions on issues irrelevant to the courses he is teaching. On controversial issues within his proper field he should fairly present the evidences on both sides—or on every side—and should not exercise his powers of sarcasm on those who hold opposing views. He should recognize the limitation of his knowledge and the fallibility of the knower. Particularly if his work lies in the social sciences or in other areas where human values and human interests are involved, he should be very careful that his own valuations do not color his presentation of the facts of the case. He should not hesitate to state the conclusions to which he believes the evidences point, but he should be

eternally on his guard against bias. Nor should he attribute baser motives to those who differ from him, for motives are always mixed, and
nearly always they are precariously inferential. He cannot claim the
primary right of the scholar, academic freedom, when he abandons the
approach of the scholar.

Academic freedom is an *institutional* freedom. It is the freedom
claimed by the educator within an institution of higher learning. In his
relations outside his institution the educator has the same liberty as other
men, except that he should be careful not to associate his institution in
any way with his extra-academic utterances or actions. There is the
further discretionary proviso that he should avoid any public behavior
that would tend to bring discredit on his institution.

Again, academic freedom is a *professional* freedom. It is the freedom
claimed as a right by the members of a guild. Just as the doctor or the
lawyer needs a special area of freedom if he is to carry out his duties and
serve aright his clients, so does the educator. In the safeguarding of
academic freedom the educator has obligations to other members of the
guild. An educator violates these obligations if he does not defend the
academic freedom of his colleagues, contented if his own freedom is
unimpaired. The guild of the educator is a very large one, and in this
work we are directly concerned with only one branch of it. The school
teacher needs the fundamental freedom of the profession no less than
does his colleague in university or college. But the conditions under
which he operates and the problems he faces are different in significant
respects and need to be separately treated.

We have stressed the point that academic freedom is essentially the
freedom of the student within his field of study, and particularly the
freedom of the educator to investigate, to draw conclusions, and to impart his knowledge. Anything that interferes with this freedom, either as
a direct curb or by its indirect repressiveness, comes within our purview.
We shall be concerned with "security" measures as well as with censorship, with tenure and status conditions as well as with authoritarian controls and the penalization of nonconformity, with the regulation of the
academy as a whole as well as with interferences and charges directed
against the individual teacher.

In its stricter—or narrower—sense, academic freedom is taken to
have reference only to the teacher and the collectivity of teachers, the
faculty. Our main concern throughout this book lies there. But we shall

also have something to say regarding the freedom of the student body and its individual members. The two freedoms, the intellectual freedom of the teacher and the intellectual freedom of the taught, though certain specific distinctions must be drawn between them, are closely associated and are interactive. Just as the guild includes its apprentices, so does the academy include its students. From this perspective the academy is a community of older and younger scholars, united in the common enterprise of learning and alike requiring certain opportunities, certain freedoms, for its pursuit.

Academic freedom, being a professional one, is a *functional* freedom. Here, indeed, lies its full significance. An educator has various other professional tasks to do, subsidiary to his primary function. He plans courses and prepares materials, he sits on committees of various kinds, he examines and grades his students, he discusses their problems, and so forth. But the reason he belongs to the guild of educators, the reason he has a place in an institution of higher learning, is that he is first and foremost engaged in the pursuit and communication of knowledge. This function is a community service, and its importance can hardly be overestimated. The service of the educator is not a service to his students alone or to his institution or to his profession. It is a service to his country, a service to civilization, a service to mankind.

The fulfillment of this incalculable service depends on the healthful maintenance of the freedom of the scholar. The society he serves often puts obstacles in the way of his service, through prejudice, fear, short-sighted interest, complacency, and sheer ignorance. The scholar himself is subject to temptation from without and from within. His career may be advanced if he bends his views to those of authority, or thwarted if he disagrees. He may attain so comfortable a sense of the finality of his own conclusions that he disparages the work of those who follow another road. When he achieves a prominent position on the faculty, he may in effect require that his subordinates shall also be his disciples. If his views happen to coincide with those approved by authority, as they quite properly may do, he may forget his function so far as to take sides with that authority when it infringes on academic freedom. Scholars are men with the same temptations as other men. In countries where the democratic spirit is alert, academic freedom is safe within the institutions of learning, for the great majority of scholars are wedded to the cause they serve and conscious of its obligations. But wherever the enemies of academic freedom are in the ascendant, the true scholars are cast out, and corruption from within joins hands with intolerance from without to destroy the institution that embodies one of the greatest vitalizing forces of human society.

That the open search for truth has rendered great services to mankind can scarcely be denied—although the magnitude of that service is not sufficiently appreciated by society in general. The institution distinctively dedicated to this service is the university, with such adjuncts as the special organizations of science, philosophy, and the humanities, themselves mainly composed of faculty members. From this function the claim to academic freedom derives. This freedom is not to be thought of as a privilege, not as a concession, nor as something that any authority inside or outside the institution may properly grant or deny, qualify or regulate, according to its interest or its discretion. It is something instead that is inherently bound up with the performance of the university's task, something as necessary for that performance as pen and paper, as classrooms and students, as laboratories and libraries.

The conclusion follows, if we accept the premise, that the special function of the university is to extend and to impart knowledge. The conclusion is deflected when the university is assigned other functions in such a manner that they interfere with, limit, distort, or wholly take the place of the primary function. The extreme case is that of the university in a totalitarian state, where its primary function becomes that of promoting and inculcating the dominant ideology. The pursuit of truth is then permitted only in such areas as are wholly neutral to the interests of the structure of power. This condition requires the falsification of learning not only in the social sciences and in the humanities but also to a large extent even in the natural sciences. There are indeed few subjects that cannot be perverted the better to support the range of indoctrinations favorable to the position and the prestige of the rulers. The university in the proper sense disappears altogether. It is converted into a subservient and sycophantic agency of power. This is indeed the final stage of deterioration, but the same process of perversion occurs in degree whenever and wherever the alleged claims of any other function than the free pursuit and communication of knowledge are suffered to intrude upon the postulate of academic freedom.

Let us see how this happens and what it means. The university, like any other institution, provides a number of services arising out of or concomitant with the fulfillment of its primary function. These fall mainly into two types. On the one hand, since the university is engaged in the communication of knowledge, it may well organize and apply relevant aspects of that knowledge to the specific training requisite for the more learned professions or vocations—medicine, law, architecture, engineering, some forms of governmental service, and so forth. A cognate activity is the service rendered by faculty members as experts called in to advise or direct some affairs of the community or of particular organizations. The other type of subsidiary function proceeds from the fact that the instruction of the university is predominantly addressed to young people, who attend its courses, sometimes live within its walls, during some formative years. Actually, therefore, the university provides, directly or indirectly, some preparation for the fuller business of living as well as for the vocation the student is to pursue.

While we call these functions subsidiary, this characterization is in no way meant to minimize their importance. They are subsidiary in the sense that they fall to the university only as a consequence of its primary function and that the manner in which the university can properly meet these calls upon it is determined by the system of values for which it distinctively stands, the values implied in the open-minded quest of knowledge. In this connection we point out that the university is not the only organization devoted to the other functions with which we are now dealing, nor is its way the only way of performing them.

As for the professional training associated with the university, it has its own problems, but there seems no strong reason why this training should not be annexed to the primary work of the university. The university usually makes the holding of a college degree a condition of entrance to its professional schools. It is not interested in mere technical training divorced from some foundation in science or in the liberal arts. Its schools and departments that specialize in professional training assume at the same time a broader educational objective. So long as this relationship obtains, the carrying out of professional training should not of itself constitute any threat to the basis of academic freedom. The issue that is more likely to arise is one of academic responsibility, the responsibility that the possession of academic freedom entails. To maintain the standards of the university, these schools and departments are obligated to refrain from any undue catering to private interests, from any indoctrinations subservient to group-limited values. The same obligation holds for the expert faculty members who may be called in as consultants to private concerns or special organizations of any kind.

It is when we turn to our second type of subsidiary function that we meet the more serious danger of confusion of standards and ambiguity of goals.

Take, for example, the idea that it is the business of the university to prepare the young for more effective participation in the life of the community, to equip them better to meet the conditions or the demands of their society, or, simply, to have a more successful career. The university does serve the purposes thus indicated, but in its own way. If it made any such objective its primary function, its distinctive quality would be blurred and its distinctive contribution dissipated. Every institution, every area of experience, every set of conditions under which young people enter into social relations can be preparation for living. Many people who never enter college or university learn to participate effectively in community affairs. Moreover, there are institutions that expressly devote themselves to this kind of training and make this objective their sufficient reason for existence. The university cannot and should not seek to be a substitute for them.

Let us consider what happens when it tries. There was a time when it seemed to be the chief preoccupation of the ancient English universities to be a kind of finishing school for gentlemen. It gave the matriculant— he could hardly be called a student—a sort of cachet. Scholarship was secondary, and the advance of learning was more promoted outside than inside the gates. The authorities were relatively content if the matriculant passed a rudimentary examination in "divinity," memorized some tags of Latin, and so forth. Social life at the university was generally deemed the thing that mattered. It could indeed be maintained that this kind of residence at the university was a fair enough preparation for the kind of life which its gentlemen alumni would later pursue. Here indeed is the rub. If the university sets out as its objective the preparation of its students for living—then for what kind of living?

As soon as we pose this question we see the danger to university standards inherent in any unqualified assertion that its business is to prepare the student for his place in society. Consider, for example, the case of a university in a society that practices racial segregation. Would it not, if it accepted the mission thus assigned to it, inculcate in the student the mores of segregation? And, apart from other consequences, would this not mean that scientific knowledge concerning the question of racial inequality would be rejected or distorted and that any educator who ventured to contradict the prevalent myths would be dismissed? The case is put hypothetically, but every reader must know that the type of situation presented is a commonplace of academic history.

Moreover, the danger exists in degree even where the social value inculcated does not need to be buttressed by a rejection of scientific evidence. We would feel uneasy, for example, if the business of the university were said to be "to educate for democracy." The point here is that men can be educated for democracy in various ways and through various agencies, including not least the experience of living in a democracy. The university cannot without distortion become an agency *designed* for indoctrination, no matter how great or good the cause. The university is a body of scholars of very diverse scholarly interests, chosen because of their respective competence in and devotion to some field of knowledge. On most of the issues that divide other men they, too, are likely to be divided. On one issue they must sound a clear unanimous note—unless there be any among them that betray their calling—and that is *the intrinsic worthwhileness of the knowledge of things,* the moral and spiritual value of the integrity of mind that steadfastly seeks the truth, refusing to yield to biases within and pressures without, determined, so far as may be, "to strive, to seek, to find, and not to yield."

If the university makes the inculcation of this virtue its special concern it will at once be true to itself and make its best contribution to the moral life of the community. When, instead, some academic authority, say a college dean, announces that his institution puts "character building" first among the goals of education, or when some university alumnus demands that his alma mater devote itself to the propagation of Christian principles, there is always an implicit or explicit rejection of the creed of the scholar, the creed by which alone a university lives. The university is not the church or a missionary society. It is sheer confusion to ask it to do the work of either of these. Those who make such demands generally do not appreciate the primary service the university renders and are likely to have scant respect for academic freedom.

The university may well provide *opportunities* for its members of different faiths to meet and worship within its walls, but it should not identify itself with any particular faith. It may well provide for religious instruction, but it should not make it a requirement. Why, for example, should the Jewish student or the Hindu or the Mohammedan be not equally admitted to the brotherhood of learning? To deny it, except in denominational institutions, is the sheerest intolerance and is outrageously in conflict with the meaning and the purpose of academic freedom. It may well provide, without commitment, occasions for any kind of edification to which student groups may be responsive, but it should not, institutionally, become committed to any kind of "ism."

There is one specific faith, and one only, that animates the university as an association of scholars. It embodies a high ideal. It offers a great contribution to the moral quality of society, to its spiritual as well as its material advancement. In asking for academic freedom, the members of a university are simply asking for the right to make this contribution without having conditions imposed on them that would interfere with their so doing. That right is not the enemy of any other worthwhile goal, for no value, no faith, deserves man's enduring allegiance if it shrinks from the consequences of the open quest of knowledge, the disciplined search for the relationships between phenomena and for the laws that they obey. In the ancient trinity of intrinsic values truth stood beside beauty and goodness. They were allies and never enemies.

Indeed, it may be claimed that the truth-seeking virtue is itself a condition of other ethical qualities. The sincerity of mind that is the mark of the genuine scholar is a moral as well as an intellectual attribute. In our own days the need for it is peculiarly great, and correspondingly great the service of the institution that seeks to enshrine it. For we live in the midst of a multitude of organized interests and pressure groups, economic, political, and ideological. The air is full of their solicitations. Organizations of every kind and of every size live by their powers of persuasion. Successful distortion of the truth has often a high market value. Strong inducements are everywhere at work to lead people to accept as truth what it is to their own interest, or to the interest of the propaganda makers, that they believe. In this whirl of biased voices a body of men pursues the primary goal of discovering and communicating the knowledge of things as they are, of sifting the evidences to reject error and reveal the actual relationships between things. They, too, may reach wrong conclusions, but they never rest with them, they keep on testing, checking, inquiring. They seek to convey to their students not only knowledge but the spirit of the search for knowledge. Thus the university constitutes the rallying ground for the intellectual integrity of the community, and without intellectual integrity all other virtues are insecure.

Instead, therefore, of seeking to divert the university from its primary function by demanding that it direct its teaching and its research to the service of some social or religious culture pattern, that it proclaim the virtue of democracy or, perhaps, of "free enterprise," that it stand for religion in accordance with some dominant group's conception of what religion means, it is far wiser to let the association of scholars make its own saving contribution to the moral well-being of the community.

In his famous work on *The Idea of a University,* written in the middle of the nineteenth century, Cardinal Newman, addressing himself specifically to a Roman Catholic audience, pointed out that "knowledge is its own end"; that the function of the university is "intellectual culture" and that it "has done its work when it has done as much as this." Observe particularly that he added: "Liberal education makes not the Christian, not the Catholic, but the gentleman." Since the word "gentleman" was coming to be identified with an "antiquated variety of human nature and remnant of feudalism," he proceeded to explain that for him it meant "to have a cultivated intellect, delicate taste, a candid, equitable, dispassionate mind, a noble and courteous bearing in the conduct of life." These he regarded as the virtues that the university breeds. "These are the connatural qualities of a large knowledge; they are the objects of a university." They are by no means all the qualities a man needs, but they are those that the university can develop. The others must be sustained by other institutions.[2]

In Newman's idea of a university the stress was laid much more on the communication of "universal knowledge" than on its advancement. To later writers this aspect of his definition has seemed inadequate. The vast new horizons modern science has revealed and the growing sense of our need for a fuller understanding of man himself and his ever-changing society have led to a greater emphasis on the role of the university in the expansion of knowledge, on the need for research as a concomitant of teaching. Unfortunately, the term "research" is sometimes taken as signifying merely a kind of routinized hunt for disconnected "facts," but in its proper signification it includes the full bent of the equipped scholar who seeks evidences in order to reach conclusions,

[2] Cardinal Newman, *The Idea of a University,* Discourse v.

who investigates in order to better comprehend the relationships of things. In this sense research and teaching are or should be inseparable. Following this line, a recent book that has received much attention in England defines a university as "a corporation or society which devotes itself to a search after knowledge for the sake of its intrinsic value." [3] The last phrase of the definition has a special importance for us here. It by no means belittles the value of vocational training or the utilitarian applications of knowledge, whether pursued at a university or anywhere else. But it properly distinguishes the university from the technical school. It asserts that the education a university contributes is worth while in itself, that its service is not to be estimated by the practical applications of the knowledge it provides, and that the spirit of the quest to know and to comprehend is an aspect of the fulfillment of life.

Nowadays, in the prevailing climate of opinion within the United States, there are many who are unwilling to let our colleges and universities be themselves, who are constantly agitating to make them agencies for the propagation of particular causes. Such people do not understand the principle of academic freedom. Some of them already are calling it a superstition. They do not know the meaning of the university. Unless we make some such distinction as that elaborated by Newman, unless we appreciate the value of the primary function that distinctively and in a sense uniquely characterizes the university and refuse to let it be jeopardized by the conformist demands of special groups, then the community will suffer two grievous losses. It will lose the light of intellectual freedom that shines from the untrammeled university, itself a freedom on which the very being of democracy depends. And it will lose the great contributions that the free university can bestow—the example of open-minded inquiry, the substitution of reason for passion in the treatment of controversial issues, the spirit of fair play that listens to the arguments on all sides of a case, seeks to discover and to interpret the evidences instead of rushing to conclusions, and thus leads to understanding and wiser decisions on matters where the miscalculations of prejudice may have grievous costs. To quote Cardinal Newman again, "the special fruit of the education furnished at a university" is "a habit of mind which lasts through life, of which the attributes are, freedom, equitableness, calmness, moderation, and wisdom."

While no university may fully live up to the ideal set by Newman,

[3] Bruce Truscot, *Red Brick University* (Pelican Books, 1951), Part I, Chapter 2.

nevertheless it is the ideal at which every genuine institution of higher learning aims. To pursue this ideal is the simple obligation of the scholar, for it is the condition that alone gives meaning to his chosen task. Aside from this, individual scholars have their particular creeds, as all men do. They have their dividing values and their variant interests. They have their particular likes and dislikes, their quarrels, their ambitions, and their vanities. At times their impulses may be at war with their scholarly obligations. But the university itself, the collectivity of scholars, sustains and reinforces in each member the standards requisite for the fulfillment of its primary function. It can do so, however, only if it is *free* to pursue that function and thus render to humanity its inestimable services. Its indispensable requirement is academic freedom.

Part One

THE CLIMATE OF OPINION

I: THE STRUCTURE OF PUBLIC OPINION
IN THE UNITED STATES

I am often amazed at the lack of faith which Americans seem to have in the solidity and vitality of democratic institutions or of the values of free discussion and controversy. In many an American's mind there is an unacknowledged mental reservation that only that speech should be free which agrees with our point of view.

PRESIDENT VIRGIL M. HANCHER

STATE UNIVERSITY OF IOWA

IN THE COURSE of this work we present many evidences of attacks on and violations of academic freedom. In the period from 1945 to 1950 the American Association of University Professors has had before it a total of 227 separate cases, aside from a number of "situations" that were not classified as cases.[1] There are indeed few institutions of higher learning, and none of note, that have not been subjected to complaints and charges brought against one or more of their faculty members or against whole departments. This state of affairs seems to be peculiarly characteristic of our society. Why it should be so is an intriguing question. Why should a people that prides itself on its democracy and its love of liberty be so embroiled in troubles where the liberty of learning and of teaching is concerned? Why are there so many more cases here than in the democratic countries of Europe?

Is it, perhaps, because American colleges and universities are, to an extent not found elsewhere, folk institutions, many of them of relatively recent origin, drawing their students and their instructors from all strata of the population, and offering them educational services of every variety, by no means confined to what are called the "liberal arts," unlike the older "aristocratic" universities of Europe? And would that

[1] W. T. Laprade, "Academic Freedom and Tenure," Report of Committee T for 1950, *Bulletin of the American Association of University Professors,* XXXVII (Spring, 1951), 79.

mean that the American institutions are of greater concern to the people, more responsive to them, and thus more subject to changing demands and to the tides of opinion that move through the people?

This type of explanation is sometimes offered, and it contains a useful lead, though we cannot accept it in the simple form stated above. There are, for example, some smaller countries of Western Europe—Scotland is a good example—where for a number of generations the universities have drawn their alumni from all ranks, including the humblest, and where the highest importance is attached to them by the people generally —but without any sign of the encroachments and demands upon them so characteristic of this country. Besides, the folk character of our universities is itself a relatively recent development, having become more characteristic since the influx of students following the First World War. Moreover, the argument assumes too readily that the troubles of our institutions of learning come from the people generally, whereas we shall presently see that it is nearly always particular interest groups, and not infrequently relatively small groups, that carry on the attack. The chief exception to this state of affairs is found in the South, where a racial issue dominates the mores and leads to somewhat severer controls, now beginning to diminish, on the freedom of the universities.

A full exploration of our question would itself be a major undertaking, but our study of the sources of many of the charges brought against our educational system leads us to infer that a large part of the answer lies in the relation of two distinctive phenomena of American society. One is the special form of academic government that prevails in this country. The other is the character of public opinion. Without an appreciation of the manner in which these two conditions operate and cooperate, we cannot arrive at the most pertinent conclusions for the safeguarding of American freedom.

Public opinion is a much more complex and interesting phenomenon than the usual picture that is presented of it. A considerable amount of investigation is directed at it, but attention is turned to questions of sampling and so-called measurement rather than to the study of its structure. Yet from long back astute observers have been aware that the public opinion of any country has its own special characteristics and have sought to point out the distinctive qualities of public opinion as it is generated in the United States. In 1840 Alexis de Tocqueville drew some interesting contrasts between the expression of public opinion in America and in Western Europe. He attributed the difference to the spirit of equality that prevailed in this country. One consequence, he said, was that people here are less prone to put their trust in one another or in any one set up in authority. In turn they are more susceptible to the judgment of the crowd. There is less reliance on reflection, and Tocqueville portends that, given certain circumstances, the very democracy that proclaims freedom for everybody may actually extinguish itself under the weight of mass influences.[2]

Tocqueville's account may have contained some inaccuracies and certainly would have to be modified in important respects if applied to our own time, but it is highly suggestive. And it is a pity that we have so little serious investigation along such lines to reveal the lineaments and special characteristics of our public opinion. We can therefore offer only a general sketch of its features.[3]

Let us for our immediate purpose distinguish three major components of a public-opinion system.

First, there is the ground of generally held expectancies and assumptions that give, as it were, the tonality of public opinion. There is no public opinion unless an area of common ground lies underneath and supports the differences of opinion, finding expression in the traditions and conventions and behavior patterns characteristic of the folk. The coherence, strength, and universality of these traditions is from one aspect the slowly developed consciousness of the solidarity of the folk or nation. It consists not so much of a body of doctrines as of a pattern of attitudes, a broad social ethic, a way of responding to situations in which is implicit a set of values. We shall call this the *ground of consensus.*

Second, there is the *alignment of opinion,* the spread of the positions or viewpoints from "left" to "right" taken on broad issues and generally on matters of public policy. As the result of the exchange and conflict of ideas there is some canalization of opinion such that various groups or

---

[2] *Democracy in America,* Part Two, *passim* and especially Chapter 20.

[3] The statement on this subject that follows is based partly on some unpublished work by the author and partly on a number of sociological studies. For a general account, see, e.g., William Albig, *Public Opinion* (New York, 1939), Chapters 16–18, and David B. Truman, *The Governmental Process* (New York, 1951), Part Three.

blocs can be represented as occupying a particular place along a line that runs from one extreme position to an opposite extreme.

Two countries might have a quite similar distribution of opinions on any issue, with roughly the same proportion of the population holding the same position about it, and yet the impact of the controversy might be very different in the two. Thus two countries might have the same distribution of opinion on the question whether communists are qualified to teach in universities, and in one of them the universities would be allowed to deal with the matter in their own discretion while in the other strong indiscriminate outside pressures would be brought to bear. The hypothetical case we have taken is in fact directly relevant to our subject here. A false conception of the amount of intolerance in the United States is promulgated by some commentators in this country and abroad. To gain a proper perspective on the state of academic freedom, to diagnose the situation aright and to assess the ways of meeting its dangers, it is not sufficient to cite instances of violation and to denounce the offenders. It is essential that we understand the special conditions out of which these troubles arise. It is essential that we relate our problem to the other components of public opinion, particularly to the "ground of consensus" and to the third component, which we shall call the *structure of communication*. On the second component, the alignment of opinion, we need not comment, since its role is obvious enough.

Both the ground of consensus and the structure of communication, to which we shall give special attention, are profoundly affected by the unique multigroup character of the American people. Some European countries are multigroup in a different sense, since their constituent ethnic elements are associated with particular areas. But in the United States, aside from a racial concentration in the South, the elements are mostly dispersed throughout the country, and the distinctions that tend to insulate groups in each locality are not only ethnic or racial. Religious, cultural, and occupational differences conspire to create strongly self-assertive subgroups with a quasi-communal existence of their own. One might think that the remarkable degree of mobility that characterizes life in the United States would operate to limit this tendency, but actually it seems to have a contrary effect. The displacement that is the other side of mobility induces people the more to seek out their immediate "likes" wherever they move. If we take the ancient Greek saying, that "God always leads the like to the like," we may add that in the mobile society the like is identified more by his group affiliation than by his personal qualities. Mobility may perhaps stimulate the belief in equality, but the man who moves from one environment to another seeks the more quickly the social shelter of whatever group he particularly feels to be his own. With mobility there is a sense of detachment, of the loss of roots, and against this insecurity the group identification is the nearest refuge.

The United States thus presents the picture of a remarkable diversity of groups loosely conjoined into one great national community partly by virtue of their sharing in the same strong if inarticulate sentiment of being American and partly because of the particular ties and interests, habits, responses, and modes of living, that identify them with the American scene. But the various groups, with their different derivations and different cultural backgrounds, cherish their different traditions, struggling to keep their place or to advance their status, seeking to maintain some values of their own against the jostling mores of the larger society. This semi-insulation of the group has been greatly fostered by the economic and social discrimination to which many of them are exposed and by the rank antigroup prejudices through which the earlier settled ethnic groups asserted their established position and their economic advantage against the later arrivals.

These conditions obviously affect the ground of consensus. Common traditions take time to mature, and the discrimination of group against group retards the process. The sense of common interest is more shallow. It depends less on the appreciation of a common cultural heritage and more on the utilitarian perception of the chances for individual and for group advantage that the common environment provides. The remarkable technological advancement of the United States and the greatness of the resources at its command, providing so many opportunities for "rising in the world," stimulate this tendency.

The ground of consensus still exists, still plays an essential role, but its foundations are less deep. Suppose we ask: What does America—the United States of America—mean to its citizen body as a whole? The indications are that the dominant note would be that of belonging to a great country, the greatest country, rich in opportunity, vast in resources, with unexplored potentials, not too heavily trammeled by government, permitting men to a large extent to go their own ways and advance their own fortunes. Along with that there is a body of usages, in part associated with the continuous advance of and interest in technological devices, certain ways of living, characteristic modes of speech, and so forth, all of which tend together to create some sense of a common heritage. This whole system of things is loosely identified with "democracy" and with "freedom." But "democracy" is interpreted mostly in an individualistic way, as a form of government that lets everyone be as good as his neighbor, if he can. And "freedom" becomes the freedom of the market place and the right of every man to be master of his own establishment—important attributes if properly related to other freedoms and their corresponding obligations, but totally lacking in ethical or spiritual content if viewed in isolation from these. It is this ethical denudation of the stronger traditions of America that enables demagogues to identify "Americanism" with the circle of narrow interests that sustains their power.

It is in keeping with these things that education should be widely regarded as essentially utilitarian or instrumental. Education has of course always a great utilitarian function. It equips men for careers and for a place in society. It helps them to understand the world they live in and thus, in some sense, to be more successful in it. But this indispensable utility has always been associated with and in some measure derivative from the intrinsic values of education, from the worthwhileness of the acquisition of the culture of the folk, from the enrichment and fulfillment of the whole being that is inherent in the study of the arts, from the liberation of the mind and the widening of horizons that come with the knowledge of science. As science has extended its territory there has arisen an increasing realization on the one hand of the exceeding proneness to error of the untutored human mind and on the other of the amazing possibilities for the discovery of undreamed-of truth that depend on the faithful and clear-eyed search for and investigation of the data.

If, on the other hand, education and the knowledge it imparts are regarded as *essentially* instrumental or functional, then there will be strong impulsions to adapt it, regardless of its intrinsic deliverances, directly to this function. From this pragmatic viewpoint the pursuit of truth can be sacrificed to the goal of indoctrination. This is in effect what the pressure groups and embattled special interests want and intend to achieve. And in this way we interpret the anomaly that so much importance is attached to education in this country and yet so many groups are more concerned with gaining control over the educator than with advancing the cause of education.

The view of education as essentially instrumental is greatly encouraged by another characteristic of the multigroup society of the United States. We have spoken of the semi-insulation of groups. This condition holds particularly for ethnic groups, and to some degree for religious groups. With the crumbling of the older type of social class hierarchy, group prestige has to a considerable extent taken the place of class prestige— or, rather, perhaps has become the basis of a more amorphous kind of class system. Within this system there is, however, another kind of grouping that also has a hierarchical aspect. This is the occupational grouping. Occupational groups differ from the others in that the higher levels are accessible to the members of any group. In the earlier days of what was the "newer immigration," entrance to the more honorific callings was very much the prerogative of the old-established groups. Some remnants of this situation still exist, but broadly there has come about a great deal of occupational mobility. The immigrant himself could move only within a narrow occupational range, though he could with good fortune and intelligent direction win financial success. But his sons could "rise in the world" in another sense. The way up was the educational ladder. It gave access to the professions and it provided the first steps from which a man might move much more easily to such careers as those of business executive or politician. Education thus became greatly prized as the gateway to success and to prestige. Its utilitarian service was paramount.

Correspondingly, the value of those branches of education—the humanities, the liberal arts—that are not direct avenues to careers in the world of affairs has been minimized. As one commentator has put it, "there is a strong tendency to discount the importance of learning unless it is 'practical,' particularly in the fields of literature, the arts, history, philosophy, and religion." [4] In consequence, our colleges and universities have had inadequate opportunity to perform an important part of their function, that of sustaining, reinterpreting, vitalizing, and enriching the cultural heritage of America and so helping to give a deeper and more spiritual basis to the ground of consensus.

Now let us see how the third component of public opinion, the structure of communication, fits into the picture. We have spoken of the semi-insulation of groups in the expansive American society. The vast development of the facilities of communication has not obliterated but on

[4] Victor L. Butterfield, "Learning and Religion in the American College," in Amos N. Wilder, ed., *Liberal Learning and Religion* (New York, 1951), p. 131.

the contrary has rather facilitated this condition. For it makes contiguity less important as a basis of social relations. It increases the range of like-to-like association. Neighborhood counts for less. In urban areas the only real neighborhood that remains is where a group of "likes" come together in a kind of colony or enclave surrounded by the habitations of "unlikes."

There is still some sense of the greater community, but it is less deep-searching, not being rooted in neighborhood feelings. In the United States there are like ways of living that are nationwide, like ways of spending leisure, like foci of popular interest, like working habits, like modes of expression and of self-expression, and like prejudices. Thus there is bred the sentiment of the larger community, but these conditions are less likely to evoke the sentiment of the local community. In the latter, for the reasons here indicated, specific group attachments tend to dominate.

These group attachments stimulate group competitiveness. There is the constant assertion of the status of the group and the constant struggle for group recognition and group advancement. Group organizations are highly developed, and it is the business of their leaders and professional agents to promote and magnify the function and the prestige of their respective bodies. To keep the membership stimulated and to keep the group in the limelight, conventions and conferences and reunions of every kind and variety are held. The more mobile the population, the more external or the more superficial the bond that suffices for the evocation of the group spirit. Thus in a city like Los Angeles the fact that residents have migrated thither from a particular state in the Union is sufficient to make them foregather in "picnics" that stretch out over miles of territory.

Group competitiveness, group rivalry, and group self-assertion is sustained by publicity. Prestige is largely a matter of public recognition, and that means advertising. Consequently it is not only commercial advertising, in the usual sense, that is highly developed but also advertising by noncommercial organizations and interests. Experts in "applied psychology," professional organizers, opinion sounders, "opinion engineers," recruiters, fund raisers, and "boosters" find a ready market. To know which way opinion on this or that question is tending, to learn which of two or more methods of appeal is more effective, to learn what kinds of people prefer to hear what kinds of things through what media, and so forth—such information is eagerly sought after. Agencies set up in the first instance to "measure" opinion change over into the more lucrative business of "producing" opinion. Status comes by publicity rather than by the more ancient methods of more stable and generally more class-conscious societies.

No matter what the objectives of the group may be, the promotion of the group organization is often stimulated by the economic interest that is inevitably associated with its advancement, the economic interest of organizers, promoters, agents, and leaders. Thus the staff of an organization is likely to regard the rise or the success of a similar organization in the same general field as a threat alike to their own prestige and to their economic prospects. They are spurred thereby to seek greater publicity for their own organization and to magnify yet further its particular services or merits. To win favor, the organization may go outside its proper field to espouse some cause that has strong public support or is in line with some popular prejudice. Again, many types of organizations feel it is incumbent on them to keep a watchful eye on social and political developments which may work out to their advantage or disadvantage. A good deal of their propaganda is then directed to the promotion of or the resistance to such developments. The American Medical Association, for example, or a veterans' organization can be as active in political propaganda as, say, a utility company that is seeking to raise its rates.

Even a quite small group can exercise an influence far out of proportion to its scale. In the fluctuating balance and sway of many competing forces any compact minority can become a potent pressure group. In the political arena the winning or losing of the support of a small group, with its penumbra of influence, may be sufficient to turn the scales. The leaders of major groups are therefore anxious not to alienate any such minority if they can avoid it—for who knows when in the ups and downs of political fortunes they may not need its aid?

Moreover, there are a number of nation-wide organizations, generally of a fraternal character or united by some bond that is common to all sorts and conditions of men, such as an organization of war veterans. A lodge or a branch, a local or regional unit of such an organization may take a stand on a particular issue. A post of the American Legion, for example, may voice a protest against some speaker who comes to town.

It acts on its own but its voice is so much more resounding because of the large membership of the total organization to which it belongs. Yet it does not follow that the organization as a whole shares its opinion.

In a similar way vocal minorities seek to parade under the banner of great causes. One of their favorite devices, for the advancement of their own interests, is to wield some big "moral" bludgeon. They identify their private advantage with the country's eternal well-being. Thus, for example, certain groups which dislike academic freedom because it permits some professors to indulge in economic "heresies" clothe their objectives in the robes of "patriotism" and "Americanism" and proclaim that they are warding off some grave menace such as communism or "statism."

These appeals and alarms are the more effective because of the absence of any well-established set of traditions permeating the population as a whole, traditions rooted in the history of the country. The heterogeneous elements that constitute the population have not yet acquired any common understanding. There is still a considerable amount of alienation, of the detachment of group from group. Nor can this condition be laid at the door of the newer groups, for it is the discrimination and prejudice of the older groups that has been mainly responsible for keeping them thus apart. At the same time the education they receive in "Americanism" has been mostly superficial and denuded of spiritual vitality. Thus the very words "American" and "un-American" can be employed by thoughtless or self-seeking leaders to exploit their lack of understanding and to instill sentiments of intolerance.

This condition of things helps to account for a phenomenon on which many observers have commented, American susceptibility to certain kinds of mass appeal. It is relatively easy to whoop up publicity with loud-ringing words. This susceptibility is exploited by publicity seekers, including some politicians.

The mode in which at the present time charges of communist infiltration are being leveled against our leading colleges and universities is a case in point. Under the guise of patriotism the makers of these charges arouse the primitive emotions that lurk in the hearts of men, the unreason that hates difference and demands conformity, the superstition that shuns the light of truth, the fear that in its blindness confuses enemy and friend. These emotions are "all too human" and come to the surface in the time of troubles. For the reasons we have suggested our public has fewer safeguards against them.[5]

The danger is increased by the lack of critical standards in various groups, groups that in a less egalitarian society would have less public influence and certainly less opportunity to give organized expression to their views. Fundamentally the trouble here lies in the lack of a civic education adequate to civic rights and powers. Since the days of the great westward expansion there have been anti-intellectualist know-nothing-and-know-everything tendencies in some areas, often associated with a simple kind of evangelism. The influence of these tendencies still endures. When, for example, the country is facing formidable danger, such as the Soviet challenge has become, these groups are very susceptible to distorted appeals to their genuine patriotism, and when these appeals are accompanied by attacks directed against the seats of learning they are all the more ready to respond. This spirit is less inhibited because college and universities in these areas have had no time to establish a tradition. Some of the colleges are immature. Their teachers have little prestige in the community. In what other country, outside of the dictatorships, would the members of college faculties be regarded, and treated, as hired men whose job it is to teach whatever and howsoever they are bidden to teach by their comparatively uneducated employers?

[5] Various commentators have noted that incidents or events that have aroused no agitation in other democratic countries would have led to public outcries and protests in our own. Thus in the Ober-Conant-Clark correspondence (see pp. 196–97). Mr. Grenville Clark contrasts attitudes in England and in the United States. When, he says, Professor Blackett of Manchester University published his book, *Military and Political Consequences of Atomic Energy* (London, 1948), in which he gave grounds to justify the Soviet position on this question, there was no impugnment of his loyalty, whereas "in our more tense and excited atmosphere" the charge of disloyalty would no doubt have been raised.

To take other examples, in England you can find in more than one university an avowed communist, but so long as he does not make himself obnoxious in some flagrant manner no group starts an outcry for his dismissal. It is not that his presence is inoffensive to people generally, but simply that the idea of ousting him for his opinions is not seriously entertained—it is regarded as contrary to the ways of democracy. A most notable case is that of the "red dean" of Canterbury. There was widespread irritation and strong displeasure felt against him, especially since he swallowed the Soviet "evidence" accusing the U.N. forces in Korea of practicing germ warfare. But when the question of his continuance in office was raised in the British Parliament, Winston Churchill said for the conservative government that no action would be taken, since the burden of free speech must be accepted if its benefits are to be reaped. He further remarked that to set up a special tribunal to investigate him would give his activities "an importance they do not deserve"—a comment that might well be taken to heart by some of our own patriots.

We have offered this broad sketch of the characteristics of public opinion in the United States because we need this background in order to understand why academic freedom is exposed to so many attacks in a land that is pledged to the principles of democracy. Otherwise we shall misjudge the strength of the forces on both sides of the struggle and particularly we may underestimate the strength of the resistance that can be marshaled for the defense. It is sometimes maintained that educators are more timid than other occupational groups in repelling assaults on their integrity or on their status. Whether this be so or not, it is well to realize that there is no necessary relation between the noise and vehemence of the agitation and the size of the forces that back it, that the intolerant and narrow-minded are always more clamorous than the friends of liberty, that the men who rise to the leadership of certain types of organization are usually more aggressive and more authoritarian than the membership in whose name they claim to speak. As we point out elsewhere in this work, many of the more violent proposals to curb academic freedom made by political and other leaders who claimed to represent the views of their constituents have been repudiated by the people themselves.

Unless we comprehend the peculiar structure of our public opinion, the real dangers that threaten our basic liberties will not be viewed in the right perspective and the proper measures to meet them will not be applied. For lack of this perspective some of our educators and not a few commentators, including foreign ones, exhibit a lurid picture of the state of democracy in this country. They take, for example, a particular incident that happened in some small college, or even in some more important institution. They present it out of context, probably with exaggerated coloration, and say in effect: "This is America!" [6] They do not appreciate that there are hundreds of institutions in which no such incident has occurred, and that nearly all the greater ones have rebuffed any attacks on their integrity. They do not appreciate that the American scene is continent-wide and in its ramifying diversities contains all kinds of situations. Nor do they take into account the numerous instances in which the obscurantists and the authoritarians have been discomfited and academic freedom upheld.

The dangers are real enough. To bring out their derivation and their

[6] We could cite examples, and we have followed up more than one such story to discover gross distortions in it, but it would be invidious to give chapter and verse.

mode of impact is part of our problem. We adduce here one further consideration that has a bearing on the strategy of the defense.

Many of those who follow the lead of the enemies of academic freedom are not themselves hostile to the free search for truth. They believe too readily what they are told. Their leaders often themselves proclaim their respect for "genuine" academic freedom, and disguise their enmity to it, or at the least their disregard for it, by appealing to the highest motives—patriotism, the love of God, the protection of youth, and so forth. Their relatively inert following are easily deceived. It is always so when any essential freedom is being undermined. For this the educators themselves must share the responsibility. The education which our youth, and through them the people, receive in "civics" and kindred subjects is often conventional, superficial, and pseudo-historical. The meaning of democracy and of democratic liberties is not, for the most part, brought home to the conditions and problems of our modern multigroup society. It is not made significant for the texture of our lives.

It is true that the campaign against intellectual freedom, openly carried on by pressure groups and conducted in more insidious and more menacing ways under the form of congressional and state investigations, has begun to evoke strong protests not only from educators but from public-spirited citizens in every walk of life. It is well also to report that in quite a few places from San Antonio, Texas, to Shaftsbury, Vermont, the attempts of embattled groups or local authorities to censor books have been stoutly and successfully resisted. These are encouraging signs, but large portions of the public are still apathetic, unable to see through the specious disguise of patriotism and "Americanism" under which the enemies of democratic liberties conceal their designs.

II: THE NEW WAVE OF INTOLERANCE

I believe that that community is already in process of dissolution—where nonconformity with the accepted creed, political or religious, is a mark of disaffection.

LEARNED HAND

At the opening of the twentieth century there was little mention in the United States of serious perils to academic freedom. The prospect seemed rather that the area of freedom would constantly be enlarged and that the democratic tradition would spread over the face of the earth. It was recognized that in certain areas of the country, where religious orthodoxies of a narrow type held sway, there were curbs on freedom of thought and freedom of investigation. But, after all, these were the "backward" areas. In 1902 John Dewey expressed the opinion that there was little danger to academic freedom in this country.

Fifteen years later the philosopher had changed his mind. The crisis of the First World War evoked a wave of intolerance. The censorial activities of Attorney General A. Mitchell Palmer went far beyond any reasonable considerations of national security. In New York State the Lusk Committee was set up and inaugurated a series of police raids on radical or socialist organizations. Even to play the music of the great German composers came to be regarded as an offense against loyalty. Among the other signs of the times there were disturbances in the universities, and Dewey was much concerned over what happened in his own university, Columbia, where distinguished scholars were dismissed over charges of pro-Germanism, while others resigned in protest, notably the distinguished historian, Charles A. Beard.

With the coming of the "Cold War" and its accentuation since the Korean War, a new wave of intolerance has arisen. This new wave has taken on formidable proportions and has some quite distinctive features that for the sake of our later analysis we must briefly describe. Former

The sentence at the head of this chapter is quoted from *The Progressive*, Vol. XVI (December, 1952).

Chancellor Robert M. Hutchins has said that "the miasma of thought control that is now spreading over this country is the greatest menace to the United States since Hitler." [1]

The evidence of the magnitude of the wave comes from many sides. There has been a vast increase of suppressive controls, unofficial and official, over books, public addresses, and generally over all forms of the expression of opinion. Minute Women are out to purge the libraries, American Legion posts are at work to prevent unorthodox speakers from being heard, members of a post of Veterans of Foreign Wars hunt for "subversives" in their locality, textbook committees find "subversiveness" in unexpected places—perhaps the most notable discovery being that of a member of the Indiana Textbook Commission who revealed the communist line in Robin Hood. This is something different from the older but still sufficiently vigorous censorship carried on in the name of morals or religion. It does not usually go so far as the book-burning affair that occurred in a town in Oklahoma, but it exhibits the same spirit. [2] The favorite charge is that of being "subversive," an accommodating label to stick on any doctrine that deviates to the left. [3]

There is the frequent assumption that any kind of liberalism or non-conformity is a step on the road to communism, and that any attack on the proponents of such ideas is a blow against communism. It is, however, hard to know how far a genuine if misdirected alarm about communism is responsible for the situation and how far the charge of being communist or procommunist is used by various pressure groups as a heaven-sent device for the "smearing" of their adversaries.

One of the most insidious aspects of this whole campaign is the proliferating censorship of books. It takes two main forms. One is the attempt to control libraries and librarians. The other is the screening of the school and college textbooks and reading lists.

[1] In testimony before the Illinois Seditious Activities Investigation Commission, *Report of Proceedings* (1949), p. 21.

[2] The incident occurred at Sapulpa, Oklahoma, after a committee of women appointed by the local Board of Education to examine textbooks and reference materials had criticized certain books for their attitude to socialism and to sex. The books were burned with the active approval of the vice-president of the Board of Education.

[3] It is not even necessary to deviate to the left. For example, a member of the Illinois Seditious Activities Investigation Commission declared that a teacher could be subversive even in the teaching of mathematics: "inadequate and improper teaching of any subject could be considered as subversive," Commission's *Report* (1949), p. 372.

Dr. Luther H. Evans, former Librarian of Congress, has reported that librarians everywhere are being subjected to demands, protests, and attacks emanating from groups and individuals who attempt to keep off the shelves any books of which they disapprove. Librarians were being influenced or coerced "far more than has been recorded in the newspapers." The trouble was "growing to formidable proportions." "The historic spirit of America" was being poisoned.[4] This report was confirmed by Dr. David K. Berninghausen, for a number of years chairman of the American Library Association's Committee on Intellectual Freedom. The *New York Times,* in a summary based on nation-wide information, has stated that librarians were being intimidated by outside pressures in their choice of books and other materials.[5] Representative Velde of Illinois proposed that the Librarian of Congress make up a complete list of all "subversive matter" in the Library of Congress. The city council of Burbank, California, recommended that all California libraries be required to label as such all books considered to be "subversive" or "immoral." In Illinois the *Peoria Star* did even better. It wanted to clean up the local library. It did not trust the librarian and it had grave doubts about the American Library Association. So it advanced its own tests for effective communist propaganda. The first test was that most people would not know it was propaganda. For example, if a Peoria audience were asked whether the U.N. film, "Of Human Rights," contained red propaganda, they would emphatically deny it. That just showed how cunning the propaganda was![6] The ignoble character of the fear of books is seen in the fact that in the city of Baltimore, at whose distinguished university Owen Lattimore was a professor, strong pressure was brought against the Enoch Pratt Library to take from an exhibit the book, *Ordeal By Slander,* in which he defended himself against his accusers. The library in question had the courage to resist this pressure.

One of the most deplorable features of the situation is the subservient manner in which so many officials and administrators have played safe in order to find favor with or at least to avoid the attentions of the Congressional inquisitors. Where books are concerned, the only way to be safe is to keep off the shelves everything "controversial," that is, everything that does not wholly conform to the notions of the champions of

[4] *New York Times,* October 21, 1951.   [5] *Ibid.,* May 25, 1952.
[6] *Peoria Star,* November 29 and December 1, 1951. We take the citation from "News on Intellectual Freedom," issued by the American Library Association, which has done admirable work in the defense of the integrity of public libraries.

orthodoxy. So we have the abject exhibit of a letter written by the State Department to the book publishers of the country requesting them to *certify* that the books they send abroad in cooperation with the information program of the department are not written by "communists, fellow-travellers, or *persons who might be considered controversial.*" [7] And the same department, the department that beyond all others represents the United States before the world, decreed that all books by "controversial" authors be removed from the libraries of the information service in foreign countries. Among the things the senators and representatives who are responsible for this condition of unnerved apprehension among our officials do not understand is the debasement of the image of the great democracy of the West that they are sedulously promoting in the minds of foreign peoples.

The spectacle of the banning of books by the State Department has struck a grievous blow at America's claim to be the standard bearer of democratic liberties. The list of the purged books has been kept secret, but among those mentioned are included Alan Barth's *The Loyalty of Free Men,* Robert and Helen Lynd's *Middletown,* Clarence Streit's *Union Now,* and, curiously enough, Whittaker Chambers's *Witness.* We cannot take exception to a policy which would exclude from governmental libraries abroad any books that contained communist propaganda or that maligned the United States. But the insidious disease that has vitiated the extremist anticommunist group makes its appearance here again. The Department has not been content to ban specifically communist propaganda, it has extended its directives to include the unobjectionable works of men who once were communists and of authors who might be classified as "fellow-travellers et cetera." Moreover, it has done so in the blaze of publicity so beloved by the political junta that has spurred on its action. Consequently, any authors who have received any kind of unfavorable mention in testimony before the House Un-American Activities Committee or been cited by it as being or having been members of some "subversive" organizations are liable to suffer from the ban. The list of such authors reads like an honor roll of American letters.

But it is the libraries of schools and colleges that are subjected to the strongest onslaughts. In various localities throughout the whole country charges have been raised that the local libraries harbor subversive works. Sometimes the cry is raised by a local individual or organization, some-

[7] Italics ours.

times by a columnist, sometimes by one of the pressure groups that specialize in this kind of activity. Controversy swells, and committees of investigation are appointed. On occasion the assault is successfully resisted, as in the case of Scarsdale, New York, where the Board of Education rejected the censorial demands of a local "citizens' committee" and the voters of that city gave the Board overwhelming support when election time came around, or in the case of Englewood, New Jersey, where the community after a public hearing exonerated the teachers and their texts. But often enough the end of the affair is the banning of the books.

The assault on the textbook front has been even more formidable. The number of textbook censors, local, regional, and nation-wide in coverage, official, unofficial, and semi-official, is legion. The search for "subversiveness" is indeed a flourishing business. While no one could reasonably object to the exercise of proper care in the selection of school texts, that discretion requires the application of proper standards by qualified authorities. Under present conditions these authorities are not allowed to do their work. They are subjected to constant bombardment by "patriotic" organizations and self-interested groups. They are overridden by political committees of various kinds. Detailed evidence of how these processes of control operate and what the results are is scrappy and very partial, but enough glimpses of the ways in which the censorship operates are available to reveal its reactionary bias.

Take, for example, the case of Frank A. Magruder's text, *American Government,* a book well reputed among educators and widely used in schools throughout the country, a book thoroughly American but one that compares the American type of government with others without chauvinistic bias. The heresy hunters nosed it out. In characteristic manner the alarm was raised. *The Educational Reviewer,* an organ we shall be hearing about again, raised the war cry. A radio commentator, Fulton Lewis, Jr., gave it nation-wide publicity. In state after state the book came under fire. Among other charges the "patriots" declared that it advocated a dreadful thing called "world government." The Georgia school system banned it. Some states in which it was attacked did not yield to the pressure. Virginia, through its Superintendent of Public Instruction, rebutted the charges against it. Attempts were made in various cities to have it removed from the schools. Sometimes they succeeded, as in Little Rock, Arkansas. More often, however, they failed, as in Houston, Texas, and New Haven, Connecticut. Committees of teachers everywhere came to its support. In Council Bluffs, Iowa, the superintendent of schools did a neat and effective job by having some of the teachers prepare a refutation of the criticisms of the pressure groups to forestall an anticipated attack. Within a year the ban was rescinded in Georgia. *The Educational Reviewer* nevertheless boasted that more than one hundred revisions had been made in the text, "directly attributable" to the campaign it initiated. The editor who kept the text revised since Magruder's death informs us that this claim is a "pure fabrication," that *not one* of the revisions was affected by the campaign of the *Reviewer*. And the publishers add the further cheering information that the noisy attack has backfired and that in their fiscal year beginning May 1st, 1952, their sales have shown an increase of 30 percent over the previous year.[8]

In the course of this study we shall run into various cases in which the battle of academic freedom is fought around books or their authors. But it is on the school level, with which we are not directly concerned, that the epidemic of censorship is most virulent and most widespread. School textbooks are attacked—and often enough the attack succeeds—because they are declared to approve of "socialized medicine," or because they are in favor of the United Nations or of the innocuous organization called UNESCO, or because they point out such things as the inadequate housing or the poverty-stricken condition of certain sectors of the population, or because they call attention to the economic and social discrimination to which certain ethnic or racial groups are subjected. And even where books are not banned they may be sedulously revised to cut out offending passages.

But above all and permeating all other charges there is the accusation of "subversiveness," and with it there is invariably associated the suggestion of a communist tendency. No accusation could be more convenient or better calculated to arouse prejudice. The defamer knows that the crowd to whom he makes appeal are not going to read the book and judge for themselves. Moreover, there is no accusation that lends itself so well to the condemnation of innocent people as resort to the principle of "guilt by association." How far the principle can be carried is seen in the recent edict of the Texas State Board of Education, requiring the

---

[8] The editor responsible for the revisions is Professor W. A. McClenaghan, Department of Political Science, Oregon State College. The letter from the publishers (Allyn and Bacon) is dated January 26, 1953.

publishers of textbooks proposed for adoption to vouch that the authors thereof have not been for the last ten years members of any communist front organization or of any other subversive group on the list of the United States Attorney General.[9] Another example is the action of the school administration of Denver, Colorado, which in 1951 removed from the high school libraries a number of the pamphlets issued by the Public Affairs Committee, including "Safeguarding Our Civil Liberties," by Robert E. Cushman, "Human Rights," by Roger Baldwin, "Cartels or Free Enterprise," by Thurman Arnold, and "How Collective Bargaining Works," by the Twentieth Century Fund.

Among the bodies that are specially active in this campaign are some real estate boards. The president of the New Jersey Association of Real Estate Boards reported in 1952 that publishers of two textbooks had deleted passages regarded by his organization as offensive. The books in question are entitled *Our Changing Social Order* and *The Challenge of Democracy*.[10] The latter book has also been attacked by certain groups in Alabama, including the Birmingham Real Estate Board, and they have sought a court injunction to enjoin the State Board of Education from using the book.[11]

Concomitant with the flurry of censorship has come a spate of new enactments—over three hundred of them already by the end of 1950—emanating from state legislatures for the purpose of suppressing "subversive" activities. The example set by Maryland in this respect in 1949 has been widely followed. These acts are often hastily devised and leave room for much latitude in the identification of the new criminal offense.

Had there been an outbreak of conspiratorial mutterings or any swelling of the communist ranks within the country, there might be tenable ground for new protective legislation, even although the preexisting laws against conspiracy and treason are properly inclusive. Since any such developments were lacking, the explanation must be found elsewhere. The indications are that it lies in the tensions developed in the years that have succeeded the end of the Hitlerian war, when the yearning for a secure peace was frustrated by the enmity-filled aggressiveness of the Soviet state, followed by its seizure of the now satellite countries of Eastern Europe, its sweeping success in China, and its precipitation of

[9] Associated Press dispatch of August 26, 1952.
[10] *Newark Evening News,* October 15, 1952.
[11] *Birmingham Teachers Association Bulletin,* September, 1952.

the war in Korea. This new kind of warfare, costly, erosive and protracted, meaning so much to so many American homes, has intensified the resentments and apprehensions of the people. These emotions have been exploited by interest groups seeking economic and political advantage. In particular, they have promoted an indiscriminate expansion of the meaning of disloyalty. The primitive attitude to penalize the unorthodox, the deviant from the tribal code, is thus reasserted under the guise of patriotism.

One of the manifestations of this spirit has been the increasing imposition of loyalty oaths on people of all sorts, government employees, candidates for office, educators, speakers at public meetings on public property, applicants for fellowships provided by government grants, and so forth. A simple loyalty oath may seem a harmless, if not a very effective, expedient. But it is often complicated by the inclusion of a clause abjuring membership in any "subversive" organization, or some similar requirement—a matter on which we shall have to comment at a later stage. Moreover, the widespread imposition of the oath indicates a corresponding distrust of the processes of democracy and prepares the way for a vexatious type of investigation the conduct of which often falls, by natural affinity, into the hands of men who are animated by an antidemocratic passion for conformism. It is preeminently for this reason that believers in civil liberties stoutly oppose any extension whatever of such procedures beyond the clear demands of national security.

A case in point is the situation that arose over the fellowship program of the Atomic Energy Commission. The Commission entrusted certain funds for the purpose to the National Research Council, asking it to award the fellowships in accordance with their general practice. The recipients of these awards were to be assigned strictly for nonsecret research in biology, medicine, and physics, and there was no suggestion that any of them would later be transferred to the restricted area. There being thus no "clearance," and the basis of selection being ability, it happened that one of these fellowships went to a student who was a Party member. The revelation of this fact aroused a storm of congressional indignation, as a result of which the AEC accepted the proposal that fellowship applicants sign a loyalty oath and a non-Communist affidavit. This measure did not satisfy the critics who pointed out—quite properly —the ineffectiveness of such devices. They demanded a thorough investigation for the screening of applicants. The AEC was reluctant to accept this policy. Many leading scientists were opposed to it. Thereupon violent accusations were made against the AEC and particularly against its chairman, David E. Lilienthal. Senator Bourke B. Hickenlooper led the attack, charging him with "incredible mismanagement." So gross an onslaught on a public servant of outstanding integrity, courage, and competence was simply one of many exhibits of the manner in which a certain group of senators and representatives, for whatever reasons, fed the apprehensions of a bewildered public.

Why did so many scientists, we may ask in passing, oppose the introduction of clearance for fellowship applicants in nonrestricted fields? We shall let two distinguished atomic scientists answer in their own words. "I believe," said Professor N. F. Mott, former president of the British Atomic Scientists Association, "that the effect of loyalty checks on the vitality of pure science is wholly bad, and that science could contribute more to the nation's strength without them." [12] And J. Robert Oppenheimer, in his letter to Senator McMahon, then Chairman of the Joint Congressional Committee on Atomic Energy, wrote as follows: "My colleagues and I attach a special importance to restricting to the utmost the domain in which special secret investigations must be conducted. For they inevitably bring a morbid preoccupation with conformity, and a widespread fear of ruin, that is a more pervasive threat precisely because it arises from secret sources." [13]

Such counsel, however, could not prevail against the spirit of the times. The system of clearance for fellowship in nonrestricted areas was instituted. Those who opposed it were misrepresented and traduced, and Chairman Lilienthal, weary of abuse, resigned from the Commission.

One of the surest signs of a wave of unreason is the readiness to set up stark opposites between which all men must choose, there being no middle ground. There is the side of God and the side of the devil, and all who do not worship our God in our way are in the service of the devil. So today there is the communist way and the "American" way. And the American way is the way "we" think and act, no matter how many millions of Americans think and act otherwise, no matter how discordant "our" Americanism is with the great traditions of the country. The term

[12] "Working for a Society Where Science Can Thrive," *Bulletin of the Atomic Scientists,* Vol. VII, No. 12 (December, 1951). The whole number is devoted to "scientists and loyalty."

[13] *Bulletin of the Atomic Scientists,* Vol. V, Nos. 6–7 (June–July, 1949).

"un-American" has thus come into use to damn everything with which "we" disagree.

The charge of being "un-American" has the ominous vagueness as to the nature of the crime that makes it very serviceable to certain anti-liberal elements. It was already becoming a favorite smear word when it received considerable impetus from the activities of the legislative committee promoted and then controlled by Martin Dies, the Committee on Un-American Activities. Dies and his followers were against "unsoundness." The approach is reminiscent of the old Nazi charge against non-Nazis, that they did not have a "positive attitude" toward the Party. This mode of condemnation has of course been brought to a much higher degree of refinement by the communists. Similarly for Dies and the majority of his committee the definition of un-Americanism was a negative attitude toward the "sound" doctrines they espoused, in that sense toward the "Party." Any views opposed to their own were in all probability subversive.

Inevitably the wave of the new (or renewed) orthodoxy struck also against the schools and colleges. Whole areas of inquiry now became, in the eyes of the faithful, un-American. It was un-American to mention unpleasant facts about the social order, and so a schoolbook was revised because it said one third of the people were badly housed. It was un-American to admit that our form of government, like every other in the history of the world, had collectivistic, or socialist aspects.[14] It was un-American to plead for international organization or even, in the view of some extremists, for international understanding.[15]

[14] See, e.g., Walter Gellhorn, "A General View," in Walter Gellhorn, ed., *The States and Subversion* (Cornell University Press, 1952), p. 375.

[15] An organization calling itself The American Flag Committee, located in Philadelphia, attacked as un-American a series of pamphlets entitled "Toward World Understanding," issued by UNESCO. See the *Congressional Record* for October 18, 1951, and the rebuttal by A. S. J. Carnahan in the proceedings of April 1, 1952. In Los Angeles the Board of Education ruled that a pamphlet on the educational activities of UNESCO was unfit for distribution to the teachers in their schools. The way it happened was characteristic. First, an irate lady roused to action a curious assortment of local clubs and leagues. A belligerent Protestant clergyman followed up by fulminating against "pagan UNESCO." In the end this noisy minority had its way, and the school teachers were saved from contamination. Soon thereafter a UNESCO-sponsored high-school essay contest was also dropped. We might note by way of contrast that the Los Angeles County Public Library successfully resisted the attempt of the Board of Supervisors in 1948 to foist on it a censorship authority. The California Library Association, backed by the American Library Association, played a major role in this victory.

In this time of international tension, when a dreadful threat portends and nobody knows how soon or how late, whether it will ever be loosed at all or whether even now it may not be about to fall on us, it is natural that strong emotions should be stirred against the power that threatens us and even more against those who in our own midst seem to be conspiring with that power. If such emotions are misdirected, we must still recognize that which is wrong is not the healthy protective responsiveness against a peril but its misdirection.

It is also important to remember that the communist technique is to plot in secret, to infiltrate and undermine any organizations that tolerate or fail to discern their presence. There is an impressive record of their achievements in penetrating into positions of influence or power in certain government agencies, in certain labor unions, and in other forms of economic or social organization. It is therefore no more than proper discretion to take legitimate countermeasures against such operations. On the whole there is no evidence that they have had any power over the affairs of any of our institutions of higher learning or any significant influence in any of their faculties. But there are indications that in the metropolitan areas one or two colleges at least have owed some disturbances to their presence, and that in these places there have been communist cells operative among the students and possibly in a very small faculty group. The writer himself has had two students come to him to say that as the result of the analysis of Marxist doctrine in a course of his they were attending they were renouncing communism, and that up to then they had been engaged as "underground" workers for the communist cause. Against all such activities it is certainly desirable to be on the alert—in an intelligent way. In the vast majority of colleges and universities, however, there is no evidence of any real inroads made by communists. Statements to the contrary by Congressional committees are not backed by any proper evidence. As for the rare communist who may find a niche in any of these institutions, we shall have later occasion to deal with that question.

III: THE CHAMPIONS OF THE
NEW ORTHODOXY

To strike freedom of the mind with the fist of patriotism is an old and ugly subtlety.

ADLAI STEVENSON

WE MAY CALL IT the new orthodoxy, but it is compounded of the old intolerance and the old narrow interests. What makes it new is that it has a new form of appeal, a new mode of attack, and a new label for the heretic. Whatever he may be, a liberal, an independent, a radical, an anti-Marxist socialist, a pacificist, a nonconformist of any kind, a simple believer in the rules of evidence, a conservative who upholds fair play, an advocate of civil rights, he is sure to be classified as one of the vast phantom army who are on the road to communism and are meantime aiding and abetting it.

To assess the new intolerance it is necessary to understand the role played by a remarkable array of pressure groups. These groups enter into alliance with congenial political elements and at the same time incite to action a variety of other organizations, especially those devoted to some form of economic enterprise, to whose self-interest they can make appeal. Thus the initial pressure groups gather around them other bodies which as a whole or through special committees apply themselves to the same cause. As a result, the number of organizations carrying forward the crusade of intolerance is very large and has a formidable impact.

At the same time the clamorous publicity of these bodies conveys, as we have already noted, the mistaken impression that the great mass of the people is on their side. They are formidable because they take advantage of the state of mind evoked by our time of trouble, the impatience and apprehensiveness and sense of frustration of a people which after winning a peace at heavy cost finds itself menaced by a more por-

The quotation at the head of this chapter is from Adlai Stevenson, *Speeches* (New York, 1952), p. 82.

tentous threat than before. These pressure groups exploit this situation by associating with the threat all the causes that stand in their way. How false the association is will be made amply clear in the course of this work.

The American proclivity for setting up organizations and more organizations is well illustrated in this area. The organizations that are now busily engaged in the campaign to control or influence education or educators may be broadly classified into four categories—legislative committees, "patriotic" organizations, certain special-interest organizations and lobbies, and propagandist associations that set themselves up as having mainly or exclusively educational objectives.

LEGISLATIVE COMMITTEES

Our first category, the legislative committee, is of course not a pressure group in the usual sense of the word. We think of a pressure group as a body that preeminently seeks to have an impact, directly or indirectly, on government or on some other constituted authority, whereas here we have a governmental committee that has stepped out of its normal role and under the guise of investigation assumes through its hearings and reports a potent propagandistic function. The type of committee we have in mind is concerned not so much with lawmaking as with broad inquiries into the activities of "subversive" individuals or groups—though they may, of course, make proposals for new legislation. On the federal level there is the Senate Internal Security Subcommittee and the House Un-American Activities Committee. State organizations include the "un-American activities" committees operating, under one name or another, in California, Washington, Illinois, Ohio, and Massachusetts, together with other legislative committees concerned with educational affairs, such as the California Senate Committee on Education. We may note in passing that such groups by no means sum up the engrossment of legislators in this direction. In such matters as loyalty checks for federally provided fellowships and scholarships, in the follow-up of state loyalty oaths, and so forth, legislators and administrators combine in a series of activities that carry them into the educational field.

Obviously, a study on academic freedom is not the place for tracing the histories of these various committees, fascinating though they may be. Nor is the reader in particular need of being acquainted with their more publicized activities and methods; all those who lacked acquaintance surely have become only too familiar with them since 1954, when the nation sat still to watch and hear Senator McCarthy investigating the investigation of his investigations. What concerns us here is primarily the impact of these committees on academic freedom.

The oldest of the existing legislative investigating committees is the House Committee on Un-American Activities, set up in 1938 as an *ad hoc* committee under the chairmanship of Martin Dies and organized as a standing committee in 1945.[1] Although its professed objective was laudable, this could not be said of its methods.

Its disregard of judicial procedures, the publicity of its charges against people who might be and often were innocent, and its resort to the principle of guilt by association, set a notorious example that other propagandist organizations have only too faithfully followed. As Walter Lippmann put it, the Dies Committee became "a pillory in which reputations were ruined, often without proof and always without the safeguards that protect the ordinary criminal." [2]

Although some of the House Committee's more recent members, particularly Richard Nixon, displayed more discretion and greater competence than their predecessors, the old methods were never thoroughly reformed. There was still the itch for publicity, still the tendency to impute guilt by association, still the assumption that denunciations and expulsions were the proper way to deal with the disaffection of the relatively small body of American communists, still the disinclination to seek for the roots of the problem.

One of the most menacing aspects of the House Committee's operation has been the compilation by it of voluminous files covering a vast number of individuals, presumably persons whom it had some reason to suspect of communist leanings. Thousands of honorable citizens and not a few of high distinction were listed. Rumors, reports from biased or ignorant persons, statements of fact that omitted essential aspects of the fact, inaccuracies, allegations of membership in subversive organizations when during the period of membership the organizations had not yet been declared subversive, anything whatever that taken in isolation might be derogatory to the listed person, all such items were assidu-

---

[1] Its story is told by Robert A. Carr, *The House Committee on Un-American Activities: 1945–1950* (Cornell University Press, 1952).
[2] Syndicated column of January 11, 1940.

ously amassed. No attempt was made to sift the evidence or to include items of a contrary character. These slanted files were freely released and used by private agencies. Thus were bred new accusations and new items for the cumulative indictment. Politicians made a public and sometimes a wholly irresponsible use of it, and pressure groups took advantage of the "information" to influence employers against implicated persons.

The House Committee has taken considerable interest in university, college, and school teachers who were members of any organizations listed or regarded as being subversive or who for any other reason could be suspected as having communist connections.

A good example of the Committee's approach is the case of the six physicists of the Berkeley Laboratory (University of California) who were charged by it in 1949 with belonging to a communist infiltration group. It was entirely proper for the Committee to take special concern with the loyalty of physicists engaged in atomic research. Sufficient evidence was available, and more was to come, that communist informers were conveying to Russia the top secrets of the atomic bomb. The utmost vigilance was imperative. On the other hand, public exposure of grave charges against persons who might be altogether innocent or who, having at one time fallen for the communist lure, had entirely renounced it, was an injudicious proceeding calculated to prejudice the future of all the defendants. There was pressure to have them dismissed without proof from their university positions. A number of institutions took the proper stand of refusing to yield to that pressure prior to indictment under regular legal processes. This attitude was adopted by Princeton University in the case of David Bohm and by the University of Minnesota in the case of Joseph W. Weinberg. In both these cases a court indictment for contempt followed, based on their respective refusal to answer certain questions. On that ground they were suspended or dismissed from their academic posts. Another case, that of Professor Frank E. Oppenheimer (not to be confused with J. Robert Oppenheimer), presented some particular interest—and difficulty. He had told his university (Minnesota) in writing that he had never been a member of the Communist Party. This was in 1947, whereas in 1949 he testified before the House Committee that he had been a member from 1937 to 1939, when he had become disillusioned. Having so testified he handed in his resignation to Minnesota.

We single out this case because it exposes a problem that is aggravated by the unbridled publicity in the noise and heat of which so many of these investigatory committees operate. Here was a man who had renounced communism and thereafter had been accepted for work on the Manhattan Project. And General Groves, who knew his record, had later recommended him for the significant contribution he had made to the development of the atomic bomb. His case suggests that of not a few younger persons who in the days of the Hitlerian portent were attracted in considerable numbers to communism, with its deceiving promise of a new emancipation for mankind, only to discover, after their commitment to it, that the promise was a snare. Such persons are placed in a most unhappy predicament. If they admit their former connections, they are publicly branded and often professionally penalized—unless they once belonged to an inner communist ring and could win popular redemption and even acclaim by exposing their former associates.

Congressional investigations are nearly as old as the Union, and no question can be raised concerning their right to inquire into the condition of affairs in any field of public interest. But, like any other prerogative of government, they may be misused or abused. And here a heavy charge must lie against the procedures of the more recent committees. They have, most of them, violated the rules of decent and dignified investigation. They have browbeaten witnesses, refused them legal aid, and have not infrequently denied them access to the transcripts of hearings that concerned them. They have publicly cited the names of people against whom they had no adequate information to justify the charges they raised. They have yielded to sensationalism. They have been content to hear only one side of a case. They have allowed semiprofessional informers to denounce people as subversives without notifying these people or giving them a public opportunity for rebuttal. They have accused others, or allowed them to be publicly accused, of aiding and abetting communism, on quite flimsy grounds. Among those thus accused have been a leading Methodist bishop, men of high reputation as administrators, some champions of civil liberties, and some distinguished scholars. Finally, they have been largely responsible for the spirit of apprehension and the sense of intimidation that, according to a considerable amount of testimony, has invaded the halls of learning.

Not all of the committees we have mentioned have been guilty on all these counts, but all have been guilty on some of them. The Senate Internal Security Committee has on the whole refrained from the overbearing tactics of some others. The most judicious of them all, however, the committee that investigated the tax-exempt foundations, broke its good record in the closing days of its hearing by calling in Louis Budenz and allowing him to make indiscriminate charges against certain educators, without giving those thus accused any opportunity to appear at the hearings and present their case. There is good reason to believe that this departure from the ethics of decent investigation was an attempt to avert the threat of the McCarthy-McCarran contingent to set up a new committee on the foundations, since the first was not behaving according to their style. In due course the threat was fulfilled and the second committee, headed by Representative B. Carroll Reece, gave a remarkable object lesson in how an investigation should not be conducted. It began ominously with a report from its "research director," who in advance of inquiry stated his conclusion that a number of foundations had wandered from the true path of "Americanism" and who proceeded to name as "accessory agents" a whole array of most reputable organizations devoted to the advancement of education. Later on, after giving considerable publicity to attacks on the foundations by staff members and witnesses, it suddenly ended public hearings, over the protests of the two members of the committee, Representative Wayne L. Hays and Representative Gracie Phost, who throughout had opposed the procedures.

How then about the state investigatory committee? Foremost among these may be put the California committee that for most of its history was known as the Tenney Committee.[3] It is a curious fact that Tenney, who was then busy with trade union affairs—he was a piano player and his union was a local in the American Federation of Musicians—had been listed by the Dies Committee as a member of three subversive organizations, the test of disloyalty he himself was to apply so freely. Losing out in an internal fight in his union he blamed communist elements for his defeat. He nevertheless won the presidency of his local and from then on took over the political role he exploited so fully. Elected assemblyman, he sponsored the joint committee of senators and assemblymen that became the Senate Fact-Finding Committee on Un-American Activities, with Tenney as chairman.

[3] See Edward L. Barrett, Jr., *The Tenney Committee* (Cornell University Press, 1951), and for a synoptic account of this and the other legislative committees, Walter Gellhorn, ed., *The States and Subversion* (Cornell University Press, 1952).

Among its other investigations this committee turned attention to high school texts concerned with sex education, fastening on the school at a place called Chico. It discovered that the course given on the subject there was "a communist plot to destroy the fibre of youth." It proceeded to investigate a number of organizations and to impugn others, including the stalwart American Civil Liberties Union. It listed twice as many subversive organizations as the attorney general had discovered. It opposed a fair employment practices bill as having been inspired by the communists, although it was backed by considerable numbers of loyal citizens. (To condemn a measure or a cause ostensibly because communists are also found in the lists of those who support it has become a familiar device.) The committee also proposed a string of suppressive bills, nearly all of which were defeated in the assembly. Most of them would have given the legislature a hold over educational programs and policies, and particularly over the texts and reading materials that students use.

The committee outdid its federal exemplar in reaching "indisputable" conclusions and presenting "indubitable proof" on the basis of evidences that no work on scientific method would ever justify. To prove an organization to be a communist front it was enough that some of its members or sponsors were also members or sponsors of other organizations that were held to be communist fronts. In its hearings the committee acted as a prosecuting body and not as an impartial tribunal. It was content to hear the evidence against a person or organization without giving due opportunity for the submission of contrary evidence.

The committee's bullying methods and in particular its attempts to secure suppressive and censorial legislation led to strong attacks upon it from various groups, as a result of which Tenney was compelled to retire from his chairmanship. The existence of the committee was threatened and it was salvaged only by the substitution for Tenney of Senator Hugh M. Burns, who was understood to be an advocate of more equitable procedures.

We shall not here deal with the other state committees operating in this field. We shall have later occasion to refer to some of their actions. It may suffice to say that in their standards and methods they have been no more judicious and no more wise than the Tenney Committee. In some respects the record of these others is even worse. The rough-riding tactics of the Broyles Commission in Illinois and of the Canwell Committee in the State of Washington are or should be notorious. Indeed, even the chairman of the Canwell Committee admitted that some of his chief investigator's questioning might have been "inept."

The whole exhibit is a most unhappy revelation of the lack of perception or understanding displayed by groups of legislators at a time when the country needs high statesmanship as urgently as ever in its history. The problem of how to deal with the minute proportion of scholars who are communists is only a minute part of the master problem of how to deal with communism in the world, communism as a world power. These legislators in their treatment of the smaller issue show a pathetic inability to comprehend the major one, while at the same time they loudly offer their nostrums for its solution. Not in heat and confusion, not by disregard of the democratic principles we profess to defend, not by drawing infallible conclusions from flimsy and one-sided evidences, not by the childish identification with communism of every form of independent thought, not by denunciations and alarms, will the United States rise to the challenge. That way lies the abdication of intelligence and the bankruptcy of statesmanship.

In this matter of dealing with communism there are, as in all great historical problems, many questions of policy on which differences of opinion are inevitable. The wisest judgment is fallible. But for our legislative committees there are no such questions. They know the answers in advance and anyone who differs from them is playing the communists' game and is roundly denounced accordingly. To take an example, the Canwell Committee paid its respects to Columbia University as a hotbed of communism, cherishing "several hundred" fellow travelers. To support its contention its witness adduced the fact that this university had accepted from the Polish government an endowment for a chair of Polish language and literature. It was of course the exclusive prerogative of the university to appoint whatever scholar in its judgment was best qualified to occupy the position. But the Canwell Committee accepted without qualification the testimony of J. B. Matthews, former research director of the Dies Committee, that the university had fallen for a communist trick to have a "foreign agent" at Columbia who would not be required to register as such. Their witness proceeded to denounce the then president of the university, General Eisenhower, for having accepted the gift and for having "completely and shamelessly evaded the issue." Not a word was heard on the other side. No member of the committee, so far as the published record is concerned, asked any probing question. The prosecuting testimony, with its false implications, alone was included in the committee's report, with the charges in leaded type.[4] At no later time was mention made of the fact that a distinguished Polish scholar who is not at all communistically inclined was appointed to the position. The broader aspects of the situation, aside from the benefit to the university's program of East European studies—the desirability of maintaining a friendly interest in the traditions of an important people held in restraint behind the iron curtain, and in general the importance of assuring all the peoples of the East, so far as opportunity is given, that the democratic peoples have not abandoned their faith and created an iron curtain of their own as well, thus turning division into despair—such considerations were of course utterly beyond the range of vision of the committee.

PATRIOTIC ORGANIZATIONS

The "patriotic" type of organization is hard to demarcate. It is a matter of convenience or discretion whether we should place certain organizations here or elsewhere. In general, we include the various organizations that without specifying any particular objectives claim to stand for America or "Americanism." A number of these are usually active in campaigns against academic freedom—for instance, the D.A.R. and the groups that constitute the American Coalition of Patriotic Societies—but there is, of course, no assumption here that all groups thus classifiable are opposed to academic freedom. What we do imply is simply that antiliberal groups not otherwise specified are prone to fly at the masthead the banner of patriotism. This also applies to the subgroup of organizations that specify as their sole aim their opposition to communism, whatever their real objectives may be—e.g., the Joint Committee Against Communism.

We need not give any elaborate exposition of the ways in which the associations that fall in this category work. We shall occasionally run into their doings in the course of this study. Unlike the other main types with which we deal, the old-established "patriotic" organizations do

[4] *Un-American Activities Committee in Washington State,* Second Report of the Joint Legislative Fact-Finding Committee on Un-American Activities, 1948, pp. 44–45; see also p. 49.

not usually make a regular business of prosecuting nonconformity. They have as a rule prestige interests and considerable social pretensions, though the older organizations are aped by newer aspirants which do not have the class standing of the former. They tend to carry their native conservatism into reaction and thus are easily convinced that those who advocate any kind of social change, such as the abolition of segregation in the South, are undermining the foundations of the Republic. They are inclined to regard independence of mind as the forerunner of subversiveness. Bodies like the D.A.R. and its paler brother, the S.A.R., not infrequently initiate or join in protests or outcries or bans against speakers or educators who advocate policies they dislike or against books and especially textbooks that do not follow the prescriptive line. Thus their influence on the whole tends to be prejudicial to academic freedom.

Among the groups included in this category are some older established veterans' organizations, which no longer have any major problems of veteran benefits to fight for on behalf of their own members and thus tend to become largely social clubs. They are not inherently on the side of intolerance; on occasion quite the contrary is true; but sometimes the control of such organizations is taken over by the more fervid patriots who see subversion round every corner. This can happen the more easily in the present climate of opinion. In some measure at least this has become the case with the American Legion. Its leaders have disturbed the friendly relations the Legion previously maintained with the National Education Association. They attacked the NEA rather violently as being under socialist control. The *American Legion Magazine* is constantly calling out against educators, book publishers, editors, and others who do not toe the line. Usually the charge is that of subversiveness, but often the Legion is content with flimsy evidence, and it seems to have no remedy to propose except suppression. Again, there is good reason to believe that in this respect considerable numbers of veterans do not see eye to eye with the hierarchy. Referring to the Legion's attack on the NEA, the Connecticut Commissioner of Education, Dr. Finis Engleman, said that the Legion commander who spearheaded the attack "did not speak for him or for the overwhelming majority of veterans in this country." [5] Veterans are of course folk of every persuasion and of every walk of life. Many of them are inarticulate. Some Legion posts have taken an attitude very antagonistic to the liberty of

[5] *New York Times,* July 3, 1952.

the educator, as for example in the unhappy affair that eradicated from Fairmont State College in West Virginia many of its liberal-minded teachers, including its president,[6] but on the other hand there are some posts, such as the Ford Motor Co. Post 173, that have stood firmly on the side of academic freedom.

Moreover, in fairness to the Legion, we should add that its present tendency, especially as exhibited by its official organ, is out of accord with the more broad-minded attitude to education it has otherwise displayed. In August, 1949, its National Convention passed a policy resolution of a highly judicious character respecting the investigation of instructional materials, presenting a set of criteria, which, if generally followed, would safeguard our schools and colleges from the excesses of intolerant censorship to which they are now exposed. And the New York Convention of the Legion in August, 1952, reaffirmed its faith in the public schools as defenders of American ideals, called on its members to recognize and resist all subversive attacks on them, and paid a tribute to the teaching profession and to the NEA for the assistance they gave to the Legion's Americanism program.

CERTAIN SPECIAL-INTEREST ORGANIZATIONS AND LOBBIES

There are a number of industrial, financial, commercial, and professional groups that to protect their particular interests make the "education" of the public and above all of the educators one of their major operations. The number of special-interest groups is legion, and it is only a quite limited proportion of them that seek to bring undue pressure on educators. Moreover, it is perfectly proper that any interest should organize for its own defense and promotion. There are, however, certain quite powerful organizations which have not been content to present their case and make sure that it came to the attention of as many educators as possible but have gone so far as to demand, exerting all the influence at their disposal, the excision from textbooks of unfavorable statements and the removal of educators who take a position to which they are opposed.

One might innocently ask why certain special-interest groups should

[6] See, e.g., William Manchester, "The Case of Luella Mundel," *Harper's Magazine,* CCIV (May, 1952), 54–61.

so vigorously have joined the attack on the intellectual freedom of educators and education. Actually, however, the attempt to curb educators because a minority of them, often a small minority, entertain economic theories that displease business or occupational groups is a quite old story now. The chief difference today is that so many special organizations or branches or offshoots of larger economic organizations have been evolved or created to focus the attack. Thus the liberal economists of the United States in the generation before the First World War were bitterly assailed as socialists or anarchists and in consequence some of them lost their jobs.[7] These men advocated certain economic reforms, opposing monopoly and exploitative privilege but not the broad system of private enterprise. In a larger perspective these economists and their sociological allies, men like Richard T. Ely, E. A. Ross, and E. Benjamin Andrews, might be regarded as working to save the system of private enterprise from its natural maladies, maladies that have, where uncontrolled, led to its defeat or destruction in various countries. They were its friends and not its enemies, but they refused to accept laissez-faire and on that account were falsely charged with being socialists and anarchists and made the subject of abuse and sometimes of "investigation."

To illustrate the more modern attack we shall briefly review the modes of operation of the Conference of American Small Business Organizations, listed as a nonprofit corporation. CASBO, for short, has other interests besides its devotion to educational problems. It is concerned also with labor relations, agriculture, commerce, trade practices and monopoly, taxation and fiscal policies. It has a committee for each of these activities, including education, and does a very active lobbying business. It is maintained by membership dues and other contributions from businessmen or firms.

Its methods in various respects are somewhat questionable. The language and the layout of certain of its materials convey the impression that CASBO and its committees are working under direct congressional sanction "and that it is an adjunct of the United States Government," which is, in the words of the House Select Committee on Lobbying Activities, a "preposterous suggestion." [8] It claims to express the "de-

[7] Joseph Dorfman, *The Economic Mind in American Civilization* (New York, 1949), Vol. III, Chapter 11.

[8] House Report No. 3232, 81st Congress, 2d Session (1950), p. 7.

liberated opinion" of organizations "representing an affiliated membership of over 600,000 small business concerns." But the deliberation
consists largely of the ratification of propositions sent out to subscribers
with loaded comments. "Truly deliberated opinion," to quote from the
report just referred to, "is much to be desired but it rarely exists within
pressure groups." [9]

What, however, interests us particularly is the work of its Committee
on Education. Its major operation has been the publication of the *Educational Reviewer*. It came forth initially with a great parade of its devotion
to the Constitution and with the proud boast that it was "a new tool designed to help awaken and rearm the champions of liberty."

It rearmed the champions of liberty by damning all textbooks and
reading that suggest any flaws or imperfections in the "American
system" and particularly in the system of private enterprise. We are not
for a moment suggesting that the *Reviewer* was not perfectly entitled to
adopt this attitude—or any other. If it limited itself merely to critical
comments we would never dispute its right to make them. The *Reviewer*,
however, went beyond this. It grossly misrepresents books it dislikes.
Thus in its review of Frank Magruder's *American Government* it says,
for example, that "the treatment of race and inequality of income follows the Communist Party line." [10] This is a preposterously unfair and
misleading statement, and it is only one of many. Having thus maligned
the book, CASBO proceeded to drum up its misinformed following to
exert pressure to have it withdrawn from schools and colleges, as they
so notably succeeded in doing—in the state of Georgia, for example.
Perhaps no further comment is needed than the following quotation
from the Select Committee's report on this organization.

We all agree, of course, that our textbooks should be American, that they
should not be the vehicle for the propagation of obnoxious doctrines. Yet the
review of textbooks by self-appointed experts, especially when undertaken
with a legislative ax to grind, smacks too much of the book-burning orgies
of Nuremberg to be accepted by thoughtful Americans without foreboding
and alarm. . . . If these educators are so utterly naive and untrained as to
need help from a lobbying organization in selecting proper classroom materials, then our educational system has decayed beyond all help. This proposition we cannot accept.[11]

[9] *Ibid.*, p. 3.
[10] Eona Lonigan, "Broadcasting Collectivist Propaganda," *The Educational Reviewer*, I (July 15, 1949), 3.
[11] House Report No. 3232, as in Note 8 above.

In passing we note that a number of organizations in this field do not limit themselves to criticizing texts and readings—they obligingly supply some texts and supplementary materials of their own. The National Association of Real Estate Boards, after bringing pressure to bear for the establishment of courses in the economics of real estate, supervised the preparation of special texts for use in such courses. The National Economic Council generously arranges for free copies of its publications in school, college, and university libraries. The Foundation for Economic Education and the Committee for Constitutional Government see to it that propagandistic pamphlets and books are provided freely for teachers and for students.

These organizations obviously want to "reform" the faculties as well as censor the books they use. Thus Merwin K. Hart, heading the National Economic Council, is "quite shocked at the attitude of many of the faculty members at Cornell." It seems these offenders would "let the student make up his own mind," instead of insisting on "the right lines," and this, he declares, spells doom.[12] It is the major premise of all such groups that only their own bitterly narrow orthodoxy should be taught at our universities.

The ways of CASBO merely exemplify a pattern that with some variations is followed by various other organizations. We could also cite the work and methods of the Employers' Association of Chicago, or of the West Coast association going under the name of Pro-America, or, say, the Friends of the Public Schools. Alike they find the taint of communism on everything that is experimental, or unconformist, or liberal, or "new-dealish," or in any way critical of the divinely appointed perfection of things as they are—or rather as they were before the "radicals" began to mess them up. We do not need to accept any of the particular viewpoints they thus misrepresent when we expose the baseness of their attacks. We do not, for example, need to be advocates of progressive education when we repudiate such statements as this—to quote the words one of these groups employs: "So-called 'progressive education' and communism are one." The tactics of untruth come naturally enough to those who fear the pursuit of truth.

It is important to observe that the attack on academic freedom, under whatever banner it is conducted, is always part of a broader campaign to suppress opinion adverse to the interests concerned. We deal here only

[12] *Ibid.*, p. 502.

with organizations that focus all or a considerable portion of their efforts on education and educators. But the counterparts of these are no less active in the whole area of communication. Thus the concern entitled American Business Consultants carries on similar operations, particularly through its organ, *Counterattack,* and its publication, *Red Channels,* in the field of radio and television.

PSEUDO-EDUCATIONAL ASSOCIATIONS

The appearance of a rash of propagandist organizations claiming to have mainly or exclusively educational objectives is a sign of our times. Some of them use the term "education" in their titles. Examples are the Guardians of American Education, the National Council for American Education, the American Education Association, the Friends of the Public Schools of America, and the Foundation for Economic Education. Apart from anything else, it can be economically advantageous for such groups to profess to have primarily educational objectives, for if they can get away with the claim, they become tax-exempt. Various other bodies, which do not use the term "education" in their titles, equally announce to the world that they are interested in nothing else. Thus the very active Committee for Constitutional Government, which circulates in vast quantities the highly tendentious book of John T. Flynn, *The Road Ahead,* "regards itself," in its own words, "as strictly an educational organization." "Its position," it explains, "almost exactly parallels that of the economics department of a college or university." Some other operators in this field prefer to give themselves simply the patriotic label, such as Pro-America.

There is no discernible difference between the approach of such organizations and that of the special-interest bodies we have just been considering. Their arrogation of the term "educational" is wholly misleading. Unlike the previous groups, however, they direct their official attention entirely to bringing their influence to bear on genuinely educational institutions.

It may suffice, then, to look at one only of this new array, and we take as our example the National Council for American Education. This is the resplendent name under which Allen A. Zoll, a gentleman who claims a Ph.D. from an obscure diploma mill, carries on his campaign.[13]

[13] For information on Zoll and his "educational" activities, see the report issued by

It is not without significance that Zoll in earlier years founded an organization entitled American Patriots, whose members met at lunch to hear leading Bundists, anti-Semites, and Christian Fronters. The organization came to grief over the indictment of Zoll in connection with a certain financial transaction.

His present organization is financed, he tells us, from membership dues and the contributions of "patriotic citizens and companies." It circulates various materials, some of which are decently conservative while others strike the characteristic note.

Aside from the series of reports on "Red-ucators," Zoll puts out *The Educational Guardian,* with its incessant warnings against "subversiveness" in the schools. Among other discoveries Zoll finds a red trail in "progressive education." This contention played some part in the Pasadena affair that ended in the dismissal of Dr. Goslin. It need hardly be said that the real question of the merits and demerits of progressive education receives no illumination from the propaganda of Zoll's organization.

One of the objectives of the National Council is "to review and evaluate as many additional textbooks as possible." "Reviewing and evaluating" means hunting between the covers for anything "un-American," such as the advocacy of federal aid for education, which is part of the "master-plan" of the communists, or indeed almost any suggestion that the present scheme of things can be improved by constructive action. In the intervals of damning such nefarious designs, the Council recommends "truly American" books, including the bitterly partisan work of John T. Flynn and the still more extreme contribution of Elizabeth Dilling (*The Roosevelt Red Record*), whose true Americanism is attested by a long record of anti-Semitic and fascist agitation.

It is an unhappy reflection of the lack of public enlightenment and the dominance of narrow self-defeating interests among some influential groups that Zoll and his Council have had so much impact in certain areas of the country. It is a remarkable phenomenon that when Zoll promoted his "educational" enterprise he was able to enlist on his advisory committee six members of the House, three U.S. senators, the ex-

the Research Division of the National Education Association in December, 1950. See also Arnold Forster, *A Measure of Freedom,* a publication of the Anti-Defamation League (New York, 1950), pp. 74–79; *The Boston City Reporter,* May and June–July, 1952; and the exposure by Frederick Woltman in the New York *World Telegram,* August 25, 1948.

president of a college of good standing, and a professor from a Southern denominational university. Some of his first supporters, however, including Senator Vandenberg, Senator Mundt, Stanley High, General Jonathan M. Wainwright, and Gene Tunney, were merely deceived by Zoll's misleading propaganda, as so many members of the public have been, and honorably resigned when the facts about Zoll and his organization were exposed in the New York *World Telegram*.

Our classification is far from complete, and our information concerning most of these bodies is extremely limited. While they devote themselves to intensive publicity campaigns in the pursuit of their objectives, many of them are extremely chary of exposing their own affairs to the public view. A full-scale investigation of the great anti-academic-freedom brigade would be most illuminating. The way some of them are financed is a particularly interesting aspect. We get some glimpses of their true character from the *Report and Recommendations on Federal Lobbying Act* of the House Select Committee on Lobbying Activities [14] and from the separate reports on individual organizations issued by the same body. Among other things these reports confirm our judgment that certain of these bodies, run by a few individuals, make quite misleading claims to the effect that they speak for a large public following.

A survey made by the National Commission for the Defense of Democracy Through Education shows that attacks on the public schools have been increasing considerably in number and in intensity in the last few years, and that in many instances these attacks have been stimulated, initiated, or encouraged by the organizations whose work and character we have been sketching. Their impact on the public schools has been on the whole more serious than on the colleges and universities, and again their impact on state institutions has been greater, especially in some areas, than it has been on private institutions. In broad perspective it appears that these pressure groups make little headway where educational authority is entrusted to men who themselves are well equipped educationally, men who have knowledge of educational standards and a sincere respect for them. The significance of this simple fact will be manifest as we proceed.

We have spoken only of the centralized pressure groups that maintain an insistent drive to force colleges and schools into conformity with

[14] House Report No. 3239, 81st Congress, 1951.

their own interests and objectives. The picture of the total barrage to which these institutions are exposed is by no means thereby conveyed. We must remember that many organs of the press, through columnists and editorial writers, as well as some radio commentators and others who make use of one or another medium of communication, aid and abet the pressure groups. We must also add the hundreds of local groups that make representations to the educational authorities in their vicinity. Some of these groups are regularly constituted bodies, such as parents' organizations, and these groups, whatever their attitudes may be, can be regarded as having at least a genuine interest in education. Others are sporadic and transient formations, often stimulated into being by one or other of the larger propagandist organizations. We must remember also that important and powerful bodies of all kinds, including chambers of commerce, labor organizations, fraternal clubs, and, not least, religious organizations, particularly certain Protestant groups and the Roman Catholic Church, also bring their weight to bear. Indeed, our colleges, and even more our schools, are the target of a tremendous volume of protestations, charges, and appeals.

Straightforward criticism, based on a regard for educational values, is always to be welcomed. But the operations of the four groups of organizations we have listed do not come under that head. On the contrary, it is our deliberate judgment that their operations are a more serious menace to the integrity of our educational institutions than the machinations of the handful of communists who may still be found within them. The great body of educators and the whole structure of educational authority can take care of the latter, whenever any need arises. But these other organizations are frequently high-powered, backed by much influence and wealth, often possessed of social prestige, and above all operating in close alliance with a group of ambitious politicians. Their power to do harm is proportionately great.

We said they were not engaged in constructive criticism of our educational institutions. The sufficient testimony is the methods they employ. Let us briefly sum up the conclusions in this regard to which all our evidence points.

1. They totally ignore or misconceive the function of the institution of higher learning. They demand that all its teaching, in every relevant subject, be solely along the line of the particular viewpoint or doctrine to which they themselves adhere. They demand that all its researches, in

every relevant subject, arrive at the position from which they themselves start. They demand conformity and they denounce difference. They do not reason with those who differ from them. They condemn them. They are not interested in the *pursuit* of knowledge.

2. Their specific proposals are always of a repressive character. They endeavor to remove what they dislike, whether it be textbooks of which they disapprove or teachers with whom they disagree. To secure these ends they appeal not to educators but to a public which they misinform and to authorities on whom they can bring pressure to bear. In these operations they indulge in much misrepresentation of the issues.

3. Their main weapon is the deliberate exploitation, for their own purposes, of the fear of communism. They incite that fear the more in order to misdirect it. They pretend that our colleges and universities are overrun with communists, undermined by them, infected by them. Anyone who advocates social security, or state medical aid, or better facilities for housing, or more adequate relief for the unemployed, or more measures against unemployment, or some kind of international organization is a "statist," a "collectivist," a "socialist," a follower of the communist line, a fellow traveler, or a downright "red." Anyone who thinks the economic system can be improved is accused of seeking to destroy it.[15] The fact that these charges are false and utterly misleading does not concern them. Their appeal is to prejudice, not to intelligence.

These then are the forces that in our time most seriously threaten not only academic freedom but the whole broad freedom of thought and of inquiry. For in striving to purge the universities of all independent thinking concerning man and society, they work to desiccate the nursing grounds of intellectual and cultural leadership in this country, and without that leadership freedom of thought would lose its most effective defenders.

[15] On this subject see the argument, "The Economic Line," in Chapter 10.

Part Two

ACADEMIC GOVERNMENT AND ACADEMIC FREEDOM

IV: THE AMERICAN PATTERN

Lay government more than anything else expresses our national individ-uality—I would not call it our genius—and it lies at the heart of the academic freedom issue as it has developed in this country.

WALTER METZGER

ACADEMIC FREEDOM is intellectual freedom within the institution of learning. Like any other kind of institutional freedom, it depends at once on the government of the institution and on the spirit that animates the governed, i.e., the body of educators. In assessing the problems of American academic freedom we must therefore give attention to the prevailing mode of government, to the kinds of authority that regulate or impinge on the American college or university.

There is on the one hand the range of authority that operates within the institution itself—the governing board and the hierarchy of adminis-tration. There is on the other hand the "extramural" authority that has discretional control over the institution, essentially that of government, whether local, state, or national.[1] Back of authority there is the whole changeful climate of public opinion to which we have devoted the last three chapters. Consequently, what is formally the same system of aca-demic government may have very different manifestations according as the climate of opinion is favorable or unfavorable.

In this chapter we endeavor to point out the characteristics of aca-demic government in the United States. It is a complex subject that cries for fuller exploration than it has yet received. The main features of the American academic structure are, however, easily distinguished. What is clear in the first place is a highly distinctive American pattern —we might call it a North American pattern, since Canadian institutions,

The quotation at the head of this chapter is from the *Antioch Review,* XIII (Septem-ber, 1953), 280.

[1] One type of academic institution, the denominational, may in addition be subject to a third kind of authority, that of the ecclesiastical organization with which it is connected. For a discussion of this, see Appendix A.

while in some other respects modeled on different lines, have on the whole a similar form of government. This pattern stands in marked contrast to those exhibited by British and European systems.

The primary difference lies in the composition and derivation of the governing board. This difference in turn not infrequently reflects itself in the manner in which presidents are chosen and in the relation between governing board and faculty.

A few quotations from an article on continental European universities will suffice to accent the difference. "It would be unthinkable," we are told, "for a Rector"—who roughly corresponds to our college or university president—"to be brought into the university from the outside or to be a non-academic person, as is often the case in the United States." "Rectors and deans in Europe have no power to hire or fire faculty members, a right which is reserved exclusively for the faculty." Most of the universities of Western Europe are state universities, and there "it is the government which hires, but the recommendations of the faculty are always solicited and rarely questioned." [2] These continental European universities are "essentially self-governing groups of scholars. There are no boards of trustees, no alumni secretaries, no administrative officers who have any power over the faculty. The faculty runs the university and is the university." [3]

These statements need, however, some qualification. While in some European countries the situation is substantially as depicted, particularly in the Netherlands, Switzerland, and the Scandinavian countries, in others undue political influences have at times been brought to bear on appointments. We need hardly add that wherever totalitarian regimes took over they thoroughly corrupted university traditions. It should also be noted in passing that the European state university is generally a national institution, unlike the American state university. There is the further consideration that these universities derive most or all of their finances from state or local grants, so that the extent and, in degree, the direction of their development depends on the will of the political authorities. But,

[2] With respect to their form of government British universities differ from the typical university of continental Europe. They are all, however, self-governing with respect to appointments on their faculties, with the exception of a number of ancient Regius professorships appointment to which is formally made by the Crown, after consultation with the university concerned.

[3] The quotations in this paragraph are from Anatol Murad, "Democracy in European Universities," *The Educational Forum,* XIV (May, 1950), 459–60.

broadly speaking, the educational autonomy of the faculty is well recognized and established.

Here there is an interesting contrast with our American institutions. Consider, for example, the following excerpt from a report of the American Association of University Professors: "In the typical [American] institution in 1941 the board of trustees appointed the deans, and the deans, in turn, designated the department executives, all without benefit of consultation with teaching staff." [4]

It should be understood that this "typical" practice or, as the same report also calls it, the "statistically modal usage," is by no means universal. There are colleges and universities that exhibit a very different structure, institutions in which there is a good relationship between faculty and governing board, in which the direction of intrinsically educational affairs is fully entrusted to the faculties concerned, and in which the board is quite as anxious as the teaching staff to maintain the integrity of education and to assure the academic freedom on which that so largely depends. Moreover, in recent years a certain number of institutions have come to realize the inadequacy of the typical pattern and have sought by various devices to bring board and faculty into closer contact.

Such cases, are, however, exceptional. A survey of 1941 showed that of 228 institutions 176 had no definite plan for exchange of opinion between faculty and board, that in 177 there was no consultation with the faculty in the appointment of departmental heads or chairmen, and that in 158 the officers appointing deans entered into no consultation on the subject with the faculty. [5]

During the nineteenth century the tradition became established in the United States that the government of institutions of learning should reside in boards composed of lay trustees. There was a tendency toward the increase of alumni representation in these boards and generally of alumni influence in policy making. On the other hand there was during this period no tendency toward the admission of faculty members on boards. Instead, the accepted principle was that the teaching staff should have no participation in the actual determination of the laws that

[4] Report of Committee T, on "The Place and Function of Faculties in College and University Government," *Bulletin of the American Association of University Professors*, XXXIV (Spring, 1948), 60.

[5] *Ibid.*, pp. 59–60.

govern them. Indeed, some institutions had clauses in their charters or statutes barring active teachers from board membership. Thus the Columbia University charter has the proviso, "that no professor, tutor, or other assistant officer shall be trustee." A similar rule is contained in the basic laws of George Washington University, Lehigh University, the University of Wyoming, and the Massachusetts Institute of Technology.[6]

The operation of this whole system of academic government, essentially so different from those of European countries, has never been seriously investigated. A study of its impact on the character and direction of American education would be rewarding. That, however, is not our concern here. But anyone who follows the fortunes of academic freedom in this country cannot fail to note that the manner in which our colleges and universities are "typically" governed has much to do with the problem. Observers from foreign universities have pointed out, by way of contrast, that in their countries cases involving academic freedom are of comparatively rare occurrence. Our own study leads strongly to the conclusion that the difficulties that beset the maintenance of academic freedom in the United States depend very largely on the particular ways in which the manifestations of group opinion impinge on our distinctive form of academic government.

The scheme of government, as will be brought out in the chapters that follow, is specially exposed to the impact of interest groups. The composition of the governing boards, in many instances, is such as to render them less qualified to resist external pressures or even to understand the danger of these assaults on the integrity of education. State institutions are peculiarly vulnerable in this respect, at least in those areas where no strong tradition favorable to academic freedom prevails.

By way of developing this thesis we shall now consider the main aspects of this scheme of government.

[6] See E. C. Elliott and M. M. Chambers, *Charters and Basic Laws of Selected American Universities and Colleges* (New York, 1934).

V: THE GOVERNING BOARD

There is no natural antagonism between trustees and professors. To suggest it is to suggest failure in their proper relation to one another; to suppose it is to provoke failure; to assume it is to ensure failure.

A. LAWRENCE LOWELL

THE BOARD OF TRUSTEES of the college or university is normally invested with full authority over all institutional decisions. All matters of policy come within its jurisdiction. We need not concern ourselves here with certain complexities or modifications of this principle. As a minor complexity there is, for example, the case of Harvard, with its Corporation of five officials and its Board of Overseers composed of alumni. Again, there is the matter of state institutions and their relation to the legislature. Seven state universities are sometimes spoken of as "constitutional," because of the renouncement by their respective states of any right of managerial control over them on the part of the legislature. In effect, however, in these as in other state universities, the control of the legislature over the budget can be a potent substitute for direct authority. In the case of denominational institutions there is also, depending on the type of affiliation with the religious body, some question as to where final jurisdiction may lie.

But the general rule is that the board of trustees has full authority to determine the affairs of the institution, to direct its educational policies, to elect its president and other officers, to appoint its faculty members, and to prescribe its discipline. The board is so empowered by charter. In the eyes of the law the board *is* the institution.

This principle is necessary and proper. The university is a corporate body and as such must possess a final source of authoritative decision. At the same time, as with other types of institutions, the legal formula may be far from expressing the operative process. The right to make final

The quotation at the head of this chapter is from A. Lawrence Lowell, *At War with Academic Traditions in America* (Harvard University Press, 1934), p. 290.

decisions need not and should not involve the actual determination of all policies. The obligation it entails will be best fulfilled by the ratification, in matters requiring special competence, of policies made by those who have the requisite qualifications. The role of trustees is in the first place to assure that the standards of the institution are sustained and advanced. They can fulfill this role only if they jealously protect the integrity of education itself and highly respect the collective judgment of the body of scholars who constitute the very being of the institution. Where this spirit prevails in the board it will render services as valuable as they are necessary and will leave to the president, the officers of administration, and the faculty the respective initiative that their various functions require.

Only so can the institution of learning be welded into a unified harmonious structure. Only so can academic freedom be safeguarded against the assaults of groups that value their own narrow advantage more than the light of knowledge. Wherever we find a board that dictates to the administration and sets at naught the judgment of the faculty, we find an institution that is divided against itself, that has lost academic standing, and that suffers gross violations of academic freedom. Some flagrant examples will be given in the course of this work.

It is no coincidence that the universities of highest repute—and usually those with the longest established traditions—have boards that fully recognize the prerogatives of the faculty. Such boards, when the occasion arises to choose a president, seek for one who is acceptable to the faculty and who understands their problems, frequently enlisting, formally or informally, the advice of the faculty in making their selection. When, as occasionally may happen, the board of a university of high standing takes a step that creates serious faculty dissent and disruption, as happened at the University of California in the famous decision to impose a "loyalty" oath, it is usually because the board does not properly understand the viewpoint of the faculty—an institutional defect that we must presently consider.[1]

On the other hand, gross violations of academic freedom occur much more commonly in areas where educational standards are lower or where

---

[1] In approving the oath requirement, the majority of the regents were moved by strategic considerations—to ward off threats of legislative intervention and to prevent a reduction of the university's budget—but they did not count on faculty reactions.

the institution of learning is itself dominated by a board that has little respect for or understanding of educational values. Under such conditions the governing board is still ready to think of the faculty members as its employees, its hired men.[2] Under such conditions a board may dismiss a faculty member without consulting or contrary to the advice of the president of the institution, as happened at Fairmont State College.[3] Or it may choose a new president against the strong protests of the faculty, and sometimes even of the alumni, as happened at the University of South Carolina in 1944. Or it may dismiss a president who opposes high-handed action by the board in the treatment of faculty members, as happened to President Rainey at the University of Texas and at Fairmont State College, or one whose educational viewpoint is uncongenial to it, as that of President George D. Stoddard was to the Illinois trustees. Boards of this type naturally seek presidents who will be subservient to them.

In the cases just cited the scheme of institutional relationships is a faulty one. There is no proper understanding between the components. The assignment of functions between the board, the president, and the faculty is not such as to promote educational standards, the objectives to which every institution of learning should be directed. Under such conditions the institution has little power of resistance against the demands and assaults of pressure groups.

An institution cannot be well governed unless each of its components clearly recognizes its obligations as well as its rights in the promotion of the common end. Throughout this chapter we endeavor to set out the conditions of relationships that are requisite for the maintenance of academic freedom—which itself may be regarded as an index of the intellectual health of the institution. Already it should be clear that governing boards should accept the following limitations in the exercise of their authority:

[2] During the controversy at the University of Texas between the board and the administration which led to the ousting of President Rainey, several regents spoke slightingly of the system of tenure and jeeringly called the American Association of University Professors "the professors' C.I.O. union." During the University of California controversy a leading pro-oath regent made a vicious attack on the AAUP.

A signal statement of the "hired man" theory was provided in the famous Scopes case in 1926 in Tennessee, when William Jennings Bryan advanced it as a defense for the dismissal of Scopes.

[3] See William Manchester, "The Case of Luella Mundel," *Harper's Magazine,* CCIV (May, 1952), 54–61.

1. Boards should consult with their faculties in the search for a new president and should in no instance appoint to the office anyone who does not meet with the general approval of the teaching staff.

2. Boards should not make appointments to academic positions or promotions or transfers or dismissals except on the advice of the president,[4] who in turn should previously have consulted the appropriate sectors of the faculty or the faculty as a whole, according to the nature of the appointment.

These provisos follow logically from a recognition of the ends of the institution of learning, but they can be amply supported by an examination of the cases in which the discretion they would impose on governing boards has been transgressed. To take the first proviso, it needs little imagination to perceive how essential to the well-being of any college or university is a good understanding between president and staff, and how destructive of morale it is when an undesired president is imposed on the staff. To the faculty the scholarly qualifications of their president and his all-round comprehension of educational needs are primary desiderata. Some boards, however, appear to be less impressed by such requirements than by more extraneous considerations, such as the nonacademic prestige or the political importance of a candidate for the presidency. A number of cases can be cited where this difference of viewpoint has led to the appointment of a president whose selection aroused bitter resentment on the part of the faculty, to the serious detriment of the institution. A recent instance occurred at the College of William and Mary over the appointment of Rear Admiral Alvin D. Chandler. The faculty protested against the manner of election, especially as it claimed that it had been promised a voice in the matter. The Dean of the College, Dr. Nelson Marshall, resigned by way of protest and in his letter of resignation characterized the manner of election "as a studied insult to our faculty" and as showing "a lack of responsibility to the greatness of our college." [5]

[4] This principle has been approved by various accrediting agencies. See, for example, the statement of the Southern Association of Colleges and Secondary Schools in the *Southern Association Quarterly,* XII (February, 1948), 365; also the *Revised Manual of Accrediting* of the North Central Association of Colleges and Secondary Schools (January 1, 1938), p. 14.

[5] For a report of the case—which like so many others has overtones that the record does not reveal, in this instance leading back as far as the football arena—see the *Alumni Gazette of the College of William and Mary,* September and December, 1951.

No less essential to the well-being and harmony of the institution is the second proviso. On the whole it is scrupulously observed in the leading colleges and universities, though there have recently been cases in very reputable institutions where under the influence of a public opinion rendered excitable by the fear of communism it has been violated. Academic freedom always suffers grievous injury when a board takes it upon itself to dismiss or discipline educators in opposition to faculty judgment. This type of transgression was back of the disturbances that shook the much-troubled University of Texas when Dr. Rainey was president. A precipitating factor was the request of the majority of the board that the president do not renominate the Dean of the School of Medicine. Again, the board in 1943 removed the Director of Public Relations in the name of economy, though the next day one of the regents inquired of another man if he wanted the job; the dismissal was made against the advice of the president and the vice-president. No type of action on the part of the board could have been better calculated to lower the prestige of the university and to rouse a spirit of bitter resentment in faculty and in student body alike.

Implicit in the two limitations on the direct activity of the governing board is a broader principle, that of autonomy of the faculty in the area of its own special competence. The mode of instruction, the direction of research, the laying out of the curriculum, the content of courses, the assessment of student performance, and the determination of admission and degree requirements are matters properly belonging to particular departments, to particular faculties or schools within the institution, and to the teaching body as a whole. Situations occasionally develop where through some kind of mismanagement or excessive inbreeding a whole school or faculty within an institution becomes narrow and self-enclosed, fails to maintain adequate educational standards, and is lamentably behind the advancement of scholarship in its field. Under such circumstances we suggest that the wise course for the president of the institution is to seek the advice of leading scholars in this field from other institutions and to arm himself with their counsel and moral support before introducing whatever changes may be deemed necessary.

This autonomy is of primary importance for the status of the teacher and of the teaching profession on the collegiate level. But, even more, it is an essential condition of the advancement of education. The assumption that a board of trustees, no matter how devoted to their institution, a body not chosen because of their experience and reputation in the profession of teaching, is qualified to direct the procedures or overrule the conclusions of those who have made education their lifework runs counter to intelligent practice in every area of human endeavor. Only where the profession of the educator is held in low esteem would the assumption be made. In all universities of high standing the autonomy of the faculty, as above explained, is taken for granted. And it is not without significance that in West European universities, where governing boards themselves contain a considerable proportion of educators and therefore might claim a degree of competence in this field that our own boards lack, faculty autonomy is thoroughly established.

We therefore set out as a third principle of self-limitation for boards of trustees the following:

✓ 3. Boards should assure to their faculties full autonomy over all matters specifically relating to the curriculum, the content of courses, and the conduct of teaching and research.

It is hardly too much to say that this principle alone, were it fully observed, would remove many of the major perils that beset academic freedom in this country. At the same time it provides a foundation on which the status of the profession of educator can be upbuilt. In conjunction with the second of the two principles enunciated above, it provides a safeguard of tenure. If, for example, a professor of economics incurs the displeasure of his board because of his "heterodox" viewpoint, he would no longer incur the danger of some kind of unfavorable board action which might render his position precarious.

So far we have dwelt only on certain limits proper to the exercise of authority by governing boards. It is not on that account to be inferred that the functions of the board are of secondary importance in the promotion of the ends of the institution. On the contrary, the role of the governing board is always highly significant and can be eminent. No university can attain to greatness if its board lacks high quality and fine discretion, and no university can maintain its greatness long except under the same conditions. However, it lies in the nature of our task that we must search out the weaknesses in the defenses of academic freedom. There is therefore less need for comments on cases where boards have taken the proper stand than for scrutiny of situations in which they have failed to do so.

Nor would we draw a line and say that the functions of the board are simply the control and direction of the external or material aspects of the university. It should be noted that we have not taken the position sometimes held, that the board should keep its hands altogether off educational policies. There is a broad area of forward educational planning in respect to which the board can give signal and essential service. This subject, however, lies outside our sphere, and we merely state here that one great service the board can render, is to sustain and reinforce the morale of the faculty and in particular to ward off all attacks on the freedom of teaching and inquiry.[6]

To accomplish these services the board should be constituted of persons alert to appreciate the needs and values of higher education, and the board itself should have some direct way of keeping in touch with the faculty. In both these respects it is necessary to raise some questions regarding certain distinctive features of governing boards in the United States. We shall reserve consideration of the latter of these requirements until we deal with the role of the faculty.

Various investigations have been made into the occupational distribution of board members. Broadly speaking, the control is in the hands of businessmen and lawyers. A relatively recent study showed that on the boards of thirty universities, 41.5 percent of the members were engaged in business or finance.[7] For 16 nongovernmental universities the percentage was 47.4, but for 14 state universities it was only 29.4. On the other hand, members of the legal profession constituted 38.6 percent for the nongovernmental institutions. There is a scattering of members drawn from other professions. Out of 734 board members, 34 were *technically* classified as educators, nearly all of them in nongovernmental universities. But 15 of the 34 were university presidents, mostly ex-officio members, and all of the others were administrators—vice-presidents, deans, and so forth. Not one of the thirty-four was a regular member of the teaching staff of a college or university.[8]

The prominence of businessmen (including bankers) on boards is a relatively modern phenomenon. According to a study by Earl J. McGrath, clergymen constituted in 1860 39 percent of the membership of

[6] Some public figures—the late Senator Taft was a notable example—have been exceedingly helpful in this way. As examples of other trustees whose services have been eminent, we cannot refrain from mentioning Laird Bell of the University of Chicago, Carleton College, and Harvard University and Grenville Clark of Harvard.

[7] Hubert P. Beck, *Men Who Control Our Universities* (New York, 1947).

[8] *Ibid.*, pp. 56–57. See, however, below, pp. 102–3.

his list of nongovernmental boards, considerably exceeding the representation of businessmen and bankers.[9] Even in those days, however, the proportion of clergymen on state boards was quite small. Today there are very few clergymen on any boards except those of denominational institutions. The same author reports that for his list of nongovernmental universities the percentage of bankers rose between 1860 and 1930 from 4.6 to 20.3, while for his state universities it rose between 1860 and 1910 from 4.4 to 22.2, dropping however to 13 percent by 1930.

The boards that govern our universities are thus drawn predominantly from two occupational groupings. The selectivity is somewhat different for nongovernmental and for state institutions. In the nongovernmental institutions the typical board member is associated with large-scale business, as banker, manufacturer, business executive, or prominent lawyer. His income falls in a high bracket.[10] He is in the neighborhood of sixty years of age.[11] In the governmental institutions lawyers are more numerous, and there are some public officials as ex-officio members and usually also some persons who have previously held a political office. The trustees of state universities are on the average younger, less wealthy, less identified with the greater industrial or financial corporations, and more closely associated with the political arena.[12] In the state universities the absence of educators is even more conspicuous than in the nonstate institutions. A few women appear on the list, but the state universities are no more receptive than the others to persons who have won distinction in literature, art, or any other form of cultural achievement.

The differences in composition between the state universities and the others arise partly from the respective modes of appointment but they reflect also differences in tradition, in geographical distribution, and in the socioeconomic conditions that determine the character of the student bodies and the alumni of the respective types. There is the initial fact that one type is largely dependent on endowments and private benefactions while the other is largely dependent on subventions voted by state legislatures or other public authorities. In the nonstate universities cooption is the dominant method of selection, whereas the state universities depend primarily on appointment by state governors, usually "with the advice and consent of the senate," or else directly by the state

---

[9] Earl J. McGrath, "The Control of Higher Education in America," *Educational Record*, XVII (April, 1936), 259–72.

[10] Beck, *Men Who Control Our Universities*, pp. 66–69.

[11] *Ibid.*, Table 9.   [12] *Ibid.*, pp. 120–21.

legislatures. A few universities, particularly those of Michigan, Illinois, Nebraska, Colorado, and Nevada, depend instead on a system of public election. State appointments are for a term of years whereas cooption is generally associated with life tenure.

Our evidence makes it clear that a major factor in the disturbances of academic freedom that occur so frequently in various parts of the country is the frequent lack of *rapport* between governing boards and faculties consequent on the character and attitudes of the boards themselves. Where a good understanding exists between the two, outside pressures hostile to the freedom of the educator can generally be successfully resisted, as has recently been shown, for example, at Harvard, Yale, the University of Chicago, Vassar, Roosevelt College, Sarah Lawrence College,[13] and a number of other institutions. Where such understanding is lacking these attacks on academic freedom are either given sympathetic hearing by the board or are not properly resisted, as has been the case, for example, at Ohio State University and in degree at the University of California. Sometimes indeed, the attack is conducted by the board itself, as occurred, for example, at the University of Texas. Moreover, where the board is not in sympathetic relationship with the faculty, it is the more likely to appoint presidents and other officers of administration selected without reference to the views of the faculty and thus less qualified to establish a liaison between faculty and board.

These considerations make it desirable that we assess the methods in present use for the selection of board members. On nonstate boards a considerable majority of the members are usually chosen by cooption, while in four important institutions this method accounts for the total membership.[14] There are generally also a few representatives of the alumni. On behalf of cooption the argument is made that it provides for stability and the maintenance of institutional traditions. It can also be claimed that, given a good board to start with, the principle of cooption is likely to assure a good succession. On the other hand, the question

[13] The following statement, jointly issued by President Harold Taylor and Chairman of the Board Harrison Tweed, admirably illustrates the best kind of understanding: "It is an essential part of good educational policy that a college ask for no orthodoxy in its teachers as to religion, politics, or philosophical theory. If it were otherwise, teaching would be done not by the faculty but by the governing board of the institution. The teacher would be a mouthpiece for the preconceived philosophy of the institution rather than a seeker for the truth about problems in his field of learning."

[14] For details, see Beck, *Men Who Control Our Universities*, Table 25.

may be raised whether the stability and conservatism attributable to the method of cooption are unmixed blessings. A modern university must be many-sided. It must be responsive to the ceaseless advance of science and humane scholarship as well as to the changing conditions and needs of society. Nowhere is it of more importance than in the educational process to combine a devotion to permanent values with a readiness continuously to adjust institutional provisions to new requirements and to new insights. Colleges and universities are more and more the breeding grounds of discoveries that change the face of the world and the proving grounds of dynamic ideas that change the minds of men.

Cooption tends to limit the occupational and social range from which trustees are drawn. Beck found that of coopted trustees in sixteen leading universities "four-fifths were directors or major executives of business concerns, and two-fifths carried such responsibilities for one or more of the 400 largest corporations in the country." [15] The question at once presents itself: Why so narrow a basis of selection? Why, in particular, should the various groups whose occupational interests lie closer to the field of education, groups whose work becomes part of the very substance of education—scientists, artists, authors, creative scholars, inventors, leaders in various associational activities, architects, and so forth—be deemed so little qualified to share in the direction of the institutions of higher education? And why, conversely, should prominence in business affairs be presumed to confer so preponderant a capacity to guide these institutions? We have direct knowledge of the fact that some business leaders and some lawyers are excellently fitted to be members of boards, entirely aside from their special qualifications to render certain services, such as the management of the university budget. But universities have many aspects, and universities do not live by bread alone. And there is the further consideration that the members of these groups live in a very different atmosphere from that of the educator—as well as on a much higher income level—and that their engrossments often leave them little time and opportunity to acquaint themselves adequately with university needs. Thus there is created in too many instances a certain remoteness—sometimes even a gulf—between trustees and faculty, a condition of things that contains some particular perils for academic freedom.

When we turn to the boards of state institutions, we might anticipate that the more public and presumptively broader-based mode of appoint-

15 *Ibid.*, p. 117.

ment would assure a more representative membership. This is so to a limited extent. There is certainly not the same concentration of an economic hierarchy on these boards. They contain on the average more agriculturalists, more middle-rank businessmen or executives, and a few more women members, occupationally classified under the unrevealing designation of "housewives." It is only in women's colleges that we find any important proportion of women board members.[16] The charters of some institutions require the representation of one or more particular groups. Thus the Cornell charter was amended in 1945 to require three representatives of organized labor, while the University of Wisconsin at one period required representation of agriculture, the manual trades, and women.

On the other hand, the composition of state boards has some questionable aspects, especially when one bears in mind the responsibility of boards for the protection of academic freedom. In the first place, a large percentage of trustees nominated or elected to these boards are present or former holders of some public office, suggesting that political expediency has priority over educational qualifications. When governors or state legislatures make appointments, they are tempted to use the occasion in order to reward or honor or placate political friends, just as boards with a strong political complexion are likely to select college or university presidents for political reasons. The appointees in such cases are usually men of substance and of standing in their communities, but that is not enough. They are likely to "carry to the board the savor of politics and their attitude toward the university is inevitably wrong." [17]

In some states, as we have mentioned, trustees are publicly elected. Direct election of trustees has sometimes been hailed as laudably democratic, but this claim is based on a false though very prevalent conception of the nature of democracy. Where special training, expertness, or background qualifications are essential for the proper performance of a particular function, popular election is a hit-or-miss method. Here there is no need to resort to it. It is not enough to be a "good citizen." In this respect we disagree with a writer who claims that the role can be effectively filled "by a good citizen of any occupation"—"farmer, railroad worker, miner, druggist, or haberdasher." [18] It is not a question

---

[16] An exception is the University of North Carolina, where at least 10 of the 100 board members must be women. *Ibid.,* p. 43.

[17] R. M. Hughes, "College and University Trustees and Their Responsibilities," *Educational Record,* XXVI (January, 1945), 27–32.

[18] Claude Eggertsen, "Composition of Governing Boards," in Harold Benjamin,

of whether he is a railroad worker or a banker—and, for that matter, it is undesirable that the board should be identified with any social class. But "good citizenship" is not enough. No one would regard it as desirable that the direction of an atomic laboratory, say, or of a museum of fine arts, or, if you like, of a great industrial corporation, should be determined by popular vote or on grounds of political expediency or party service. The standards of fitness for board membership are similar, whether the institution is a state university or a private corporation. Whatever the type of institution or whatever the method of appointment, there should be agreed-upon standards of eligibility in terms of the qualifications appropriate to the office. We have learned not to choose our regular civil servants by political nomination or by popular vote—why then choose in these ways trustees whose task demands a mature understanding of the complex problems of higher education?

The need for high trustee qualifications is in one important respect even greater for the state universities than for the others. For the state boards are subjected in greater degree to the pressures of interest groups. Conflicts over academic freedom are more conspicuous here and often more aggravated than elsewhere. We may note, for example, that of the nineteen institutions that in the period 1935–1950 were censured or "blacklisted" by the American Association of University Professors—an action resorted to only in flagrant cases—eleven were in state institutions, five in nonstate, nondenominational institutions, and three in denominational ones. Incidentally, we remark that the only major area in which no such action was taken was New England, where traditions making for academic freedom have on the whole been longer established.

Some governing boards have shown an admirable spirit; others have been lamentably deficient. How boards should be constituted if they are to serve best the cause of higher education is a difficult question that lies outside our province. But one point is sufficiently clear. Unless the boards are composed of men who have a real perception of educational problems and who at the same time can enter into sympathetic relations with the faculties they control, the vital issues of academic freedom will frequently cause strife between educators and boards, a strife that today as in the past threatens the integrity and retards the advancement of our institutions of higher learning.

ed., *Democracy in the Administration of Higher Education* (Tenth Yearbook of the John Dewey Society, New York, 1950), p. 121.

VI: THE PRESIDENT

"What we want," said the Chairman of the Board of Trustees, "is a man in his middle forties with a fine record of scholarship, a good speaker, with an attractive wife, an easy manner in dealing with people, a good business head, the capacity to win the confidence of his associates, an experienced administrator with sound views on public affairs, and lots of energy—lots of it."

"What, no vision?"

"Oh, of course, that goes without saying. In fact, not simply vision, but plenty of BROOOOAD *vision."*

"I think," broke in the third speaker, who had already been a college president for two years, "that your man should also be a licensed plumber."

THE AMERICAN SCHOLAR

CONCERNING THE PROBLEM of being a university president much could be written, but again our task is limited to those relationships and functions of his that are important for the fate of academic freedom within his institution.

The president is the executive head of the institution and *ex officio* he is a member of all faculties and generally presides over faculty meetings. He is the direct and sometimes the only means of communication between faculty and trustees. He is responsible to the trustees for the general administration of the institution. He reports faculty and departmental recommendations to his board. He frequently possesses a veto on faculty decisions but in many cases where he does not formally have this right, or where, having it, he does not exercise it, he still has substantial control over them, since practically any decision concerning which he has any misgivings can come before the board, where his views will have considerable weight. Most presidents, however, are not dis-

The quotation at the head of the chapter is from an editorial in *The American Scholar*, XVIII (Summer, 1949), 265.

posed to veto any strongly supported faculty resolution. Every good administrative officer, whether he be president or provost or dean, knows that his major function is to enable the teaching staff to carry forward its work more effectively. "Throughout my university career," said Vice-President and Provost Emeritus Monroe E. Deutsch of the University of California, "I never forgot that the faculty is the university and that administrative officers exist to help make wise choices for the faculty and then to do everything possible to aid them in their work. We are not 'bosses' with 'employees'; we are colleagues in the cause of education." [1]

A university president has a highly strategic and often very difficult position. He can be overwhelmed by a multitude of details. Besides his more immediate obligations he has to represent the university on numerous occasions, preside at all sorts of functions, make speeches before all sorts of assemblages, sit on various boards, travel to various conferences, attend the celebrations of other universities, and generally maintain the public relations of his institution. He has budgetary problems to wrestle with and is expected to be a good money-raiser. In the state universities he has to justify his institution to the legislature, to make them understand its needs, to meet the various allegations, criticisms, and attacks that from time to time are made by unfriendly groups. Sometimes, depending partly on the scale of the institution, it is hard for him to keep in touch with his faculty. Moreover, the university has so many subjects, departments, and schools that many of these, even if he himself has been an educator, are remote from his ken. Yet he must not show partiality to those with which he is more familiar. He must have a broad educational insight and a sympathy with every kind of scholarly enterprise. [2]

To succeed he must know how to delegate tasks and he must assuredly know when not to compromise. In the larger universities the president

[1] Presidential address before the Western College Association, Spring Meeting, 1950.

[2] For a summary of the statements made by forty-six state university presidents concerning the endless tasks they are called on to fulfill, thus making it exceedingly difficult for them to concentrate on the major problems of their institutions, see the article by President I. D. Weeks of the University of South Dakota in *School and Society*, LXXII (November 18, 1950), 321–24. President Weeks concludes: "The presidents of state universities have a task that would challenge the energy and ingenuity of a superman. It is a difficult position to endure, to say nothing of filling it efficiently and with credit." On the difficulty of the president's role see also the Editorial in *The American Scholar*, XVIII (Summer, 1949), 265–70.

has become the head of an upper hierarchy, with vice-presidents and sometimes a "provost" or other officials above the rank of dean. Columbia University, for example, has now two presidents (respectively of Teachers College and Barnard College) and various vice-presidents besides the president of the whole university. Chicago has a chancellor with four vice-presidents. But whatever responsibilities the head of the institution may thus entrust to senior officers, he still must retain two primary functions that are of the utmost importance for the maintenance of academic freedom. He still must be the focal point for the formulation and promotion of general educational policies, and he must be strong enough and persuasive enough to enlist the sympathy and support of the board for his program.

Our present concern, then, is with the relations between the president and the faculty on the one hand and his relations with his board on the other. In principle the educational policies of an institution of learning should express the best available consensus of its own body of educators. In practice this rule does broadly apply to particular curriculum arrangements, requirements and standards for degrees, and so forth. But the fields of learning are wide and numerous; the interests and attitudes of educators are diverse, and each group is highly concentrated on the pursuits of its own area and understands relatively little about the problems of the others. To the outsider, to his colleagues working in fields remote from his own, the devoted seeker after knowledge may seem to be exemplifying the sentiment of Hamlet: "I could be bounded in a nutshell and count myself a king of infinite space." Each is intent on discovering the secrets of his own province, whether his province be a speck of dust or Cepheid variables, cuneiform inscriptions or the eighteenth-century novel, the nature of the virus or some quirk of the human mind. Communication between them is not much easier than it was with the builders of the Tower of Babel. They have little enough in common, except perhaps the scholar's faith, the scholar's mentality, and a regard for academic tenure.

It falls then to the administrators, headed by the president, to run the institution. From the faculty standpoint, the first responsibility of the president and the administration is to assure conditions as favorable as possible to the evocation of their contributions to teaching and to knowledge. The function of the administration is to enable the scholars to fulfill their function. Its authority is not authority over educators except so far as authority is needed to promote the cause for which the educators stand.

It is the president who mainly must deal with serious charges and complaints and therefore who has the primary duty of warding off attacks on the liberty of teaching and research. So often some disgruntled alumnus or some "patriotic" organization is raising an alarm, or perhaps some business club complains about a faculty member who has expressed doubts about some manifestation of private enterprise, or has sympathized too openly with the workers in a local strike, or has some left-wing affiliations. It is for the president to take the lead in interpreting to the public—and even, perchance, to his own faculty—the values and goals of higher education, the primary importance of free inquiry and what it means to the well-being of the community.

But it is not only from the outside that attacks on academic freedom originate. In more subtle and disguised ways they may arise from within, from the action of lower administrators or of department heads. While the members of any faculty will resist external and direct attacks on academic freedom, they are not always so regardful of the more indirect repressions that occur among themselves. A dominant departmental group, for example, adherents of the same school of thought, may prove intolerant of divergent views entertained by younger members of their staff and by refusing to recognize the scholarly merits of the latter may themselves violate the academic freedom they profess to defend.

It is usually up to the president to accept or reject nominations for appointment or promotion before referring recommendations to his board for final approval, and generally to have oversight of department usages. He does not normally raise any question concerning faculty nominations—provided they are within the allotted departmental budget—but when he submits a list of nominations to the board he has, if need be, an opportunity to make whatever comments he sees fit. In this way occasions may arise when he is in a position to vindicate or to betray academic freedom in the face of these more subtle but sometimes serious dangers.

Thus, for example, a senior department head may show a notorious preference for his own yea-men, for candidates who are diligent disciples of his own school, hold back from promotion subordinate professors who do not follow his line, and thus in effect make his department a sounding board for his own doctrines. It is all very well for a teacher of distinction to seek to enlist as colleagues men whose views are congenial to his own, but when this is done so flagrantly that difference of viewpoint is discouraged and even punished, then it is a threat to the liberty of thought and to open-minded inquiry. Possibly this situation is more likely to occur in departments of economics, anthropology, sociology, and education, where it carries the greater danger, because it is the area of social studies that most frequently suffers from the external attacks on academic freedom. To deal with cases of this kind is a delicate matter, in which the administration can be wisely effective only by making judicious use of some appropriate faculty agency. It would be some safeguard if the principle were generally adopted that the chairmanship of a department be held only for a limited term.

Another typical situation may occur when a candidate has been nominated for a position in some department and objections are raised against him on grounds other than his professional competence. There are sometimes reasonable grounds of this nature and it is no doubt proper to take into consideration such matters as the nominee's personal characteristics if these could seriously interfere with the efficiency of his service or the establishment of good relations with his colleagues or with his students. But sometimes objections are raised on prejudicial or irrelevant grounds, and in disposing of these, especially when they are made by some outside group—or perhaps by some members of his own board—the president can show himself a true defender of the faith. The objectors, for example, may be animated by social or racial prejudice, bringing pressure for the rejection of a thoroughly qualified scholar because of his national origin or color. Or they may raise a hue and cry against the candidate because he is not sufficiently "orthodox" according to their economic or political standards. In such situations the issue lies with the president.

If the president is called upon to guard academic liberty when controversies arising over appointments occur, he has obviously much more occasion to do so in the matter of dismissals. In recent times this duty has taken on a new dimension, owing to the character of the campaign against "radical" educators and particularly to the pressures that are stimulated by certain congressional investigations. Some presidents have stood out nobly against these pressures, while others have shown an unhappy spirit of concession. But we shall deal with this matter at length elsewhere.

We turn to the relation of the president to his board. This relationship in a sense antedates his appointment as president. So we may include here the role of the board in selecting a president. We have already pointed out the proper approach of the board in this respect, but since it performs no function more crucial to the well-being of the institution we shall look now at some other aspects of it.

There are three serious mistakes that boards may be tempted to make in appointing a president. First, they may choose a man because of his distinguished career in a noneducational field, without due regard to his lack of understanding of the needs and the ways of a university. We are not suggesting that a qualified president must invariably have had an educational career. There are men whose life-work has lain in other areas but who have at the same time a deep appreciation of learning and feel at home in the company of scholars. Such men, however, are most rarely available at the right age, and the mere fact of eminence in another direction is itself no warrant whatever of eligibility here. Second, they may choose a man with the thought uppermost in their mind that his financial connections and his own business standing will enable him to redeem the institution from its usual financial straits. No one would deny that this is an important consideration, but the price is too high where intrinsic fitness to preside over a company of scholars is at all doubtful. Thirdly—and this is the most deadly of all sins against an institution of higher learning—a board in its efforts to control the faculty may appoint as president a man who will be subservient to its will, with little regard to qualifications of leadership or of scholarship. There is strong evidence to suggest that this attitude has at some time prevailed on the boards of some state universities, particularly in certain areas of the country. It is clear that no graver blow could be struck by a board at the cause of academic freedom. A less heinous but still a grievous offense is to appoint a man primarily because of his friendship with some members of the board or, in the case of the state university, in order to confer a reward on a worthy politician.

It is hardly necessary to add that many boards, and particularly those of colleges and universities of high standing, take their responsibilities very seriously and would never stoop to the practices mentioned under our third head. They occur only where boards are constituted of men who have no understanding of the life of the campus and no devotion to the spirit of learning.

The choice of a president is certainly no easy matter, as many boards have found. Besides a broad devotion to learning he requires high administrative capacity. He must be apt in public relations, have a good presence, and be an effective speaker. He must be willing to turn aside from his former interests—something the true scholar finds hard to do— and give himself entirely to an endlessly exacting round of duties. Too many boards are anxious, instead, to secure a "sound" man, one who does not entertain ideas or cultivate habits that might offend any important group.

The most frequent choice is an academic administrator who, if he is not already a president elsewhere, is a dean or acting president or vice-president or other officer, drawn roughly in the same proportion either from the same institution or from some other. Exceptionally, this administrator may have had no professorial experience, but nearly always he is or has been a faculty member. A study made a number of years ago showed that of 300 college and university presidents 149 had faculty experience and that 68 more were active faculty members, frequently department heads. Of the remainder, 27 were clergymen, 12 business executives, 22 were in public service, national or local, and 12 were superintendents of schools, leaving a small number drawn from other fields.[3] A survey of 80 important institutions brought out the interesting fact that the presidents of 9 of them had had no teaching experience while 11 had only from one to three years. There were 17 who had experience in private enterprise, 12 who had been in public service, and 12 in the teaching or practice of law.[4]

The president brings before his board the proposals and resolutions of the various faculty divisions and of any general faculty council. He submits to them the budget prepared, with or without the direct aid of the faculty, by the administration. He lays before them any important problems or issues that arise, including cases concerning academic freedom. It is for him to explain these various matters to a body that must finally pass on them but often has little enough familiarity with their nature. Any board that trusts its president, and as a matter of course the boards of the most reputed universities, will readily accept purely educational proposals submitted in the name of the faculty or faculties concerned.

Since the board is not itself composed of educators, the quality of

[3] R. M. Hughes, "A Study of University and College Presidents," *School and Society,* LI (March, 1940), 317–20.

[4] Survey made by Joan Moravek, research assistant on the American Academic Freedom Project.

leadership is all the more important in a president. His own success and the advancement of his institution will depend largely on his ability to give his board a lively sense of the values of higher education. It should be for him to interpret to its members the role of the faculty and the primary importance of the freedom of teaching and of fearless inquiry. There is reason to fear that too many presidents do not succeed in doing so. In one instance, where a board made a ruling that occasioned widespread faculty revolt as being a direct attack on their educational autonomy, the chairman of the board intimated to the writer that he and his colleagues had been completely surprised by the faculty reaction. The president had failed in his responsibility to understand his faculty and to convey their sentiments to the board. In the crowded agenda of board meetings, appropriate opportunities for the fulfillment of this task may be hard to come by, but the task itself is essential and there can be no doubt that were it more generally accomplished the distance that too often separates faculty from board would be reduced and the cause of academic freedom would be advanced.[5] For there is in this country no greater obstacle to that cause than the failure of governing boards to appreciate its meaning and its service.

On the other hand, the board may be of such a caliber that the wisest and most persuasive of presidents must fail in his efforts to maintain educational standards. This is the penalty we pay for a system under which, all too frequently, educational considerations do not enter into the appointment of board members. What headway, for example, could a president have made with the board of Fairmont State College during recent disturbances there or with the board of the University of Texas at various times in its history? Under similar conditions many presidents have gladly welcomed a call elsewhere or have been so frustrated that anyhow they have resigned when they have not been "eased out" or actually dismissed.

The most notorious recent case was the forced resignation of President George D. Stoddard of the University of Illinois after a six-to-three vote of "no confidence" by his board. In the judgment of his faculty and generally of educators throughout the country, Stoddard had proved an excellent administrator, constantly seeking, in the face of

[5] How rarely the task is accomplished is emphasized by President Henry G. Harman of Drake University in his statement, "Effective Organization of the President's Office for University Service," *Proceedings of the Institute for Administrative Officers of Higher Institutions,* Vol. XIX (1947).

opposition from his board, to uphold and advance academic standards. We shall have occasion later on to refer to his firm stand in a controversy concerning the School of Commerce at that university. One of the counts against him was that he had taken an important part in the development of UNESCO! The board told him, when he returned from a Paris meeting of that institution in 1950, that he had better attend to his proper business. Another source of friction was the curious Krebiozen affair. A cancer drug named "Krebiozen" was taken up by Dr. Andrew C. Ivy, vice-president of the university and head of the university's Medical, Dental, and Pharmacy Schools, who sought to advance research on it at the university. This drug was branded as useless by the American Medical Association and the American Cancer Society, and Dr. Ivy was temporarily suspended by the Chicago Medical Society as acting contrary to medical ethics by "promoting a secret drug." President Stoddard under these conditions denied university facilities for further research on it.

The resolution of "no confidence" was moved by "Red" Grange, the famous ex-footballer, an alumnus but not a graduate of the university— his scholastic grades at the university were, to put it softly, minimal. A perhaps sufficient evidence of the quality of the board is the fact that its chairman, Park Livingston, published thereafter in the *Chicago Tribune* a series of charges against Stoddard, among them a statement made on the authority of a member of the legislature that he had harbored at the institution "fifty reds, pinks, and socialists." When challenged to name the "reds," the legislator in question retreated and said that if they were not reds they were at least "ultra-liberals"!

In this cursory survey we have not dwelt on the fact that, whatever and however numerous may be the tasks that fall to the president of a privately maintained university, his confrere of the state university has an additional load to carry, arising out of his relationship to the state legislature and the political system in general. Here a special combination of diplomacy and firmness is called for. We shall touch on this subject in our chapter on political controls. The problems that beset the head of a state institution vary in magnitude with the particular climate of opinion that prevails in the area. Above all, he has the task of protecting academic freedom against a number of indirect as well as direct attacks. Among the things he must chiefly guard against is the erosion of scholarly standards through compliance with suggestions or requests that come from important politicians or from politically influential sources. Wherever these standards are undermined, academic freedom is also insecure. Sometimes the requests are made by people who are more concerned with the athletic standing of the institution than with its educational integrity. Sometimes they take the form of nominations of unqualified persons to administrative or even to teaching positions. "In one of our most outstanding state universities . . . the president had to warn a legislative committee that they could not make a broken-down politician the dean of the school of agriculture without a change in the presidency of the university as well." [6]

What makes such requests so embarrassing is that there is often an implicit threat that any serious resistance to them may have adverse effects when it comes to the annual vote on the university's budget. The really skillful president knows how to conciliate and to persuade without sacrificing standards or goals, and there have been and are today some fine examples of this kind of leadership. But occasionally the intransigence of dominant groups is such that the president must choose between his office and his honor. At the same time, we must admit that there are a few examples of presidents who have yielded only too readily. A president of this type can easily rationalize his subservience by claiming he is acting for the welfare of his institution as a whole. The president of one state university declared to the writer that had he known in advance that a certain educator who had somewhat radical (but entirely noncommunist) views had been invited to speak on the campus, he would have prohibited his appearance. The speaker in question was objected to by a part of the local press. The president emphasized the point that this was damaging to the welfare of the institution. In fact, he went on to say, if that speaker had visited the university some months earlier, "it might have cost us three million dollars."

The attitude thus exhibited is unhappily not so rare. Another manifestation of it appears in the following statement by the former president of two Mid-Western universities: "Boards are made up chiefly of conservative men and women. They are sensitive to criticism regarding radical statements or actions by the faculty. The writer believes the

[6] J. Hugh Jackson, "The Private University in the History of American Education," *Proceedings of the Western College Association* (1942–1943).

able president will see that such persons are not appointed to the faculty." [7]

In other words, when the competent faculty group nominates as a colleague anyone who might be deemed "radical" by some members of his board—and we shall see in the course of this work how freely that epithet can be applied to anyone who is the least bit nonconformist—the "able president" will avoid trouble by vetoing the recommendation. Intellectual independence would wither in our institutions of higher learning if all presidents followed the advice of this one.

[7] Raymond M. Hughes, in F. L. McVey and R. M. Hughes, *Problems of College and University Administration* (Iowa State College Press, 1952), p. 54.

VII: THE FACULTY

Teachers must fulfil their functions by precept and practice. By the very atmosphere which they generate, they must be exemplars of open-mindedness and free inquiry. They cannot carry out their great and noble task if the conditions for the practice of a responsible and critical mind are denied them.

FELIX FRANKFURTER

THE UNIVERSITY exists to pursue knowledge and to impart it. It is the faculty that carries out this mission. It is the faculty that needs academic freedom and best knows what difference it makes. If the control of educational policies were in the hands of the faculty, academic freedom would on the whole be secure, save for minor infractions that can best be dealt with by its own discipline, conjoined with that of its administrative officers.

In saying so we are not at all suggesting that the whole management of university affairs should be assigned to the faculty, thus doing away with lay boards. There are good reasons why this should not be so, not only in state institutions but in the others as well. A university faculty is exceedingly heterogeneous. Each department and each school always wants more—more staff, more equipment, more courses—and each is apt to magnify the relative significance of its own field and its own contribution. For this and other reasons the disposition of the budget—not to speak of the raising of it—calls for some general perspective that other than faculty members might be more likely to exhibit. Moreover, were the allocation of the budget left solely to the faculty, it would tend to breed dissensions and jealousies, and the larger departments and schools might become too dominating. As it is now, the budget demands of each department and division are screened by the administration, but the board is back of it as a final control, and not un-

The quotation at the head of this chapter is from Justice Frankfurter's concurrent opinion in the Oklahoma Oath Statute Case, December 15, 1952.

commonly one of its tasks is to insist upon the necessity of having a budget that does not run the institution into debt, or deeper into debt.

There is also a considerable amount of general direction and administration in connection with endowments, properties, equipment, and a variety of other problems in which men of business experience and executive ability can be of great service.

But there is an intrinsic area of educational policy that should be the exclusive prerogative of the faculty, as we have already pointed out. Broadly speaking, what they teach and how they teach, what they investigate and how they investigate, what books they prescribe and what studies they assign, what they add to the curriculum and what they withdraw from the curriculum, these and all kindred matters fall properly within the area of professional competence and should be determined only by the educators themselves and by their committees and councils. This indeed is the practice of American universities at their best—we are speaking here of institutions of higher learning, not of schools for younger students. The statement of former President William Rainey Harper of the University of Chicago holds true of other great institutions. "It is a firmly established policy of the trustees," he said, "that the responsibility for the settlement of educational questions rests with the faculty . . . In no instance has the action of the faculty on educational questions been disapproved." [1] Wherever this principle prevails, academic freedom keeps it company.

This happy situation is unfortunately far from being attained in a considerable proportion of American colleges and universities. Infringements of proper faculty autonomy vary from relatively mild interventions, such as the demand, made occasionally in state institutions, that the faculty set up some additional program or supply some particular service, contrary to the judgment of the scholars in the field, to gross arrogations of control over educational processes. The board of the University of Texas has been one of the most notorious in this respect, at times overruling both president and faculty. Thus in 1943 it removed the novel *U S A* by John Dos Passos from the supplementary reading list of the English Department, and frequently in the same period it rejected research projects in the social sciences that had been promoted by the faculty and approved by the president—not to mention

[1] From his Decennial Report of 1902.

a whole series of other interferences with the regular operations of the institution.

The lack of proper distinction between the responsibility of the board and that of the faculty is accentuated by the lack of effective communication between them. According to a report of the American Association of University Professors 176 out of 228 institutions had no plan for exchange of views between faculties and boards.[2] Even in some of the others the mode of communication is limited to the sporadic meeting of a faculty-trustee committee on special occasions. Otherwise, the vast majority of institutions assume that the president sufficiently serves the purpose of expressing to the board the sentiments of his faculty. The assumption, as has been shown in the preceding chapter, is a precarious one.

Various measures have been proposed to bring the faculty into closer contact with the governing board, and some of these have been tried out. One approach is directed to making the board more broadly representative. We have seen that some state boards require the representation of particular categories, such as agriculturalist and labor members and women. In one or two state surveys of higher education the recommendation has been made that institutional faculties should be entitled to offer a slate of candidates from which a certain number of board members would be selected.

Another method is the provision of occasions where faculty representatives and board members can meet to discuss matters of common interest. These occasions may be informal or they may be provided through joint committees or councils. If they are sporadic and infrequent, they are not likely to be very effective. Nor can one lay much stress— though certainly such contacts are in themselves desirable—on visits of board members to various parts of the institution they control, still less on the device of having a faculty man or two show up at a special meeting of the board. Another way of establishing some kind of contact is illustrated by a practice recently developed at Rockford College, Illinois, where a group of business and professional men called the Rockford College Board of Counselors meets periodically with the president and the secretary of the college and the trustees to discuss matters of

[2] Report of Committee T, on "The Place and Function of Faculties in College and University Government," *Bulletin of the American Association of University Professors,* Vol. XXXIV (Spring, 1948).

faculty-board relations, including questions of academic freedom. We are informed by the former president of the college, Mary Ashby Cheek, that these discussions have been very helpful.

Regular faculty-trustee committees are more significant. Various experiments of this kind are in operation. Some institutions, including Reed College, Wellesley College, and Brown University, have committees composed of faculty members and trustees. Variations of this method are also operative at the University of Denver, Hobart College, and Occidental College. Other institutions have an arrangement by which faculty committees meet regularly or occasionally with the board, as is the case at Amherst College, Mount Holyoke, the University of Washington, the University of Wisconsin, Vassar College, and elsewhere. Capital University has a plan whereby board members attend faculty meetings and vice versa. At Bennington College they have devised a system under which trustees, faculty, and students meet together through the respective Educational Policy Committees. We note in passing that leading women's colleges appear to be setting an example in the establishment of good faculty-trustee relationships.

These devices are serviceable so far as they go. Anything that helps to lessen the distance between educators and trustees is to be commended. Whether they are adequate is another question. They still leave the faculty without a voice in the final decision-making process. Matters of vital moment to them may still be determined without any knowledge of it on their part. Hence, especially in recent years, there has been a movement for direct faculty representation.[3] As long ago as 1911 Professor J. McKeen Cattell polled 299 leading men of science on the subject, of whom 233 were in favor of faculty participation in the direction of institutions of learning. A number of colleges now have some faculty members on their boards, including Haverford, Roosevelt, and Sarah Lawrence. The Wellesley faculty elects a member of the board, but so far has chosen an ex-colleague or an outsider. The highly experimental Black Mountain College has a Board of Fellows wholly composed of faculty-elected faculty members. In several other institu-

[3] On this subject see Ralph E. Himstead, "Faculty Participation in Institutional Government," in Institute for Administrative Officers of Higher Institutions, *Proceedings,* ed. by John Dale Russell, Vol. XVII (University of Chicago Press, 1946); and Paul W. Ward, "The Role of Faculties in College and University Government," *Bulletin of the American Association of University Professors,* XXXIV (Spring, 1948), 58–60.

tions—Cornell, Bryn Mawr, and Barnard—one or more faculty members sit with the boards, but have no voting privileges.[4]

At this point we may include the modern experiment known as "community government," variant examples and degrees of which are to be found at the following colleges: Antioch (Ohio), Bennington (Vermont), George Williams (Illinois), Talladega (Alabama), and Bard (New York). (The special feature is that administrators, faculty representatives, and student representatives are combined into a single body for the discussion and, within certain limits, the determination of college policies. In its full development this system integrates the governing board into the entire framework of the institution, instead of its remaining semidetached like the "governor" on certain types of machine. An unusual example of this development is provided by Antioch College. The following statement regarding its organizational structure may be of interest.

Although the Board of Trustees has the final legal responsibility and authority in the institution, the focal point for the formation of current policy in the College is the Administrative Council, which first appeared in 1926 as an informal advisory group which the president appointed. Since 1930 the Council has been provided for in the charter of the College, which prescribes that there shall be ten members on the Council, to be determined and elected as the faculty shall authorize. At present the provision is for seven faculty and three student members of whom the president, the dean of administration, and the community manager (a student) are members ex officio. The other two students and two of the faculty are elected each year by the whole community through proportional representation; the remaining three members of the faculty are elected by the faculty. After three years' service on the Council, an elected member must remain off a year before he is eligible for reelection.

The Administrative Council has the unique power to elect six members of the nineteen on the Board of Trustees, and in joint election with the Board is empowered to choose the president. If the Board and the Council fail to agree on a president, the Board may, by the same vote that is required to amend the charter, elect the president.

The Council is also the planning (executive) committee of the faculty. All major matters of College policy—such as the current building program—come to it for review and decision, or originate there. It passes on all questions of personnel. It counsels with the president concerning College finances and

---

[4] Information obtained from W. H. Cowley, "Academic Government," *Educational Forum*, XV (January, 1951), 217–29; Catalogue of Sarah Lawrence College; Certificate of Incorporation of Black Mountain College, Article 8 as amended; announcement by Barnard College; and letters received from the various institutions.

passes on the budget. It appoints faculty policy-making and administrative committees to handle admissions, student counseling, curriculum, and examinations, as well as to establish the policies of the co-operative plan.[5]

We cite this example not as a model that other institutions can or should follow but as a notable contrast to the prevalent system. We are informed by the administration that "an unusual degree of confidence exists" between the Council and the Board.

To the outsider it seems peculiar that the most highly trained profession—and the trainers of all other professions—should be so totally excluded from any share in the direct government of their own institutions. In other positions of importance and public responsibility, such as governmental commissions, arbitration boards, foundations, this profession is significantly represented; in the control of their own institutions, with rare exceptions, they are unrepresented. In *Who's Who in America* we find that educators constitute roughly twenty percent of the entries. But this type of distinction is not thought to be relevant for the guidance of educational institutions. There is a fair representation of alumni on governing boards, but not of those who have educated them.

What is perhaps even more surprising is that some university administrators and educationalists have strongly opposed faculty representation. Thus the late President Draper of the University of Illinois declared roundly, and rather patronizingly: "The business of university faculties is teaching. It is not legislation and it is not administration— certainly not beyond the absolute necessities." And he added this remarkable statement: "It is true that teachers have great fun legislating, but it is not quite certain that, outside their specialties, they will ever come to conclusions, or that, if they do, their conclusions will stand. The main advantage of it is the relaxation and dissipation they get out of it." [6] The same negative conclusion, without the sarcasm, is reached by George G. Bogert, who writes that university government "must follow the business corporation model, with trustees in the position of directors and with administrators, teachers, and research workers as employees." [7] He proceeds, however, to say, that it should nevertheless

[5] Algo D. Henderson and Dorothy Hall, *Antioch College: Its Design for Liberal Education* (New York, 1946), pp. 206–7.

[6] Cited by George G. Bogert, "Historical Survey of Faculty Participation in the United States," in Institute for Administrative Officers of Higher Institutions, *Proceedings*, ed. by John Dale Russell, XVII (University of Chicago Press, 1946), 114.

[7] *Ibid.*, p. 118.

be a partnership of equals—as though the relation of directors to employees was ever such. In the same work Ernest Cadman Colwell makes various suggestions for communications between faculty and dean or president but regards these methods as satisfactory without any faculty participation on boards.[8]

With respect to the matter under consideration, there is no proper analogy between an institution of learning and a business corporation. In the latter the top management are experienced in the business they conduct. While the board of directors may contain one or two members chosen for their connections or their prestige—qualities that here have also business value—at least the great majority of the members have been appointed because of their wide experience and established competence in the area in which they operate. Various members of the board are also executive officers engaged full time in the operations of the business. But the trustees of our institutions of higher learning are not experts in education in the sense in which the directors of a business corporation are experts in their own field. We do not suggest that university trustees who lack this expertness may not nevertheless be admirably qualified for their special function as trustees, *if that function is properly delineated and integrally related to the work of the educators.* But this integral relationship is surely more difficult to achieve without the presence of educators on the board. It is elementary that the direction of any great or complex undertaking needs the participation of those who are familiar with its conditions and with its needs. Higher education is certainly an undertaking of this kind. Here is an area of endless complexity, endless growth, and endless change. Its problems are as great as its potentialities. If expertness is needed anywhere, it is needed here—not the *expertise* of the mere specialist but the maturity of comprehension that must be sought in the collective judgment of the faculty and in the particular qualities of those whom its members themselves choose as their representatives, spokesmen, or leaders.

It is hardly possible for anyone who seriously reviews the situation to fail to observe that the potential contribution of the faculty to the guidance and advancement of higher education in this country is quite inadequately evoked and is generally denied the opportunity to express itself in the higher ranges of policy making.

[8] *Ibid.,* pp. 126–28.

Nor is it reasonable to claim that the sentiment of the faculty is conveyed through deans and other administrative officers, as well as directly, to the president, who in turn presents it to his board. We have already touched on this point and here will be content to cite a leading authority on the problems of academic administration.

I am mindful of the arguments *pro* and *con* as to the wisdom of faculty representation on the board. But one thing seems to me clear; it is less than accurate to assume that the president can and will voice *faculty* sentiment in board deliberations. He can no doubt report it, if some effort has been made to find out what it is. Hence, I hazard the prophecy that within ten or fifteen years it will become a far more usual practice than now to have direct faculty representation on trustee bodies. And the benefits of this, I believe, will be substantial both in trustee discussions and in faculty understanding. I do not say that such a measure will of itself break down the barrier or gulf which so often exists between trustees and faculty; but it should be a gesture of some benefit in that direction.[9]

We dwell on these considerations not with the object of presenting a case for any form of academic government as such but solely because of their relevance to the problem of vindicating academic freedom against the menaces to which it is subjected in various parts of the country. The relation between the prevailing scheme of control and the not infrequent violations of faculty integrity in the quest of knowledge is not hard to find. For so long as the faculty is denied any participation in academic government on its highest level, so long conditions are likely to arise that are definitely inimical to academic freedom.

In the first place this denial tends to confirm the relatively low status the educator holds within the occupational hierarchy. If educators are preeminently the kind of people who need to be governed by others, if they are not judged competent to share in the government of their particular institutions, this subordination must react upon the popular esteem for the services they render to society. In the second place this exclusion creates that distance and lack of understanding between faculty and board which so often has unhappy consequences for the liberty of teaching and research.

The views we have here set forth are those of the staff of this study. We recognize that well-informed opinion is divided on the subject, and this holds for our own Panel of Advisers. Various arguments are brought

[9] Ordway Tead, *Trustees, Teachers, Students* (University of Utah Press, 1951), p. 7.

forward by those who reject our position, as follows. The faculty is already represented on the board by the president of the institution. No one should be on a governing board which has control over his own promotion, his salary and other emoluments. A faculty is a group of very diverse specialists and "it is almost impossible for a man who has been concerned with one branch of learning to be objective about it and those other branches of learning that he may consider as rivals." Besides, "it is very doubtful wisdom to have members of a faculty present during discussions that may affect the disposition of the university's funds." [10] They cannot be expected to be dispassionate or impartial about it.

We do not find these reasons so cogent as those that sustain the contrary position, nor do we see why such arguments should be conclusive with respect to educators when they are not applied in other areas of responsibility—the membership of the boards of industrial corporations, for example. Perhaps, however, the best argument on the other side is the general experience of the colleges that have adopted faculty representation. The writer has a fairly wide acquaintanceship with such insituations abroad and has not heard any objections raised on any of these grounds. He has also communicated with the presidents of the colleges in this country that are now experimenting with faculty representation, asking specifically how far such objections have been confirmed in practice. In every instance the response has been highly favorable. President Millicent C. McIntosh of Barnard College reports that the plan "has been very constructive from the point of view of both the trustees and the faculty." President Gilbert F. White of Haverford College says: "About one fact I feel entirely clear. That is that faculty representation on the board has not in any respect been harmful. Personally I feel that it has been an excellent provision, and that it is a provision which should be generally adopted across the country." Among its other advantages President Edward J. Sparling of Roosevelt College mentions that "it does stimulate faculty thinking about the financial implications of educational policies and board thinking about the educational implications of financial policies." President Harold Taylor of Sarah Lawrence strongly supports the practice, seeing only one difficulty it creates, viz., that a faculty representative may make a different report on the proceedings in controversial areas from that delivered by

---

[10] Quotations from a letter from a distinguished trustee of Yale, written by way of comment on our position.

the president—but he adds that there are ways of meeting this difficulty. President Margaret Clapp of Wellesley holds that, while in this college the good relations already established between board and faculty make representation less essential, "in principle it is highly desirable." President Deane W. Malott of Cornell states that "faculty representation has worked out very well indeed."

What most concerns us here is that several of these responses refer to the improvement brought about in the understanding between board and faculty and particularly state that representation is beneficial when questions involving academic freedom arise. While we do not ourselves regard it as of itself enough to close the gap that so often exists between trustees and educators, we submit that it definitely helps to diminish it and may well prepare the way for other approaches to a more complete solution of the greatest weakness in our present pattern of academic government. We note, for example, that in the institutions which have adopted faculty representation there is also a tendency to set up faculty-board committees on important issues.

Finally, let us point out that our main argument in favor of faculty representation can be satisfied *even if no present member of the staff of the institution is placed on the board.* While on other grounds we find it preferable that members of the faculty most directly concerned should be eligible, yet so far as the assurance of academic freedom is concerned, this end is equally well advanced by the presence of educators drawn from other institutions. This provision cuts away the basis of the various objections we have mentioned, and where it has been tried it has worked notably well. For example, Dean Frederick Woodbridge of Columbia was a most valued trustee of Amherst, and Monroe E. Deutsch of the University of California has given fine service to Mills College.

Certain broad conclusions we have now reached will be considerably reinforced as we dwell on particular problems and refer to particular cases.

VIII: THE ALUMNI AND THE PUBLIC

Never overestimate the information of the American people. But never underestimate their intelligence.

RAYMOND CLAPPER

As ACADEMIC GOVERNMENT in the United States was taking on the typical pattern we sketched at the outset, it was natural that former students should frequently be cast in the role of trustees. There was also a movement toward formalized participation by alumni in institutional affairs. This movement was advanced in two ways. One was the setting up of regulations, sometimes as the result of concessions made by boards to bodies of alumni, assigning a specific percentage of the membership of boards to alumni elected or nominated as such through their own organizations. This method has been adopted particularly in the nonstate universities and colleges, such as Princeton, Columbia, Amherst, and Dartmouth. In such institutions it is usually supplementary to the method of cooption. The other way has been the closer organization of alumni in the form of alumni councils that effectively bring their views before the trustees.[1] Some universities have again made arrangements for special visiting committees of alumni, which concern themselves with particular areas of the institution, especially the more professional schools such as medicine, law, engineering, and business administration. Princeton has in operation a successful plan for conferences on subjects of broad importance which bring together in a new kind of reunion the alumni of its School of Graduate Studies.

Under such conditions it is not surprising that the boards of more than a few nonstate institutions are predominantly composed of alumni members. Harvard is an outstanding case, since its Board of Overseers

[1] For the character of alumni councils see W. H. Cowley, "The Government and Administration of Higher Education," *Journal of the American Association of Collegiate Registrars,* XXII (July, 1947), 477–91. On the role of the alumni see Monroe E. Deutsch, *The College From Within* (University of California Press, 1952), Chapter 24.

has since 1866 been constituted almost entirely of Harvard alumni.

Recently pleas have been made for alumni control in a different sense. It has been claimed that the alumni as such have, and should exercise, the right to determine the educational policies of the institution. This claim raises some interesting questions.

Let us take the Harvard situation. Its Board of Overseers is composed of alumni, but that does not mean that Harvard University is run by its alumni. Still less does it mean that the educational policies of Harvard are dictated by its alumni. The Board of Overseers does virtually nothing about educational policies. Like other high-ranking universities, Harvard entrusts to its faculty the major voice in the specification of its educational procedures. Furthermore, when particular alumni are nominated or elected to the Board of Overseers, they are not chosen by virtue of their representativeness as alumni but because of their interest in and qualifications for this office.

The alumni of any large university are very numerous and highly heterogeneous. It is doubtful that there is any such thing as a representative alumnus. Every year a new crop of alumni leave the halls of learning, having pursued during their course of four years or so one or another of a great variety of programs with more or less edification or success. For some it has been mainly the gateway to a career; for others it has been also worth while intrinsically. When they leave, their ways of life go widely apart. To many the sense of the university, in whichever of its aspects they once knew it, grows dim or takes on a merely sentimental aspect. When they return for a tenth-year reunion, or a twenty-fifth, or, with luck, a fiftieth, they know little or nothing of what now happens within its walls. It is indeed the few who have had both the opportunity and the desire to keep in touch with educational affairs. Consequently, alumni reunions are less conspicuous for the educational content of the discourses than for the revival of old anecdotes, reminiscences of escapades, characterizations of departed worthies of the campus and retold tales of the football field. With the lapse of time the bonds of common interest that endure to unite the alumni are often only a lively concern for the success of the institution in the realm of sport and a pervading sense of the gray glory of the grand old walls.

In so saying we do not depreciate the importance of the alumni for the well-being of the university. They can be, and not infrequently are, a great source of its strength. They help to maintain its continuity, they are of primary value in giving it roots in the community. For the privately endowed institutions they are an ever-necessary financial support, and for the publicly supported institutions they are often very influential in assuring that the legislature will vote funds reasonably adequate to meet educational needs. More generally, alumni can play a considerable part in upholding and advancing the public relations of their institution. Under good guidance alumni associations can also be valuable defenders of the intrinsic values for which the university stands —though their record in this respect is two-sided. Thus against the recent infringements of academic freedom at Ohio State University the leadership and the official organ of the alumni organization took a strong and most helpful stand.[2]

In this connection we should mention also the excellent services rendered by a number of alumni journals. Among those whose contributions we have noticed, besides the *Ohio State University Monthly,* are the *Princeton Alumni Weekly,* the *City College Alumnus,* the *Harvard Alumni Bulletin,* the *Lafayette Alumnus,* the *Brown Alumni Monthly,* the *Sooner Magazine,* and notably also the inclusive *AAC News,* organ of the American Alumni Council.

This recognition of the services alumni render is, however, a very different matter from the acceptance of the role for which the alumni as such are cast by some recent advocates of their "rights." The claim thus made is that the alumni ought to determine what their successors, the present generation of students, are taught, and particularly that the content and above all the doctrinal slant of the teaching should be brought into accord with their ideas.

This is the burden of a book devoted to the exposure of the "superstition of academic freedom." [3] Its author directs an assault against Yale for departing from the ways of the fathers. Its teachers of economics are guilty of gross heresies against the principle of free enterprise, and many of its professors have abandoned Christianity and take a godless line. So he summons the alumni to action and bids them purge the university of those miseducators who have strayed so far from the true path.

We have been referring to the important services alumni can render to the cause of academic freedom, and here it is well worth noting that the

[2] See the *Ohio State University Monthly,* Vol. XLIII (November 15, 1951).
[3] William F. Buckley, Jr., *God and Man at Yale* (Chicago, 1951).

Yale Alumni Magazine has exposed the fallacies and misrepresentations of Mr. Buckley and that an alumni committee has refuted the charges he made against the faculty.

Let us listen to Max Eastman upholding the new definition of academic freedom. "Buckley's most original and challenging idea," he says, "is that essential freedom is the freedom of the customer to buy what he wants in the market. The alumni of a college who support it, and the parents who pay their children's tuition, are customers, and the commodity they are buying is education." He sums up as follows: "In the last analysis, academic freedom must mean the freedom of men and women to supervise the educational activities and aims of the schools they oversee and support." [4]

There is an unhappy lack of clarity in these statements. To begin with, academic freedom has undergone a strange transformation. It is no more the freedom of the scholar to inquire and to teach. That freedom becomes a "superstition." It is now the freedom of the non-scholar to dictate to the scholar what and how he must teach. It is no longer a freedom inside the academy but outside it. The scholar is still perfectly free, or free enough, according to the Buckley doctrine. He is free to go elsewhere.

The freedom of the scholar becomes the freedom of the alumni to "supervise" the scholar. But even this proposition is unhappily vague. We have pointed out that the alumni are numerous and highly diversified. They are not a compact body with one viewpoint or one set of values. In many instances, where violations of academic freedom occur, the majority of the students have been on the side of the educators. Within a year or two many of these students themselves became part of the alumni body. In more than a few institutions the governing board itself is largely or mainly composed of alumni who have defended academic freedom against outside assaults. Is it the idea of the Buckley contingent that a poll be taken of all alumni to determine from time to time just what the content of, say, economic instruction should be or just what should be done about Professor X, who is alleged by someone to have shown leanings to "statism"? And if, say, fifty-five percent of those who take time off to answer the questionnaire want something done to change the situation or to discipline the professor, would that be enough?

[4] Max Eastman, "Buckley Versus Yale," *American Mercury*, LXXIII (December, 1951), 22–29.

Would any educator be allowed to carry on if his views found favor with only forty-five percent or thirty-five percent, or must all the faculty take a position that is full square with the views of whatever majority may emerge from a series of polling operations? The Buckley school ought to give us some information concerning the mechanics of the system of control to which they are committed.

Let us look now at the proposition that universities are the department stores of learning, offering a variety of subjects to the public. Since the customers do the paying, it is for them to decide not only what goods they want but also what styles they prefer. In one respect the analogy holds. Unless the public want and are willing to pay for higher education, the doors of the universities must close. And if there is no demand for this or that subject, there will be few or no teachers employed to expound it.

Beyond that point the analogy breaks down. Mr. Buckley's "most original and challenging idea" does not support the conclusion he and his supporters draw. Customers do not claim the right to dismiss the salesmen whose goods are not to their liking—they go elsewhere. There is no reason why any parent should send his son to Yale, if he does not approve of Yale's economics—which, incidentally, is on the whole on the conservative side—or of Yale's provision for religious instruction. Yale has plenty of "customers" who are very happy to take advantage of the "commodities" it offers.

Aside from this, however, the analogy is quite superficial. It is only in one quite limited area of the immense field of higher knowledge that even its proponents dare apply it. The man in the street would never claim that he should give orders to the physicist on how to teach the atomic theory or on how to run a cyclotron. He would never dream of suggesting to the botanist or the geologist or the chemist or the mathematician how he should go about his job. He would not think of instructing the engineer how he should allow for stresses or wind pressures. He would not ask the philosopher to change his method of interpreting Spinoza or the classical scholar to modify his views on the development of the hexameter.

But when it comes to economics, or social studies generally, or any subject that has a direct bearing on group values or group interests, the situation is entirely different. The demand that the scholar must reach conclusions in conformity with prevailing conceptions is as old as the quest for knowledge. In an earlier age the astronomer, the geologist, the biologist, were the particular victims, sometimes the martyrs, of this ban on discovery. More recently the evolutionist was forbbidden to teach a doctrine that did not chime with the Book of Genesis. Today it is the social scientist who is most exposed to attack. The customer does not prescribe the brand of physics he wants, but he is entitled, according to Mr. Buckley, to order and get the kind of economics he wants and to dismiss the economist who fails to meet the demand.

Observe that the progress of social knowledge, of all knowledge that touches directly on human affairs and human relationships, is thus rendered doubly difficult. In the first place there is the difficulty inherent in the subject matter. Like every other searcher after knowledge, the social scientist seeks to discover the connection between things. Why does the delinquency rate rise? Why are there more divorces in this area than in that? Why does this political party grow strong and this other one dwindle? How can a high level of employment be maintained? How can the business cycle be controlled? What are the major effects of this or that piece of legislation? What steps can be taken at a given time that are best calculated to diminish the danger of war? Numerous questions of this kind, of lesser or greater magnitude, questions that are of interest to every thoughtful citizen, challenge the social scientist. It is his business to study them. It is important that they should be studied. But the problems are complex and tangled and, while considerable light can be thrown on the situations with which they are concerned, solutions are never final. At best they are conclusions of the well-informed judgment, and judges will still differ. This is the way with all problems of policy or of strategy. But strategy is still necessary, and the more significant the problems, the more we need to be enlightened about them. Every social scientist who is worthy of the name seeks to learn and to enlighten, not to propagandize. And here he meets his second difficulty. For he works in an area in which it is hard to avoid bias, and as he strives to do so he is beset by influences and pressures that subtly or overtly would bring his conclusions into conformity with group interests. In this area then, perhaps more than in any other, it is essential, alike for the advancement of knowledge and for the wise direction of policy, that the accredited scholar be suffered to follow his own road, wherever it may lead, in the quest for truth. What the customer wants, often enough, is indoctrination.

What the scholar seeks is not so easy to attain—enlightenment. The type of alumni control advocated by Mr. Eastman and Mr. Buckley would put indoctrination first, with enlightenment a poor second. Happily, so far at least as the greater institutions of learning are concerned, the good sense of the alumni—their respect for the integrity of the university—saves them from responding to any such appeals.

The customer-commodity argument we have been refuting is sometimes made with reference not to the alumni but to the public at large. The public supports the college or university. In the case of state institutions they pay through taxes the major costs of their maintenance. Therefore, it is claimed, it is for the public to say how these institutions should be run. We find an argument of this kind put forward, in a somewhat ambiguous way, even by some educational groups. One such statement runs as follows: "The people have the right, through their duly elected representatives and within a given constitutional framework, to determine the policies of educational institutions which they support—whether independent, church-related, or state-supported." It is the function of the governing boards, the statement proceeds, as representing the public, to lay down the "broad policies" of these institutions.

A statement of this sort seems to imply that the public elects representatives to constitute governing boards; that it chooses them because they hold views concerning educational policy which the public, or the majority of the electors, approve; that the boards thus elected are in turn instructed or obligated to carry out the policies in question. These implications are not in accord with the manner in which governing boards are set up, even for those state universities where trustees are elected by popular vote. In any event, the formula that the governing board lays down the "broad policies" of the university is acceptable only if the range and limit of such policies are clearly specified.

The public may well claim the right to ensure that any institutions they support are properly organized to fulfill educational objectives and are efficiently directed. But when it comes to all matters bearing on educational standards and educational methods, we enter the area of professional competence. Only those who possess this competence are qualified to pass on such matters. What applies to educational institutions applies equally, say, to publicly supported museums, art galleries, institutes of technology, and training schools of various kinds. It is a false theory of democracy that speaks of the "right" of the people to prescribe to the expert how he should do his particular job. The man who buys shoes does not tell the shoemaker how to stitch leather.

But the danger of undue interference with educational standards does not come so much from the public at large as from special groups which claim to represent the public and which may, by meretricious appeal, succeed in obtaining enough votes to give them the necessary power. One authority who has for a long time devoted himself wholly to problems of academic freedom declares that "at no time in the history of higher education in the United States has the public as a whole sought to dominate the university." [5] Whether this conclusion needs to be qualified or not, it is sufficiently evident that the main threat to the integrity of educational standards comes from the drive of special interests of one kind or another.

The university serves the community. The service it renders is of inestimable value. It has a responsibility to the public at large as well as to its own students. Its responsibility extends as far as its capacity to serve. But this responsibility is betrayed, not fulfilled, if it suffers any bias or any influence to deflect it from the sincere pursuit of knowledge, if it yields in any way to the demands of aggressive groups that would turn education into an instrument of propagandism for their particular beliefs or their particular interests. Such demands are not more justified, but only more dangerous, when they are made in the name of the people or by its representatives. Only those who misconceive the meaning of democracy would claim that either consensus should move or the suffrage compel the university to swerve from the direction that the honest search for unbiased knowledge alone should determine. Its function and its first obligation must always be to educate alike the public and its own students, according to its own standards and in the light of its own ideals.

[5] Ralph E. Himstead, "Faculty Participation in Institutional Government," in Institute for Administrative Officers of Higher Education, *Proceedings*, XVII (University of Chicago Press, 1946), 139.

IX: POLITICAL CONTROLS

No one ought to meddle with the universities who does not know them well and love them.

ATTRIBUTED TO THOMAS ARNOLD OF RUGBY

Any adequate treatment of the ramifying subject of academic government would include not only certain varieties and complexities of regulation we here omit but also some special features to which we have made no allusion. There is, for example, an increasing amount of what one writer calls "super-academic government." [1] A particular form of it is the accrediting agency, an organization which undertakes to rate college and universities in terms of some set of scholarly standards and which, though of a voluntary character, is widely recognized and influential. A large number of organizations of this sort have arisen.[2] Any comprehensive study would include also deviant or exceptional cases, such as those where the student body participates directly in academic government. The highly experimental Black Mountain College, for example, has a "student moderator," elected by the student body, who sits on the all-faculty Board of Fellows. But our concern here is solely with the impact on the freedom of teaching and learning of the major controls exercised in or

[1] W. H. Cowley, "Academic Government," *Educational Forum,* XV (January, 1951), 217–29.

[2] These agencies are broadly of two kinds, those established on a regional basis by the colleges themselves and independent agencies that attempt to prescribe standards for particular fields of training, such as medicine, law, engineering, dentistry, and music. The latter have greatly proliferated in recent times. In consequence, a National Commission on Accrediting was set up. Its secretary, President Cloyd H. Marvin of George Washington University, reported that these "independent" agencies were interfering with faculty freedom, that too often their standards were quantitative and superficial, that they were forcing colleges to sacrifice cultural objectives for professional ones and generally creating a "guild pattern" in our educational system. Accordingly, the commission recommended that all accrediting should be left to the six regional agencies and should be done on the basis of institutional qualifications taken as a whole (*New York Times,* January 9, 1952). For a summary account of these agencies see the excellent report, *Higher Education in the Forty-Eight States,* issued in 1952 by the Council of State Governments, Chicago, Illinois, pp. 55–59.

over the colleges and universities of the United States, and with that in view we turn to the one highly important group of controls we have still to deal with, the controls imposed by political authorities of one kind or another. It is unfortunate, and a little surprising, that no serious attempt has been made to explore this subject, although the American Civil Liberties Union has made overtures to various educational associations in the hope that one of them would undertake the task.

We may broadly divide political controls into federal, state, and local. For our immediate purpose their nature may be sufficiently indicated by a conspectus of the main ways in which federal and state authorities operate in this sphere.

The aspects of federal control that chiefly interest us here arise, first, from measures and processes concerned with matters of security or again of "loyalty," and, second, from the conditions associated with federal grants made to institutions of learning for special purposes or services.

It is unfortunate on various counts, and not least for the cause of academic freedom, that issues of security and of loyalty cannot be more clearly separated. The question of security is involved only where the scholar works on "classified" problems, in the special areas where research is developed of a kind that the proper authorities adjudge should be kept secret because of its potential military or strategic significance. Where the line should be drawn must remain a matter of judgment. Since a major objective is to keep this knowledge from being conveyed to communist circles, it is obviously important that the candidate for clearance should be proven to have no communist leanings. But with the prevailing climate of opinion, the scrutiny employed to secure this end is not infrequently of a sort to deter the scholar who is in any respect nonconformist or of an independent turn of mind. Such nonconformity becomes suspect, even where it is associated with an entire aversion to communism. To have unorthodox views of any variety subjects the holder to suspicion and even to a kind of inquisition. Thus many of the ablest scholars shy away from the protracted processes of screening that lie between them and acceptance for work in this area. This attitude was illustrated by the falling off of applicants for postdoctoral fellowships awarded through the National Research Council. Funds were provided for such fellowships by the Atomic Energy Commission. There were thirty fellowships in the physical sciences and twenty in the biological sciences. In 1949, when no clearance was involved, the applications were ample. In the following year, when the work became wholly classified and clearance was required, there were only twelve applicants for the fifty fellowships.[3]

The requirement of clearance extends far beyond the area of classified research. It is entirely proper that candidates for governmental jobs should be subjected to careful scrutiny with respect to their trustworthiness, and in the light of the notorious development of communist tactics of infiltration we must have considerable sympathy with those whose duty it is to pass on the *bona fides* of applicants. But the prevalent fear of making a mistake in this respect leads people to confuse conformism with loyalty and to regard initiative as an index of instability. Thus an atmosphere is created unfavorable to the true scholar, to the spirit of open-minded investigation that is certainly as important in the service of government as within the walls of the academy.

Ambiguities and confusions perhaps inevitably arise where clearance on a wide scale has to be instituted as a safeguard against communist wiles. The situation is much aggravated, however, by the clamors and charges of politicians and partisans who trade on popular suspicion and fear. Considerable sections of the public are not educated enough to appraise these men. Thus a new kind of vigilantism is bred. It bears far more on loyal citizens of independent mind than on the few who have subversive intentions. The latter are usually too well schooled to commit indiscretions or to express unpopular opinions. Vigilantism is not vigilance but often is its enemy.

The screening of scholars who may be called on to work on classified problems or generally who are candidates for governmental positions is dictated essentially by considerations of security. The loyalty hunts presided over by the House Committee on Un-American Activities and the various nonjudicial state bodies that have followed its example are another matter altogether, and their impact on academic freedom has been much more serious and pervasive. But this subject receives treatment in other parts of our investigation.

We must, however, call attention here to one incident which ominously reveals how a body like the House Committee, if not restrained, might come to exercise direct control over educational standards. This was the action of its chairman, Representative John S. Wood, requesting more

[3] Philip N. Powers, "National Security and Freedom in Higher Education," *College and University*, Vol. XXVI, No. 1 (October, 1950).

than seventy colleges and universities to submit lists of their textbooks and supplementary readings for the year 1948–1949. This request arose out of representations made by the California and Georgia offices of the Sons of the American Revolution. The reaction of many of these institutions was prompt and spirited. Some ignored the request, some rejected it. Chancellor Edmund E. Day told the committee they could find out by coming to Cornell University to matriculate. President Harold W. Dodds called the action of the committee "an intrusion by government into an area of education that ought to remain independent and not political." President Lewis W. Jones of the University of Arkansas offered to send the lists requested but declared that if the information they contained were used "as a springboard in any attempt to interfere with freedom of thought or freedom of discussion or to censor books in this or any other institution of learning the University of Arkansas will resist such encroachment on the high ideal of academic freedom with every resource at its command."

It soon appeared that the chairman had sent out the request without consulting his committee. He proceeded to explain that the committee had no desire to interfere with academic freedom and no intention to censor textbooks.[4] He did not explain what possible motive he could have had other than those he repudiated. The matter was then allowed to drop.

There is a further aspect of federal control over education that has become of growing significance in recent times. It is the mainly indirect control that depends on the grants made to educational institutions for special purposes and particularly nowadays for research operations commissioned by the Army, Navy, Air Force, State Department, and various other agencies or brands of government. Since practically all universities and colleges, aside from a few state universities, are finding it hard to make ends meet, this source of funds is the more welcome.[5] It has, however, some disadvantages. The conditions imposed and the nature of the problems to be investigated are apt to deflect promising scholars from more productive work in their proper fields. In effect government determines the direction of a considerable portion of present-day research.

[4] Bernard A. DeVoto, "Colleges, the Government and Freedom," *Harper's Magazine,* CIC (September, 1949), 76–79.
[5] In the year 1947 federal expenditure on higher education rose to $1,750,000,000. See E. V. Hollis, "Federal Aid for Education," *School and Society,* LXIX (January 8, 1949), 17–20.

University authorities and distinguished scholars have become increasingly concerned over the influence exerted on institutions of learning by the preponderance of governmentally directed research. They fear not only the diversion of scholarship from the functions congenial to it and from the free initiative that leads to important advances in science but also the growing financial dependence of the structure of higher education on the subventions thus provided. Above all they fear the intrusive if indirect controls that accompany governmental research contracts. For example, in the summer of 1953 it was announced from the American Council on Education that fourteen universities and colleges had refused to sign a contract with the United States Armed Forces Institute because the wording of the contract gave the government the power to dismiss any educators not approved by it from any participation in the performance of services within the contract.[6] The Council had previously recommended, through its Committee on Institutional Research Policy, that the government remove classified military projects altogether from the colleges and universities.[7]

On the whole, the federal system has avoided any direct intervention in educational affairs. Claims have been made that the land-grant colleges, in the areas of their operation which are specially supported by government, are dominated by the Department of Agriculture.[8] These claims have been officially denied, and we have received favorable reports from some competent sources, though our own evidence is insufficient on the subject. But situations have not infrequently arisen in these colleges, as the records of the AAUP reveal, which strongly suggest that the freedom of the agricultural investigator is restrained by certain controls and influences. In some Midwestern states, and possibly in others, the dairy interests have limited, if not suppressed, research work on the respective claims of butter and oleo-margarine. Such interference is facilitated by the fact that generally in these institutions research has to be cleared with the top administration. There is also some evidence that research work has been redirected from more important problems to minor issues of practical concern to particular interests and that the competent investigator has had to bow to these requests or run the risk of being dismissed on the ground that he is not cooperative. We have no

[6] *New York Times*, August 22, 1953.   [7] *Ibid.*, March 22, 1953.
[8] Cf. Schiller Scroggs, "The Nature of Administration," in P. F. Valentine, ed., *The American College* (New York, 1949), pp. 468–69.

reason, however, to regard the Department of Agriculture as implicated in such cases.

More broadly, as we have shown, every expansion of federal aid means an increasing danger. As that aid is called upon in larger measure, fears are expressed, not only in this country but also in England, that it may lead to serious encroachments and eventual governmental control. The former head of a private college declares that "in proportion as education accepts governmental aid . . . it must expect an effort to establish political domination." [9] The same writer asserts that the only way to avoid the peril is for the teaching profession to organize its forces to resist at every point all political pressures for the appointment to local school boards, state education boards, or a possible national Department of Education, of persons who lack educational knowledge. The selection of the members of such boards should in the first instance be made by people who are themselves educationally qualified and not by politicians. The author in question is himself, however, highly pessimistic concerning the readiness of the teaching profession to rise to the need.

We are not taking the position that federal aid to institutions of higher learning should be totally discountenanced because of the danger it may entail. On the whole, the federal government has a much better record in this respect than some of the state governments. With the increasing costliness of higher education and the consequent parlous condition of many of our colleges we may be faced with the alternatives of a rise in educational fees that would be prohibitive to some able students—which might mean at the same time the closing down of some good institutions—or the resort to federal aid. In many other democratic countries large-scale governmental aid to higher education is the rule, and yet they are less troubled with assaults on academic freedom than we are in the United States. The danger attendant on federal aid may be greater with us. Certainly any intrusion of such aid calls for the utmost vigilance, and we must continue to look on the nonstate institutions as the chief standard-bearers in the vindication of intellectual independence.

We turn next to the controls over higher education exercised by the individual states. Since a large proportion of all our institutions of higher learning are state institutions, these controls are obviously of great moment, and some of the most serious menaces to academic freedom stem from this source. Private colleges and universities are normally

[9] Bernard Iddings Bell, *Crisis in Education* (New York, 1949), pp. 197–99.

corporate bodies, chartered under the general incorporation laws of their respective states. In some states, however, and notably in New York, the incorporation of these educational institutions is entrusted to a special body—in New York State to the Board of Regents of the University of the State of New York. Private educational bodies mostly fall in the category of nonprofit charitable institutions. As such they are the custodians of endowment funds and consequently subject to the regulations relevant to corporate trustees. They have at the same time important rights of tax exemption. In spite of the historical importance of the Dartmouth College case, modern charters usually have a reservation preserving to the state the right to amend or repeal them. The rights and immunities these bodies possess may be forfeited if they fail to live up to the conditions and implications of their charter. In New York State, for example, a suit for the withdrawal of tax exemption was brought, though unsuccessfully, against Columbia University for alleged anti-group discrimination in the admission of students to certain of its component schools.

Such broad political controls are, however, of quite minor significance compared with those that apply specifically to state institutions. The latter fall into three classes. In former times and, in one or two instances, even in the early years of the twentieth century, some state courts placed them, rather curiously, in the category of private corporations. Now they are all legally as well as actually public bodies. The first group has a special status as constitutionally independent corporations. This means that they are given under their state constitution an educational autonomy with which the state executive or the state legislature cannot interfere. Thus their governing boards can use their own discretion in the allocation of university funds for educational objectives without being subjected to the approval of any outside fiscal officer—a right fully confirmed by court decisions. The number of institutions within this class is small, comprising the universities of California, Colorado, Idaho, Michigan, Minnesota, and now the university system of Georgia with its single Board of Regents.

The second and far the most numerous group have the status of public corporations but without special constitutional protection. Consequently they are subject to restrictions and obligations which may be imposed on them by legislative or executive action. The nature and extent of such controls vary considerably in different states, but sometimes they have been irksome and vexatious, as in Nebraska, for example, where the governing board was at one time compelled to add a new branch to the university and at another time to go into the business of making and distributing hog-cholera serum.

The third class is, if anything, even less secure. These do not possess, in legal terms, a corporate character of their own but are simply agencies or instrumentalities of the state. To this category belong the universities of Iowa, Kansas, North Dakota, and the Ohio State University. Under this condition the university has little recourse against political intervention, and it is the more liable to be drawn, willy-nilly, into the wrangles of party politics, to the detriment of its integrity and its prestige.[10]

We must not assume, however, that the standing and the autonomy of the state university are mainly dependent on the kind of constitutional or legal character it possesses. A university falling in the third category, say the University of Iowa, may be relatively more secure from political attacks on its academic liberty than a university belonging to the first category, say the University of Georgia. No state university can have any security unless the public has a respect for it as a home of learning and an appreciation of the services it can render. There are various ways in which, no matter what its constitutional position, it is still subject to the control of the political forces that are dominant in the state. Only a strong body of public opinion can resist such gross abuses as have been witnessed in areas where the tradition of academic freedom is not well established.

Sometimes, in states where public opinion is much divided, the governor has taken a strong stand on behalf of academic freedom. This attitude was shown by Governor Adlai Stevenson of Illinois in his opposition to the recommendations of the Broyles Commission and by Governor Warren of California during the controversy over the oath prescribed by the Regents.

Aside from the power which may be vested in the executive, there are various controls possessed by state legislatures that can be highly restrictive wherever reactionary groups are influential. Foremost among them is the voting of the annual budget of the university. Since there is often enough some group that frowns on this or that member of the faculty

10 On the legal aspects see M. M. Chambers, "Colleges and Universities," in Walter S. Monroe, ed., *Encyclopedia of Educational Research* (New York, 1950), pp. 231–32.

because he is "out of line," it will seek to discipline the offending institution by proposing a cut in the budget. Thus the administration—and particularly the president—of many a state institution is under strong pressure all the time to play down all nonconformity. The president has to justify his budget to the legislators and since often enough in these years he must ask for an increase in the appropriation, his task is hard enough under any conditions and his success is jeopardized if he has to defend "heretical" members of his faculty. Under such conditions only an able, strong, and devoted president can—as, for example, Frank Graham did—both safeguard the integrity of the university and persuade the legislature to make proper provision for its needs. The successful president of a state institution must, in most situations, be a skillful diplomat as well as an effective administrator.

The legislature has other ways of bringing pressure, if it is so minded, to bear on the university. In the name of loyalty it can pass laws that directly or indirectly affect freedom of speech and often have a particular impact on faculty members. This is a topic of such major importance that we give it special treatment elsewhere.

In sum it is clear that the direct and indirect modes of political control, operating mainly on the state and the local level, have, taken together, a powerful impact on education. The more they are utilized the greater the peril to academic freedom. State institutions are particularly exposed to them, but in degree they affect private educational institutions as well. The degree to which these types of political control are employed is an index of the unhealthiness of public opinion. For they are invoked in order to coerce educational authorities and to reduce educators to conformity. All this is done in the name of loyalty or patriotism, as a "protection" against communist inroads. A highly significant aspect of this situation is that it impinges on the local autonomy that has been so important a feature of American educational systems. State prescriptions mean that state officials acquire a power of supervision, armed with rights of enforcement and penalization, over local boards. The perils to freedom of this developing condition have been pointed out by eminent educators, not least by former President Conant of Harvard.[11]

[11] President Conant's Statement before the Joint Committee on Education, Massachusetts Legislature, February 9, 1948.

Part Three

THE LINES OF ATTACK ON ACADEMIC FREEDOM

X: THE ESTABLISHED WAYS

See you to it that no other institutions, no political party, no social circle, no religious organization, no pet ambitions, put such chains on you as would tempt you to sacrifice one iota of the moral freedom of your consciences or the intellectual freedom of your judgments.

ISAAC SHARPLESS

THE ECONOMIC LINE

ANYONE who examines the numerous and not infrequently successful attempts to censor textbooks and to discredit their authors cannot fail to observe that the main objective of the promoters of these attacks is to penalize and if possible to silence criticisms directed against the unfettered freedom of particular economic interests. A broad survey of the various forms of present-day attack on academic freedom bears out the same conclusion. Academic freedom is felt to be a threat to some kind of economic freedom. There are extremely few out-and-out collectivists in our institutions of learning, but there is a sizable number of educators —as there is of people outside the academic walls—who are critical of some aspects of the operation of the system of free enterprise. This is, of course, to be expected. The scholar is the questioner. In all fields of his investigation, he is not unlikely to question something old in his endeavors to discover something new. In so doing he may become offensive to those whose interests and emotions are bound to the *status quo*.

The extent to which special economic interests form the incentive for attacks on educators and educational systems is somewhat disguised by the fact that the charges brought against them are garbed in propagandistic terms. We have commented already on the tendency of pressure groups to label economic nonconformists as "fellow travelers" or "pinks" or "reds." Or they become "statists," "collectivists," "socialists"—the

The quotation at the head of this chapter is from Isaac Sharpless's address to the graduating class of Haverford College, June 26, 1888.

enemies of a free society and of a true democracy. Or they are "un-American," addicted to alien doctrines, subversive of the American way of life, disloyal. Or, since they are presumed to be on the side of Marx, they are anti-Christian, according to the Dies alternatives, Christ or Marx; and it is significant that some of the more outright enemies of academic freedom, such as the author of *God and Man at Yale,* denounce simultaneously the "godlessness" and the economic heresy they find rife in our universities.

Our sole concern here is with those forces that seek to curb the freedom of thought and of investigation. We make no distinction whether the threat comes from the right or from the left. It happens that in this country, so far as the universities are concerned, the organized attack comes almost entirely from certain right-wing groups, just as in some other countries it may now come more often from the left. The difference reflects a difference in the character of the socially and politically dominant interests. Wherever this dominance may lie, it sets in motion various indirect controls to assure that social institutions of all kinds, including universities, shall be preponderantly staffed by those whose doctrines are in accord with its own. That this should be so is in the very nature of things. The point of resistance comes, however, when these dominant groups resort to methods that violate the fundamental liberties on which the pursuit of truth depends. This is done when, by gross misrepresentation of what they stand for, educators—or other men—are condemned as disloyal or subversive, and again when they are ousted from their positions because they reach conclusions that are not palatable to some influential or power-holding elements.

These considerations have special relevance for such subjects as economics, political science, social psychology, and other branches of what are sometimes called the behavioral sciences, since these subjects are bound up with the preconceptions and established ways of a society and with the conflicts of interest and ideology within it. In the first place, there is a certain difference in the composite of factors that determine the recognition and appointment of educators in these fields from that which holds for subjects relatively remote from the marketplace, the forum, and the pulpit. In the former fields, the scholar whose position and conclusions are nearer to the viewpoint of the appointing authorities is likely to be more acceptable than another whose position is less conformist, aside from the weighing of the intrinsic scholarly qualifications of the respective candidates. In the latter fields—unless for the quite exceptional case of a man who is publicly on record as espousing unpopular views on matters outside his professional interest—there is less danger of bias in the assessment of scholarly qualifications. The only kind of "vested interest" that is at all likely to interfere is the predilection of senior scholars for the established theoretical constructs, for the "school" to which they themselves belong; but the nonprofessional appointing authorities are out of this picture, and the bias of the "school" is constantly subject to challenge.

In the area of the social sciences, the problem is more difficult and the situation is more confused, partly because the standards of competence are less clearly defined, but also in considerable measure because particular interests are actively and sometimes urgently at work to deflect the assessment of scholarly qualifications. In this area particularly, though not exclusively, we run into situations where it is hard to determine whether or not there has been a genuine violation of the principles of academic freedom. Was this instructor denied reappointment, or this assistant professor denied promotion, because he was less competent than his colleagues of the same grade or because his views were not quite "sound"? We have looked into some cases where complaints were based on this kind of discrimination, but the evidences were not adequate to justify citations. Not infrequently the question mark must remain unresolved.

Yet perhaps nowhere more than in this area of question marks is it important that educators and outside authorities alike should be reminded of the principle of academic freedom and of the great social values that depend on its observance. This principle requires that, not least in an area so full of complications as the economic one, the scholar shall present as fairly balanced a picture of every situation and every problem as he can. But it also requires that, other things being equal, the heretic shall be as eligible a candidate as the conservative and vice versa. In other words, in the absence of serious personality defects or other specific impediments to the effectiveness of his accomplishment of the tasks required of him, the fitness of the candidate must be adjudged primarily by his ability to contribute to the knowledge of his field and by his ability to impart that knowledge.[1]

[1] We are speaking here solely of academic positions, fully realizing that for governmental appointments or for employment in business research and so forth other considerations may properly be invoked.

To defend his freedom, the educator in the field of economics must not only refuse to be intimidated by the threats and attacks of particular economic-interest groups: exposed to the dangers of the carrot as well as the stick, he also must guard against the inducements addressed to him by these groups in the form of certain opportunities and awards. Such inducements cannot be regarded as directly an infringement of the educator's freedom. We cannot seriously reproach the men of affairs and the propagandists who use this device to advance their cause. Nor do we suggest that the educator should sternly reject all such approaches; but we would point out that a certain discretion on his part is highly desirable for the protection of his professional integrity. For example, propagandistic organizations of all kinds seek to enlist educators as board members, consultants, and the like. Presumably their enlistment is a token of the respectability of these bodies. There is no reason why the professor should not publicly support bodies dedicated sincerely to causes in which he believes, but when members of distinguished universities have allowed their names to appear, say, as consultants on the staff of the *Educational Reviewer* or as members of the advisory committee of the National Council for American Education, we submit that they are dishonoring their calling and betraying the faith that is reposed in them. Again, we do not suggest that scholars should refuse outright the "summer fellowships" offered by a propagandist body for the study of selected business concerns, or the expense-free sojourns at their headquarters plant offered by some vast corporation—and so forth. But if and when they accept these gifts, they should be aware that the givers are not disinterested, and that the talks they hear from high executives may carry a note of indoctrination. The need for caution in this respect is, of course, just as great whether the offers come from a trade union or from an industrial concern.

So far we have been occupied with the need for the economist to maintain his own standards, and it must be added that the educator who fails in this respect is the exception. What now concerns us is the danger that sometimes faces him when he does maintain his standards. Certain special-interest groups are unwilling to depend on the strength of their case or on the influence they normally wield. They resort to methods of educational control which are wholly to be deplored and which constitute a serious threat to the freedom of the scholar. These methods are focused on the suppression of economic unorthodoxy.

No other conclusion can reasonably be drawn from the constant representation of a large variety of economic proposals and policies as tainted with communism, as stamped with the same deadly brand. Thus for the Foundation for Economic Education the Point Four Program "strikingly resembles the proposals of the official head of the communists in this country in 1944." [2] Similar charges have been brought against the Wagner Act, the social security laws, the T.V.A., the Marshall Plan, and so forth: they are all steps on the downward road, leading toward the final consummation, a communist dictatorship.

Consequently, any educators who may favor these policies are held up as dangerous or "subversive" persons, unfit to educate the young. Reading through a series of the issues of the *Educational Reviewer,* we find its commentators insistently conveying the impression that to advocate economic changes or to point out weaknesses in the working of the capitalist system is pretty much the same thing as to support communism. They level these widely publicized charges particularly against the authors of school and college textbooks. The school and college administrators to whom they appeal, and the public in general, are not likely to study these texts carefully for themselves. The author becomes in their minds suspect, and his academic career may be imperiled. In any event, his book is less likely to get on the approved list. The only writer who is safe from these attacks is one who carefully avoids using any evidence or drawing any conclusions that might not be grateful, say, to the local chamber of commerce.

Let us give one or two illustrations of how authors and their books are thus subjected to prejudice. In the *Educational Reviewer* of April 15, 1952, there is a notice of Professor Arthur N. Holcombe's National Education Association pamphlet entitled, "The Problems of Representative Government." The summation runs as follows: "There is little about 'problems' in this analysis, as only one problem seems to be of importance and that is how to persuade us Americans that we need a complete change in our form of government, a change to a government which in theory will be socialist, in form centralized and with no state or local governments as we know them."

This is a sheer travesty of Professor Holcombe's thoughtful pamphlet, and it is followed by a number of petulant comments. In the same issue there is one of the characteristic reviews devoted to "Keynesian" econ-

[2] "Illusions of Point Four" (pamphlet).

omists. The book under consideration is Paul A. Samuelson's *Economics: An Introductory Analysis*. The argument runs as follows. Samuelson's position is somewhat similar to that of Keynes. Now, Keynes holds certain economic views that are akin to those of Karl Marx. No less an authority than Earl Browder has testified to this.[3] Keynes's system is therefore "wide open to attack as radical socialism." *"Now if (1) Marx is communistic, (2) Keynes is partly Marxian, and (3) Samuelson is Keynesian, what does that make Samuelson and others like him? The answer is clear: Samuelson and the others are mostly part Marxian socialist or communist in their theories."* [4]

There is no genuine critique of the actual statements and conclusions of Dr. Samuelson. He is refuted by his presumptive associations. The reader gets no proper conception of his serious attempt to present some of the major problems of economic society. One need not be a defender of either Keynes or Samuelson to protest against such unfair representations. Similar tactics employed to discredit, say, the most extreme laissez-fairism would deserve the same kind of reprobation.

Let it be remembered that these reviews are not addressed to economists but to a public which cannot, for the most part, assess or even comprehend the economic analysis that is under attack. The charges made against these textbooks are intended to prevent their use in schools and colleges by attaching to them the opprobrium of being radical, socialist, or communist, three epithets which are used for this purpose almost interchangeably.

Let us look at this indictment of the "Keynesian" more closely, since it is typical of a whole school of thought, or rather of action.[5] Samuelson is "Keynesian," and the economics of Keynes has features similar to those of the economics of Marx. Therefore Keynes and Samuelson and all their tribe are guiding their readers along the road to communism. Let us apply the same reasoning to another group of economists. A key doctrine of Karl Marx, that of surplus-value, is based on the theory of

[3] Keynes's economic doctrine was essentially dissimilar to Marx's, and in his own incisive way he expressed his contempt for the Marxian analysis. Like many other economists he did agree with Marx that depressions and periods of unemployment can result from the natural operation of the capitalistic system, but he differed totally from Marx's prescription for these evils—which is what really matters.

[4] Italics in original.

[5] For another example of the same tactics directed against the same authors, see George Koether, "Economics of Oblivion," *The Freeman*, II (April 7, 1952), 442. This review dismisses the work of the "Keynesians" as "simply socialism."

David Ricardo, who in turn belongs, in important respects, to the school of Adam Smith. Smith and Ricardo are the classical exponents of the principle of laissez faire, which means, in effect, that the system of free enterprise is beautifully self-regulating, for the welfare of all, if only government will keep its hands off. This is essentially the doctrine to which the *Educational Reviewer, The Freeman,* and all such organs of opinion cling. But by parity of reasoning, Ricardo and Adam Smith are "part-Marxian, socialist, or communist" in their position. And therefore the modern exponents of the same doctrine are tainted with communistic ideas!

On more substantial grounds, the whole campaign to discredit economic viewpoints not congenial to a particular group or interest by smearing them publicly with the brush of communism is greatly to be deplored. And it is particularly deplorable that there are even a few persons in academic positions who have demeaned themselves by joining in this practice—they do not lack reputable ways to assail doctrines of which they disapprove. To dismiss men like Keynes and, for example, Samuelson as having communistic tendencies is sheer obscurantism, where it is not deliberate misrepresentation. Keynes himself not only made distinguished contributions to the study of economic problems, he was also a man of great practical sagacity who, among his other offices, was a governor of the Bank of England. He was much occupied with the practical questions of how to prevent the recurrence of great economic crises and depressions, and how to maintain a full volume of employment. He concluded that a major device for the attainment of these ends was the maintenance of a proper balance between consumption spending and investment, and that governmental controls were necessary to secure this balance. His objective was not to overthrow the capitalistic system but rather to safeguard it against destruction and socially costly evils inherent in its uncontrolled operation. How far he was right or wrong in his diagnosis is a question on which economists differ. It is a matter involving expert analysis concerning the interaction of various factors under alternative conditions. Anyone who has tried to face such problems will recognize the ominous character of the propagandistic attempts to discredit these authors by labeling them communist, in order that their works may be withheld from use in schools and colleges.

The groups that indulge in these gross misrepresentations are always announcing that their objective is to save the American way of life or to protect American education against insidious forces. There is often good reason to believe that their actual motivations are more ignoble. We have, for example, some evidence to suggest that when the Texas House of Representatives adopted a resolution to investigate Professor C. E. Ayres, a well-known economist who was accused of holding heretical views, it was part of a design to discredit higher education in order to bring about a reduction of the whole educational budget. In other cases a more specific motivation is clearly involved. We regret to report here that professional groups have at times allowed their particular interests to color their views on matters of public policy in such a way that they, too, have put forward highly propagandistic statements. Thus the American Medical Association passed the following resolution:

Many of our educators and many of the organizations to which they belong have for many years conducted an active, aggressive campaign to indoctrinate their students in grammar school, high school and college with the insidious and destructive tenets of the welfare state, this teaching of hatred and scorn for the American system of private enterprise having been so widespread and successful that as a result our voters are conditioned to accept all manner of totalitarian expedients in direct violation of economic law.[6]

It is indeed to be deplored that a body maintaining such high ethical standards and rightfully holding such high public respect as does the medical profession should allow itself officially to become the sponsor of this kind of manifesto.

There is here no question of its right and indeed its duty to take a stand against any proposals which in its judgment are detrimental to the interests of the profession or to the invaluable services it renders. But no good cause is served when a great profession joins in the indiscriminate attack on the educator and endorses the intrinsically false economic line taken by the defamers of social-minded and truth-seeking scholars. The whole statement is meretricious. The identification of the "welfare state" with totalitarian practices is absurd. The charge that those who advocate various types of social legislation are filled with "hatred and scorn" for private enterprise is wrong-headed, if not definitely malicious. Many educators are not in favor of socialized medicine, if we take that to be the issue here; some are in favor of it. It is reasonable to expect from the medical profession a sober and direct statement of their side.

[6] Adopted by its House of Delegates, June, 1951.

We have dwelt on these examples because they reinforce a general lesson. Governing boards and administrators in general have sometimes to listen to accusations of the sort just mentioned brought against faculty members. The more qualified administrators properly refuse to be influenced by them, but sometimes they are under pressure or are themselves deluded. The moral is that no administrator should, no matter what his own views, take any action on any charges based on reports concerning the character of the instruction given by an educator without first consulting the faculty and particularly those members of it who are competent in the same field or, in smaller colleges, some of his professional brethren at other institutions. More broadly, no administrative authority should entertain any motion that would censure, discipline, or dismiss an educator on the ground of his particular viewpoint or doctrine so long as he expounds his views without resorting to abuse of others and with due respect for law and for the decent usages of society.

The process of misrepresentation has gone so far that there are some who even accuse the whole body of educators of being biased and perverse. The great exponent of Americanism, Mr. Allen A. Zoll, says, "It can be safely asserted that ninety per cent of texts and teaching in our schools today are in considerable measure subversive" of the "basic American principles of freedom and individual liberty." [7] The charge is particularly leveled against the economics sector. *The Freeman,* for example, claims that the good individualist is shut out. "The real trouble in our universities is not that collectivists have infiltrated our departments of economics and social science; it is that they have largely taken over, and blanketed the individualist opposition." [8] In the same journal Ludwig von Mises complains that the economic collectivists in the colleges conspire to deny jobs to the true believer in free enterprise.[9] Since in their jargon a collectivist is anyone who deviates in any measure from the complete gospel of laissez faire, no doubt the accusers can make the charge plausible to themselves. But if the terms "conservative" and "radical" are taken in their proper sense as indicating relative rightness of left-ness on a continuum representing the range of opinion of the population as a whole, then there is no evidence to confirm the

[7] "They Want Your Child," pamphlet of the National Council for American Education.

[8] "Yale in Turmoil," *The Freeman,* I (November 5, 1951), 71.

[9] Ludwig von Mises, "Our Leftist Economic Teaching," *The Freeman,* II (April 7, 1952), 425.

charge that educators are markedly radical. On the contrary, such evidences as we have suggest that they tend on the whole to the conservative side. Dr. E. O. Melby, Dean of the School of Education of New York University, reports that "sociological studies have shown American school teachers more conservative than the total population." [10] Indeed, the genuine radical makes precisely the opposite charge from that leveled by our pressure groups. Thus Harold Laski deplored the supineness of the American educator and his unwillingness even to mention any facts that might be distasteful to "vested interests." [11] When William F. Buckley, Jr., cited passages from works of some Yale economists to show how "collectivist" and "statist" they were, another economist put together a number of extracts from the same authors "with the result that the texts seemed the last testaments of the economic barons." [12]

The statements made by those who thus impugn our academic economists are not backed by any evidence. Their authors cite no investigations to support their claims. From direct acquaintance with the economic departments of several institutions and from further inquiries we have made, we conclude that in the larger institutions the members of the economics staff hold diverse viewpoints on questions of economic policy and certainly do not all belong to any one school of economic thought. There are "conservatives" and "liberals," Keynesians and anti-Keynesians, and not a few who take intermediate positions. Qualified economists are seekers after knowledge and do not adopt the partisan and denunciatory attitudes characteristic of the pressure groups that attack them, though there may be occasional lapses due to personal factors—one of these we shall presently have to refer to. In the smaller institutions one or another school of thought may be dominant, but there is no pattern of uniformity.

We have direct knowledge of only one case in which a group of university economists resigned their positions because they felt themselves subjected to adverse pressure, and in that case the pressures came at least as much from without as from within. Moreover, the resigning economists belonged rather to the "liberal" than to the "conservative" side, so far as these designations had any relevance. The situation in question

[10] "Challenge to the Critics of the Schools," *The New York Times Magazine* (September 23, 1951), p. 57.

[11] *The American Democracy* (New York, 1948), p. 359.

[12] See Frank D. Ashburn, "Isms and the University," *Saturday Review of Literature*, XXXIV (December 15, 1951), 44.

occurred at the University of Illinois. As happens not so infrequently, a combination of personality differences, private ambitions, and intra-faculty divisions complicated the issue. Its history is too involved to be given here. The following facts are, however, sufficiently clear. Howard R. Bowen, then the economist of the Irving Trust Company, was invited to become dean of the College of Commerce and Business Administration at that University. The condition of the College at that time had been deteriorating, and there was a good deal of jealousy and wrangling between its departments. Dean Bowen was called in as an outsider who, being free from commitments, could better undertake to improve the morale and raise the status of the college. He brought into the institution a number of new members, arousing the animosity of some of the older group. The Executive Committee of the College, consisting of a group of businessmen, supported the latter, and so did the local newspaper, the *News Gazette*. Complaints and accusations followed, the chief precipitant being the resignation of one of the older professors to take a position at the University of Florida. The action of the head of the economics department, Professor Everett E. Hagen, and of the Dean in accepting the resignation was assailed. Charges of "leftism" and "Keynesianism" were flung at them. A bitter controversy arose, in which the President of the University, George D. Stoddard, sided with Dean Bowen. Nevertheless the pressures, particularly from the business group who formed the Executive Council and their outside supporters, were so strong that Professor Hagen resigned as head of his department and Bowen resigned his deanship. Seven other economists who stood with Hagen and Bowen also resigned to take positions elsewhere. We shall return to this case in another connection, since it raises some important questions regarding the responsibilities of the educator when engaged in faculty controversies.

For the present we offer the case merely as one piece of evidence against the sweeping undocumented charge of a general "conspiracy" against conservative economists. This charge appears along with so many other misrepresentations that we are led to the conclusion that what we have here is a concerted attempt by a body of propagandists to divert educational policies to the service of certain self-centered and short-sighted interest groups.

It is unfortunate that these pressure groups are able to pose as the vindicators of free enterprise. Only a small sector of American businessmen are associated with them. Outstanding leaders in the business world, some of them members of the boards of educational institutions, are opposed to these attacks on academic freedom. But there would seem to be considerable numbers of men of affairs who are at best neutral, probably entertaining some suspicion that the academic economist and generally the academic social scientist is "unreliable." We venture to appeal to all such that they come out squarely on the side of academic freedom. There are two strong reasons why they should. In the first place the objective of the overwhelming majority of American economists who concern themselves with deficiencies in the enterprise system is to examine ways in which these deficiencies may be remedied and their social costs avoided. They are seeking not to destroy the system but to improve it, indeed to preserve it. Unemployment and the fear of unemployment are in industrial countries the great allies of communism, and those who ignore such facts are themselves the unwitting enemies of the system they too blindly champion. In the second place, when pressure groups endeavor to curb the freedom of the thought and inquiry in our universities they are, for all their protestations, striking at the major bulwarks of democracy. In doing so they are in effect working to undermine the social structure without which private enterprise in the modern world could not long survive and, what is of still greater importance, without which the unity and the strength, the tradition and the meaning of the United States would be destroyed.

THE RELIGIOUS LINE

In these days there has erupted a new burst of charges against our institutions of higher learning as being "godless," "atheistic," "materialistic," neglectful or even contemptuous of religion; and at times particular scholars or groups of scholars are accused of undermining the faith of the students or at the least offending their religious susceptibilities. The attack on Yale's "godlessness" was regarded by its author as relevant to our universities in general—Yale was rather less infected than some of the others. A little later Vassar came into the limelight as the result of the publication of an article by one of its students in which she claimed that its atmosphere was hostile to religion and that some of its teachers did what they could to disturb her religious beliefs. Some clerical officials have taken the same stand. One of the most outspoken of these utterances occurred in the inauguration address of the president of Georgetown University, The Very Reverend Hunter Guthrie, S.J., where he referred to "the fabulous formula of academic freedom" as "that Protean pulpit whereon may mount atheist and Catholic; fellow traveler and capitalist; agnostic, liberal, dogmatist, and even an occasional teacher." [13] The same speaker in a college address derided "the sacred fetish of academic freedom." "This," he said, "is the soft underbelly of our American way of life, and the sooner it is armor-plated by some sensible limitation the sooner will the future of this nation be secured from fatal consequences." [14]

The "sensible limitation" is doubtless dictated by the particular orthodoxy of the group that demands it. And it is perhaps no coincidence that many of those who attack academic freedom along the religious line are also active in the assault on economic unorthodoxy. Indeed, it seems to be as easy for certain minds to identify the divine law with their economic predilections as with their religious tenets.

The attack on academic freedom in the name of religion rests, however, in the last resort, on a wholly different set of premises. It is therefore necessary, before we examine any bill of particulars, that we consider the broad problem of the relation of the university to religious instruction. We assume here that the question is posed for the nondenominational institution. Church-controlled universities raise a different question altogether, which we deal with in Appendix A.

The university, as we have sought to show, has its own unique function in the service of man and society. It is requisite, as the primary condition of this special service, that the university shall not be barred by an outside authority, by any authority of any kind, from the free pursuit of knowledge in any field. To limit the search for truth is also to misdirect it. Moreover, the attitude that accepts, anywhere within the unlimited area of discoverable knowledge, any conclusions that lie apart from or beyond the test of investigation, is itself at odds with the scientific spirit and inimical to the integrity of the scholar.

It should be observed in passing that we are not here identifying all knowledge with science, as that term is usually construed. We include also the great areas of knowledge that are contained in the study of the humanities and the arts and in the myriad-angled history of man's past

[13] Printed in Appendix to the *Congressional Record,* May 2, 1949.
[14] *Georgetown Journal,* LXXIX (October, 1950), 32.

doings and sufferings, achievements, aspirations, and reflections, including his philosophies and his religions. Nor again would we affirm that science itself has any answers to the questions that are of most concern to mankind, whether they be questions of his destiny or questions of his relations to his fellow man. What, however, we do claim is that no conclusions, however derived or sustained by whatsoever authority, that postulate any connection between things that are susceptible to scientific investigation should be fenced off from such investigation in the name of religion. No religious system confines itself purely to the formulation of ultimate values or to the ethical dictates that may be derived from them. They sometimes make assertions of a cosmological character which lie within the range of scientific proof or disproof. Or again, they lay down specific rules of behavior to which are sometimes annexed statements of the overt social consequences of obedience or disobedience. The connections thus asserted may also be properly subject to scientific inquiry. Authority, in short, should never be invoked against the adequate investigation of the scientifically ascertainable connection between things.

We are concerned here with limitations imposed in the name of religion. Any limitations so imposed have formidable consequences beyond the immediate circle within which they are applied. Who is to lay down the limitations? One critic demands that the faculty members be required to be men who will seek to "Christianize" their students. Another complains that "the tone of higher education is secular and the total impact upon the majority of students is, if not anti-, at least nonreligious." [15] Another asserts that a "materialist" has no place on a university faculty. Assuredly no body of educators of any standing would tolerate such requirements. Who then is to impose them? The governing boards? The alumni? In the most unlikely event that either body would or could impose such a rule on any great institution of learning, there can be no doubt the institution would be disrupted. Moreover, no general rule of this sort could be imposed by any authority but that of government. And happily we need not contemplate any such event, so long as we remain a democracy, so long as the First Amendment holds.

This point leads us to another consideration. We spoke of the university as having a unique mission, a mission no other organization can

[15] Merrimon Cuninggim, *The College Seeks Religion* (Yale University Press, 1947), p. 259.

fulfill. So also may we speak of the church. So also of the state. No one of these can take the place or preempt the function of another without serious detriment to that function. Neither state nor church can dictate to the institution of learning the manner in which it should teach or pursue knowledge. Any such dictation brings us nearer to the totalitarian way.

There was a time when knowledge was officially in the keeping of the church, officially and socially inseparable from theology. Under the same conditions no proper distinction could be drawn between the sphere of the church and that of the state. It is a prerequisite of democracy, and a distinctive development of modern society, that each primary association have and hold a place and a central mission that is properly and peculiarly its own. The state in principle does not meddle with the church. The church in principle has no arbitrament over the university.

So far as this country is concerned, we can broaden the last statement by substituting for "the university" the words "the whole educational system aside from denominational institutions." The latter, including parochial schools and denominational colleges and universities, raise difficult problems of their own which we cannot examine here. Over the rest of the system the principle of the separation of church and state presumes that no sectarian influences shall enter anywhere into the educational process. How far this principle is compatible with any kind of religious instruction is in turn a much agitated issue, especially on the school level. In some states Bible reading in the public schools is required; in others it is forbidden. The rulings of the courts on the subject are conflicting or inconclusive. The Bible itself is a sectarian book to non-Christians, as an Illinois court decision has declared. The compulsion to participate in any religious ceremony is objected to as an interference with religious freedom. Many Roman Catholics have objections to the adoption by the schools of the King James version or any other non-Catholic version of the Bible. Indeed, the whole situation remains exceedingly vexed, wherever religious exercises of any sort are maintained in the public schools. The McCollum decision (333 U.S. 203) asserted that it was unconstitutional to use the public schools for the religious instruction by the different major faiths of the pupils assigned to one or another group in accordance with the request of their parents. In the Zorach case (343 U.S. 306), on the other hand, the Supreme Court upheld the "released time" program of New York City under which the pupils were released for religious instruction in religious centers.[16]

The situation in the university is very different, there being no compulsory attendance involved. Any religious instruction that may be offered is at the option of the student. Since sectarian indoctrination is out of place in the curriculum, one question that arises is whether courses in religion in its more inclusive sense should be offered. Such courses might include comparative religion, the history of religion, the sociological and anthropological aspects of religion, the forms of religious experience, and the philosophy of religion. There can be no doubt that these subjects are important fields of knowledge, the omission of which must leave a serious lacuna in any university's program of instruction. There are, however, special difficulties that beset adequate provision for this need. If a cleric is chosen to give any of these courses, charges of sectarianism may be incurred. If a noncleric, he either adheres to a particular denomination or else to none, and either way questions of attitude or of bias may arise. For this and other reasons many institutions do not offer such courses, whereas others, and particularly some of the larger universities, are able to do so, but on a relatively small scale, without arousing much controversy.

Those who advocate that the university should take a definitely religious stand are in their proselyting zeal committing themselves to a total perversion of the function of the university. They would revert to the intellectual confusion of earlier times, when a superimposed prior "truth" retarded the advance of knowledge and thus tended to imprison the inquiring mind. To make the university a center for the propagation of any creed, of any system of values that divides group from group, is to destroy the special quality and the unique mission of the university as a center for the free pursuit of knowledge wherever it may lead.

Moreover, it confuses the role of the university with the role of the church and by removing the primary distinction between their functions takes away the great asset of universality that attaches to the service rendered by the university. For we live in a world of religious divisions whereas the university is preeminently an institution that rightfully serves all mankind without dividing them into opposing camps. The

[16] For a review of the situation in the schools, see Howard K. Beale, *Are American Teachers Free?* (New York, 1936). For the more recent legal decisions and opinions, see Thomas I. Emerson and David Haber, *Political and Civil Rights in the United States* (Buffalo, 1952), pp. 913–79.

sincere search after knowledge presupposes that no prior commitments to doctrine shall preclude or influence or limit the resort to evidences or the play of the scholar's mind in the framing of hypotheses and the testing of these by methods and processes of reasoning that are independent of any doctrinal assumptions.

Is the conclusion then that the university has no concern with religion? It certainly means that the university should scrupulously refrain from the official inculcation of any particular religion and from any discriminatory practices, applying either to teachers or to students, based on religion. Creedal indoctrination, for reasons already sufficiently suggested, is entirely outside its province. "Assuredly the discussion of religion save from an historical or philosophical point of view is not in harmony with the proper function of a college or university which is unaffiliated with a special creed." [17] Since the university is at the same time a quasi community, within which in most instances students and not infrequently some of the staff reside, and since nearly always considerable numbers of its members spend the livelong day on its premises, many institutions very properly provide opportunities through chapels and services for the religious affiliations of its members. It should do so, however, with due regard for the religious affiliations of its students and not with partiality for any one group. And in the doing of it, to quote again from the former vice-president of the University of California, "every precaution must be taken against even the slightest effort to press upon students any particular form of religion, or even religion itself." [18]

If that be so, what then of the proper attitude of the college or university educator toward the discussion of religion so far as it is relevant to the subject with which he is dealing? In stating the question so, we assume that no educator should gratuitously deliver to his classes his views on religion and least of all on any particular religion, any more than he should on, say, politics, except so far as they are conclusions based on evidences and relevant to the field of instruction he is expounding. Thus our question has special import for teachers in such fields as psychology, anthropology, sociology, and generally the whole area of the social sciences, the area that mostly provokes the complaints brought against our universities. The recalcitrant alumnus of Yale de-

[17] Monroe E. Deutsch, *The College From Within* (University of California Press, 1952), p. 203.
[18] *Ibid.*, p. 208.

clared that in the field of psychology the overwhelming majority of textbooks treated religion in a thoroughly unsatisfactory manner, some by ignoring its importance altogether, others by taking a critical or hostile attitude toward it. And the situation in sociology and in anthropology is presented as being no less deplorable. The same indictment is conveyed in a series of complaints and protests from churchmen and others evoked by an article in *The Freeman* written by a student who left Vassar in revulsion against some of the teaching to which she was exposed. She had previously written a letter to the Vassar *Chronicle,* in which she defended Mr. Buckley's "blueprint for revolution against the vested interests of agnosticism and collectivism." She resented the attitude toward religion shown by some of her teachers as well as their views on Senator McCarthy and related themes.[19]

The case of Nancy Fellers, aside from its individual complexities, illustrates the problem of instruction in the social sciences in a society where there is not only great diversity of faiths and many conflicting group-interests but where also each of these groups is well organized and highly vocal. Vassar College claims that the educational process, to be effective, must challenge the student to think for himself or herself—and what college worthy of the name would not agree? In doing so, however, it seems inevitable that one type of student will resent any questionings of the indoctrinations in which he has been brought up. The stronger student will on the other hand accept the challenge and profit greatly by it. Apart from anything else, that student will be more prepared to live in a world in which he must constantly meet conflicts of views and of interests. He will see old things in a new light, with wider perceptions. In short, he will be better educated. It does not mean that he will abandon his former system of values. If we may take Vassar as an example, many of its students testified in rebuttal of Miss Fellers that they benefited by the challenge. And certainly the students of Vassar exhibited no leaning toward the "mixture of socialism, communism, and atheism" which the heated imaginations of the propagandizing critics of that college attributed to its teaching. We quote the President of Vassar to the effect that in a straw vote the students voted two to one for Eisenhower and that the senior students divided 171 for the Republican candidate and 92 for Stevenson. We mention this fact

[19] Nancy Jane Fellers, "God and Woman at Vassar," *The Freeman,* III (November 3, 1952), 83–86.

without prejudice and making no other implication than that the students of Vassar remained on the whole staunch upholders of the values they brought to college. The training of students to think, though in some respects a disturbing process, is definitely not to be construed as a training in radicalism.

Let us look at the matter from the standpoint of the educator. Particularly if he is a social scientist, he has a difficult problem. Various groups believe in effect that his proper function is to indoctrinate his students in the beliefs that correspond to their particular interests or values and sometimes seek to put pressure on him in that direction. But the social scientists must put the search for knowledge first and encourage in his students the desire genuinely to seek it and therefore to test it. As the most distinguished sociologist of our times has said, "fundamental doubt is the father of knowledge." [20] This is not the doubt of the sceptic but the doubt of the true inquirer that leads to intellectual convictions. What the scholar investigates is not values but evidences. What he seeks to discover is the actual relations between things, and he properly believes that no truth of any kind need or indeed can depend on false evidences or on false conclusions drawn from evidences. Beyond that he does not and need not, in his role of scholar, pronounce on values at all, other than the values implicit in the search for, recognition of, and acceptance of the truth that men can find.

There is indeed an occasional teacher who shows a lack of respect for the values cherished by his students and seeks to shock or discomfit them by sarcastic or flippant comments on matters they hold dear or even sacred. We offer no defense for such conduct. It is wholly uncalled for and cannot be justified on any educational grounds. And aside from its ethical impropriety it is harmful to good public relations and gives an effective weapon to those who want to harness education to the service of their creed. The percipient teacher will not only avoid such extremes, he will sympathetically seek to understand the attitudes of his students and will work to carry them along with him by giving them a wider perspective, not by casting scorn on the perspective they already have. Any educator who treats with mockery or insults the values of any group of his students is betraying his responsibilities.

The main issue, however, lies elsewhere. The most devoted and sober-minded teacher arouses the opposition of the intolerant wherever he

[20] Max Weber, *The Methodology of the Social Sciences* (Glencoe, Ill., 1949), p. 7.

undertakes the open-minded search for knowledge within any area that touches on their doctrines or on their interests. And if this is so, it is easy to understand why a considerable number of colleges eschew courses in the area of religion. Nevertheless "more than 60 percent of our state universities and land-grant colleges offer instruction in religion on an academic credit basis" and "some credit courses in Bible and religion are available to students in 40 percent of the state teachers colleges." [21] Care is taken to appoint men who, while being religious-minded, will not offend the susceptibilities of any important religious group. It is well to observe, however, that even so students respond in very different ways. Some object to it as indoctrination, and some others resent the scholarly mode of presentation. One teacher of such courses in a state university, reviewing twenty years of experience, reported that while the majority of students were sympathetic "some, however, are shocked by their first knowledge of the literary and historical approach to the Bible, and flee from further 'contamination.' " [22] No doubt such young students are intellectually of the same kindred as many of their elders who now demand that the universities themselves be propagandists of a particular religion.

Such attitudes easily breed complaints to the effect that Professor X is sacrilegious, or blasphemous, or "irreligious," or "atheistic." Sometimes demands are made that some teacher be dismissed because of his attacks on religion. It is important here to distinguish between instances where the charge is due to the intolerance or misconception of the complainant and the rare instance where the teacher is deliberately offensive. We find extremely few cases on the college or university level where teachers have actually been dismissed on this ground. In some cases where a request for dismissal was brought before the administrative authorities, the teacher has been cleared, as in one case that occurred at Hunter College. It is well in this connection to remember that different groups have very different ideas as to what is "sacrilegious." Some are deeply offended by what others regard as wholly without offense, as witness, for example, the different views taken of the motion picture *The Miracle*.

[21] Reported by Professor Clarence P. Shedd of Yale University Divinity School; see National Council of the Churches of Christ, *Information Service*, XXXI, No. 13 (March 29, 1952).

[22] Horace T. Houf, "Teaching Religion in a State University," *Bulletin of the American Association of University Professors*, XXXVI (Summer, 1950), 308–14.

What more frequently happens is that broad charges of "atheism" are included among other counts, particularly radicalism or some degree of "redness." Such charges are usually factitious or even malicious, as in the deplorable case at Fairmont State College, where Mrs. Luella Mundel was accused of being an "atheist" and a "bad security risk" and later showered with aspersions of the same order by the U.S. Senator who appeared in court for the offending board member in the slander suit initiated by Mrs. Mundel.

Thus far we have considered only issues in which the onus is the negative attitude of the teacher toward religion. There is another side of the story, where it is the positive religious convictions of the teacher that are the source of academic trouble. There is some reason to believe that religious affiliation is a factor in the choice between candidates for academic positions, especially in certain areas. This is aside altogether from the discrimination to which Jews are so often subject. Whether or not discrimination on religious grounds, or on any ground that is extraneous to the proper academic qualifications of candidates, be regarded as an infringement of academic liberty, it is a process that is certainly hurtful to the best interests of the world of learning. For not only is superior talent denied equal opportunity, but the bias exhibited in the rejection of it makes more difficult that freedom from bias which is a prime requisite for the pursuit of knowledge. We do not contend that there may not be a few subjects for the exposition of which it may without prejudice be felt that a scholar of some particular creed may be less impartial or free-minded than one who is not so committed. But the bias to which we here refer is not limited in this way nor based on any such consideration.

The religious convictions of the teacher may under certain conditions lead to his dismissal. This can happen when these convictions impel him to refuse obedience to some regulation, whether legal or administrative, that requires him to violate his creed. It can happen also when on the same ground he refuses to conform to some generally accepted standard or to participate in some cause that is commonly identified with the national interest. These two types of situation tend to run into one another. Thus the conscientious objector, if he is liable for military service, may refuse to obey the draft law or, if he is not, may arouse even more public resentment by his antiwar stand. In times of crisis or of actual war such pacifists are likely enough to lose their academic positions.

There was, for example, the case of George W. Hartmann, Professor of Educational Psychology at Teachers College, Columbia University. Professor Hartmann's case has various interesting aspects, too long and involved for adequate discussion here. He was not only a pacifist but, so to speak, a militant one and at the same time he was well-known for his activity in another unpopular cause, having run for various public offices on the socialist ticket—it should be added, however, that he took a definite stand against the Communist Party. In line with his convictions, he opposed America's entry into the war against Hitler and after Pearl Harbor became chairman of the "Peace Now" campaign. Naturally this brought on him much public obloquy. He was on leave of absence as director of a research project for a two-year period beginning July 1, 1942, and toward its end was in effect informed that he was being dropped from the college staff. As a result of various representations, this decision was modified into "indefinite leave of absence." The AAUP took the case under consideration and through the appropriate committee declared that the college was under obligation to reinstate him. It did so, on the basis of a four-year contract. This was not renewed, although his colleagues in the division voted without exception for its continuation. The original contract explicitly stated that the college was under no obligation to employ him after its expiry. Professor Hartmann brought suit before the Supreme Court of New York State. In the course of the proceedings the judge expressed the view that the four-year contract was a valid agreement, but indicated a tentative conclusion to the effect that under the rules of tenure adopted by the college in 1948 Professor Hartmann was entitled to the same tenure rights as his colleagues above the rank of assistant professor. He suggested an out-of-court settlement—in the meantime, Professor Hartmann had obtained a position at Roosevelt College—and this was arranged on the basis of a year's salary and the payment of court costs by the defendant.

We recognize that a genuine conscientious objector may be motivated not by religious convictions but simply by moral ones, but since the two motivations are hard to distinguish, we include all such cases here. For convenience of treatment we refer here also those cases where trouble arises from the imposition of a pledge of willingness to bear arms. A notable example was the refusal of certain members of the University of Oklahoma and of the Oklahoma College of Agricultural and Mechanical Arts to swear an oath imposed by the State of Oklahoma on all its employees. The oath was of the elaborate type, requiring an affirmation not only of readiness to bear arms but also of nonmembership for the previous five years in any subversive association included in the attorney-general's list. Oklahoma University took a lead in active protests against the oath law. When it was ratified in 1951, a number of educators at the major educational institutions refused to comply and lost their positions. Some of these objected specifically to the pledge to bear arms. Seven ousted members of the Oklahoma College of Agricultural and Mechanical Arts organized an appeal to the Oklahoma Supreme Court. The appeal failed, but on December 15, 1952, the U.S. Supreme Court in an eight-to-none decision ruled the oath law unconstitutional.[23] The ruling, however, was made on the ground that under the law "the fact of association alone determines loyalty or disloyalty," even if the association existed innocently. Three of the justices—Douglas, Black and Frankfurter—wrote concurring opinions in which they expressed strong condemnation of all such oath requirements, and we take this opportunity to quote from the Frankfurter opinion: "Such unwarranted inhibition upon the free spirit of teachers affects not only those who, like the appellants, are immediately before the court. It has an unmistakable tendency to chill that free play of the spirit which all teachers ought especially to cultivate and practice; it makes for caution and timidity in their associations by potential teachers."

A general comment is called for as we review the cases in which an educator has been ousted because his religious convictions—or his conscience—impels him to violate some regulation or to set himself in opposition to some strong public sentiment. It is one of the oldest dilemmas in the history of mankind, the problem of the man who must face two clashing demands on his obedience—the law of God as he interprets it and the public authority, the law of man or his own conscience. Here, however, we meet it in one of its less extreme forms. It is not a question for the institution of learning whether or not the state should override a man's conscience. It is merely whether a man who for conscience's sake violates some rule—or merely opposes some cherished belief—should on that account be held unfit to be an educator.

Let us take the case of the convinced pacifist. We may profoundly disagree with his position, but he is standing by his own conviction of what is right, and that attitude is the very basis of all integrity. It gives

[23] 344 U.S. 183.

us some assurance that he has a high sense of responsibility. To dismiss him simply because we disavow his opinions is the very negation of all intellectual freedom, in the realm where intellectual freedom is of most account. Is he then to be dismissed because his opinions are harmful, unhealthy, for his students? Of what stuff do we think students are made, that we should feel obliged to shield them from the influence of a man whose fault is that he takes the Sixth Commandment more strictly than most of us? Or is it because he is unpatriotic? But, apart from anything else, we cannot honestly call a man unpatriotic because his views on what is good for his country are different from ours. In short, we see no ground compatible with the principle of academic freedom, or more broadly intellectual freedom, on which a man can be dismissed from an institution of higher learning because he is a pacifist. Where we are dealing with a state institution and the penalty is imposed by government, we cannot dispute its right and indeed its duty to vindicate its own law, though we may question the wisdom of a law that, to take actual cases, requires the dismissal of the chaplain of Denver University on this ground or, in another state, prevents a senior student who is a conscientious objector from receiving a teacher's license. But no such compulsion applies to the penalizations, beyond the law, that ousts a conscientious objector from a nonstate college. Indeed we are driven to surmise that when this takes place, it may well be because his views arouse enough popular resentment to cause some harassment to the administration. And while we fully recognize the troubles that academic administrations are beset with in this country, we nevertheless believe that nothing brings the high cause of intellectual liberty into greater peril than a willingness to compromise principle for the sake of this kind of expediency.

THE LINE OF SOCIAL TRADITION

We include here those interferences with academic freedom that arise from the attitudes and actions of the jealous guardians of the mores, the social conventions or standards or ideas that have the support of dominant groups or of the majority. There are of course various kinds of offenses against the established ways, including the ways of the profession, that properly qualify the offender as unfitted for educational office—the neglect of one's professional duties, the flagrant disregard of the principles and ideals of the profession, the addiction to habits that sap the mental vigor of the educator, the resort to modes of behavior that destroy the respect for him of his students. We are not concerned here with these, since there is no breach of academic freedom in the disciplinary treatment of such offenses. The situations with which we are mainly concerned are those in which an influential or power-holding group endeavors to make or succeeds in making its own predilections the official standard of fitness to teach, even though these predilections are particular to their own coterie or social class. Sometimes they identify their demand for conformism with morality, sometimes with the proprieties, sometimes with the "best traditions" of the institution, sometimes with the "American way."

Where such groups exercise control, the freedom of the educator is seriously infringed, and the more independent and freedom-loving members of the institution are likely to suffer most. It is the teacher who sets the highest value on intellectual freedom who is the most obnoxious to the authoritarians. The higher his standard of responsibility, the lower the respect in which they hold him. In being true to his own sense of moral obligation he is offensive in their eyes.

The institutions that generally suffer the most grievous damage from the authoritative enforcement of social tradition are smaller colleges which depart from educational routines, especially if they are situated in localities where there is no considerable group in the community ready to raise a protest. We have in our records several instances of such colleges the spirit of which has been broken, where governing boards have been receptive to the demands of an intolerant group.

For example, there is the case of Olivet College in Michigan. Situated in a small conservative community the college was something of an anomaly. It is a liberal arts college affiliated with the Congregational Church. In its choice of students it refused to discriminate between White and Negro, between Jew and Gentile. It believed in the tutorial system and was otherwise "progressive" in its educational methods. Some of its staff were "New-Dealish"; at least one was a socialist. Of course, the socialistically inclined member was charged with being a communist, but the charge was groundless and the board had to retract the accusation of "redness" publicly made by one of the trustees against him and three other faculty members. But the board was restive. There were various complications, and among other things the financial situation was bad—a situation that not infrequently is made the excuse for authoritative intrusion on the freedom of the faculty. The president of the college was "eased out." A new president congenial to the majority of the board was appointed, Dr. Aubrey Ashby, a corporation lawyer. He offered to take office without pay. He would "put the college on its feet" again. He was no sooner appointed than he began to wield the ax. It fell first on T. Barton Akeley, a professor of political science, and on Mrs. Akeley, who was college librarian.

Professor Akeley was one of the four against whom the false charge of communism had been leveled. That was two years earlier, in 1946. This time no charge was brought against him or against his wife. He was merely informed that "his usefulness as a member of the faculty" was "fulfilled." He was one of the mainstays of the "unified study plan" that was distinctive of the college. With an unsympathetic president and a new dean it was clear that the old order was doomed. The faculty was not consulted concerning the abrupt dismissal of the Akeleys, although a constitution adopted by the trustees called for such action. The new president was definitely going to rule. He denounced the college constitution in his first convocation speech. He declared that he reserved the right to pass on any article published in the campus periodical *Echo*. It is not surprising therefore that in its official report the American Civil Liberties Union investigation remarked that "Dr. Ashby does not understand the traditions and conditions of academic liberty." The conclusions of this investigation were in harmony with others initiated by the Michigan Branch of the U.S. National Student Association and by the Olivet Teachers Union.

The ousting of the Akeleys was followed a year later by similar treatment of four more of the liberal group at Olivet, and another was slated to go the following year. The attitude of the administration and the tradition of the community brought an end to what some had fondly called the "Olivet dream."

The offense against social tradition was clearly in evidence. The faculty was too nonconformist in a community which had too little tolerance of it. Take, for example, Professor Akeley. He liked to go around wearing a beret instead of the more conventional headgear. He had even been seen in town, in his earlier days at Olivet, wearing shorts. The secretary of the Board of Trustees declared to one faculty member, "It's not the socialism, it's the beret"; and one of the trustees complained to the acting president prior to Ashby's appointment, "We're always hiring such queer people." [24]

The situation we have just depicted illustrates a main characteristic of many such cases. It is hardly possible to assign any single specific ground of offense because of which the decision to dismiss was taken. Some objectors may refer to the "socialism," some to the "beret"; but it is the whole aspect of unorthodoxy that they find so disturbing. Aside from more personal differences—and there were those also in the relations of Professor Akeley and President Ashby—there is a whole complex of intellectual disagreement between the conformist and the nonconformist.

The observation just made applies rather to the attitude of that portion of the public which is easily incited to join the assault on academic freedom than to the objectives of the organized pressure groups which so often lead the assault. The latter are special-interest organizations and the special interest appears to be, in a majority of instances, an economic one, the apprehension that any kind of economic "heresy" is contagious and will be harmful to or even destructive of the whole system of business enterprise. In defense of this interest, however, these groups are ready enough to bring charges on noneconomic grounds against the offending educator—he is "subversive," an enemy of the "American way."

Accusations based on moral grounds are often, from the point of view of the accuser, the more effective kind of indictment. If they are couched in vague terms, as when the offender is charged with "behavior unbecoming to a member of the faculty" or "not in accord with the standards of the institution," it is hard to know how to refute them. If they make some specific moral charge, the defender is in an invidious position, even if the charge is exaggerated or is in itself not such as to justify dismissal. We have received in this connection a letter from the distinguished president of a Western university in which he states that he has made it a rule not to entertain charges of a moral character dragged up after a period of years because someone wants to get rid of a member of the faculty.

[24] The statements quoted above are taken from a report by Professor Milton Mayer in *The Nation*, November 27, 1948. The rest of the account is based on the reports of the various committees that investigated the affair. See also "Bung and Trough," *Time*, LII (October 18, 1948), 63; "Test and Tragedy at Olivet," *The Christian Century*, LVI (January 26, 1949), 102–3.

We know of no cases where an educator, clearly convicted of flagrantly immoral behavior, defended his position by appealing to the principle of academic freedom. Apart from the fact that such defense would be irrelevant, it is certain that his case would receive no support from his institution or from his colleagues. What usually happens in such situations is that the offender is himself most anxious to avoid publicity and silently disappears from the academic scene.

An example of the way in which a "morals" charge may receive impetus from quite other considerations occurred at Marshall College, Huntington, West Virginia. Professor Arthur A. Fothergill was dismissed. The charge against him arose under the following circumstances. A number of policemen raided a private club there, the Harlem Social Club. There are quite a number of these private clubs in the area, no doubt in part because liquor cannot be served in restaurants in this state. Although it is illegal to sell liquor in these clubs, there is evidence to the effect that the practice was by no means uncommon. This particular club, however, was one in which white and colored people could meet. The patrons were asked to report their names, addresses, and employers. Mr. Fothergill balked at giving his name and definitely refused to identify his employer. The other patrons were allowed to leave but Mr. Fothergill was arrested, taken to city police headquarters, and let out on a bond of $7.00. Rather than appear in court he forfeited his bond, thinking that ended the matter. Discovering his mistake, he employed a lawyer and stood trial. He was charged with "disorderly conduct by way of use of profane language." The evidence concerning the profane language was contradictory, for while the police officer in charge of the raid stated positively to the head of Fothergill's department, in the presence of a competent witness, that the accused had not used profane language, three of the accompanying police swore that, when asked his name, he had retorted: "It is none of your business what my G——d name is."

Professor Fothergill was discharged. The authorities said it was because of this offence against morals—there was also a breach of the law, but it is one that apparently quite a few highly respectable citizens committed in a state with this type of liquor legislation. The authorities denied that the presence of Professor Fothergill in a place where white and colored associated had anything to do with it.

If so, the penalty might well seem extreme. The State School Board dismissed him outright, without payment for the remainder of his contract period. They gave no consideration to a departmental proposal that at least he be permitted to remain until his annual contract expired. Not only so, but presently the head of his department, Professor Louis M. O'Quinn, was informed that his own services were unsatisfactory and that his contract would not be renewed at the end of the college year. Professor O'Quinn did not have tenure. A third member of the department, Robert W. McCall, resigned in protest.

Here, then, is the case of a man dismissed peremptorily because of "conduct unbecoming to a member of the Marshall College faculty." But back of it lay two other factors. One was the strong tradition against the social mingling of white and colored—the violation of which unquestionably arouses far more resentment in many quarters in the South than the offense of being in a club where liquor is illegally sold or the utterance under some provocation, if it were uttered, of a single profane expression. The other was the economic heterodoxy, in the eyes of a group which had authority in or over the college, of the three men whose connection with the college came to an end as a result of the affair. They all belonged to the department of economics. They all shared, more or less, the Keynesian way of thinking. Some time before the affair, the dean of the college had called in Professor O'Quinn and stated that he was "becoming more and more alarmed" about their "political philosophy."

We have given an outline of this case because it is typical, aside from the specific circumstances, of various others. It illustrates also how formidable a weapon a charge of immoral or improper conduct can be. Even if the offense is a minor one, the very attempt to extenuate it may be made to appear immoral. In this instance the gravity of the charge was much exaggerated in statements made originally by some of Fothergill's accusers. How seriously a charge of this sort is taken depends on the attitude of the judges, which may be affected by extraneous considerations.

No definite protest was raised in the Marshall College case. The local branch of the AAUP, acting on the request of O'Quinn and McCall, contented itself with expressing the opinion that the racial issue was not involved and gently suggested that the procedure followed by the administration in dismissing Fothergill needed to be improved. Other organizations looked into the case but saw no ground on which they could effectively stand.[25]

Over the whole area of morals no cases of academic responsibilities raise more troublesome problems than those that center about sex. They are not uncommon, although usually they are settled *in camera*. If the charge is serious, no defense is likely to be made, and even if it is minor, or again if it is not justified, the accused party may shrink from the publicity that would attend an appeal. Not infrequently such cases arise out of the relationship of teacher and student, or rather out of a change in this relationship in some particular instance where it becomes charged, on one side or on both, with the emotions of sex. The discussion of such cases, however, lies outside our field of interest here. On the other hand, situations arise in which an indictment is based not on what may be regarded as immoral practices but on "immoral" doctrines concerning sex relationships—views on birth control, on the instruction of the young in sex knowledge, on premarital or extramarital arrangements, and so forth. Occasions for the expression of such views obviously present themselves mostly to those who teach courses in sociology, anthropology, and social ethics. Under a strict interpretation of the concept of academic freedom it might be claimed that only cases of the kind just mentioned are relevant to our investigation. However, we shall briefly review some situations in which educators are subject to control over their private life, especially in matters where sex may be concerned, while similar controls are not imposed on the members of other professions. The character of these restrictions throws considerable light on the attitude of the public toward the educator and on the role he is expected to play in the community.

For obvious reasons such restrictions are more far-reaching in the regulation of schoolteachers than of their brethren in the academies. The Research Division of the National Educational Association sent out a questionnaire to the advisory members of its Committee on Tenure and Academic Freedom. Twenty-two percent of the respondents knew personally of teachers who had been disciplined for violating restrictions

[25] Documentary evidence for the Fothergill case was not procurable, and therefore our outline is based only on letters from Messrs. O'Quinn and McCall, on the report of the local AAUP, on a statement from the representative of the American Civil Liberties Union in Charlestown, West Virginia, and on short statements of the Dean and the President of Marshall College.

imposed on their personal life. And in answer to the question concerning topics teachers must avoid altogether in the classroom the subject of sex easily headed the list.[26] A few schoolboards even go so far as to forbid teachers to live alone in an apartment, while regulations forbidding marriage are not unusual.[27] It is wholly understandable that parents should require the instructors of their children to set a moral example, but when they impose on these instructors requirements they do not themselves accept, questions arise not only regarding the proper liberty of the educator but also with respect to his status in the community and the ability of the profession under these circumstances to attract men of independent mind. We shall have something to say on this general theme when we come to deal with the educator as citizen.

In our institutions of higher learning the degree of supervision exercised over faculty members varies very considerably according to the nature of the enclosing community. The size of the institution is also a factor. Thus the severity of control, whether stated in specific regulations or dependent on popular reaction, is generally greatest in smaller colleges, particularly state or municipal colleges, situated in those areas of the country where the tradition of academic freedom has had least time to develop or where, as in many parts of the South, the system of social relationships strongly predisposes the dominant group to put a high premium on conformity and orthodoxy.

It is under these conditions particularly that practices which may have nothing to do with actual sex relations in the stricter sense are regarded as disqualifications for teaching positions. The Fothergill case had for its background a club in which Whites and Negroes met together, and no doubt the taboo on this kind of association is primarily a sex taboo. Among other causes for dismissal we find membership in a nudist colony. One case is that of a professor of physics at Bethel College in Tennessee, whose appointment was not renewed because he belonged to the American Sunbathers Association. This college is at the same time a theological seminary, and it is not clear whether the objection was felt to be justified on the ground of religion (or theology) or on the ground of morals. Since we have another recent case where theology was not involved—that of an Ohio teacher of music—it is perhaps more likely that the offense was regarded as a moral one. However,

26 *The Freedom of the Public-School Teacher,* NEA Report, 1951.
27 *Ibid.,* Table 34, p. 60.

the evidence seems to bear out the conclusion that the people who are attracted to this kind of private nudist colony are generally scrupulous about
the correctness of their behavior. Therefore we surmise that the basis of
the dismissal was the violation of social usage or tradition, which in
matters pertaining to sex has a particularly strong public sanction. This
again is the type of situation in which effective protest or intervention
on the part of organizations interested in civil liberties is practically impossible.

Of all cases involving morals none has more significance than the
famous Bertrand Russell case. It is significant not only because of the
philosophical eminence of Bertrand Russell (now Lord Russell) and
his distinctive place among the social thinkers of our time but also
because in its setting it raised a whole series of fundamental issues pertaining to the nature of academic freedom.

In 1940 Bertrand Russell was appointed Professor of Philosophy at
the College of the City of New York, by unanimous vote of the Board
of Higher Education of New York City. The appointment was challenged by Bishop William T. Manning of the Protestant Episcopal
Church, who denounced Russell as "a recognized propagandist against
both religion and morality, and who specifically defends adultery."
Manning's protest was taken up by other clergymen of the major religious bodies and by a number of organizations, including the New York
City Council. Others sprang to Russell's defense, among them many
distinguished educators. There were also some clergymen who rejected
Manning's position, notable among them being a well-known cleric of
his own denomination, Guy Emery Shipler, editor of *The Churchman,*
who characterized Manning's point of view as "stemming from the
Dark Ages."

Some members of the Board of Higher Education weakened before
the assault, but the majority, headed by the chairman of the board,
Dr. Ordway Tead, reaffirmed the decision to appoint. Then a taxpayer
was found, a certain Mrs. Jean Kay, in whose name suit was brought
before the New York Supreme Court. The suit asked for the rescinding of
the appointment on the double ground that Bertrand Russell was an
alien and that he was an advocate of sexual immorality.

The hearings before the Court were marked by two anomalous features—at least let us hope they were anomalous. One was the attitude
of the presiding judge, John E. McGeehan, who in deciding against the

legality of the appointment decreed that the Board had no right to appoint an alien or for that matter anyone whose competence had not been tested by competitive examination. This decree is of course contrary to universal usage in all institutions of higher learning and if followed up would have called for the dismissal of every professor in every state-maintained institution in the country, not to speak of the indictment of the members of every governing board of such institutions for making illegal appointments.[28] He furthermore declared that Russell's books promulgated "immoral and salacious doctrines," that what the Board had established in appointing him was a "chair of indecency," and that its action was illegal because it sponsored or encouraged violations of the penal law, his view being that Russell advocated this violation in his discussion of sex relationships—a position which the judge later had to retract. Finally, he denied counsel's motion for permission to appeal. The denial came before the Appellate Court, which also was unfavorable. Judge McGeehan also denied to Russell, who was not allowed to be a party in the proceedings, permission to file an answer to the scandalous charges made against him.[29]

The other anomalous feature in the proceedings was the attitude of the Corporation Counsel, who is the legal adviser and representative of the Board. In the hearings before Judge McGeehan his assistant appeared and confined himself to refuting the only legally relevant argument in the petition against the appointment, to wit that an alien was ineligible. But when the judge ruled differently and when an appeal was sought by the Board, its legally appointed defender at law opposed and effectively prevented the Board from securing this permission. By this time dominant political forces in the city had taken sides against the appointment.

The decision in the Russell case highlighted issues of the greatest significance. One is the right of a court of law to void an appointment in an institution of learning because of its objection to the opinions of the appointee. On this basis the judge in question overrode the faculty that recommended and the constituted educational authority that approved the appointment. The action of this authority was stoutly supported by the most distinguished educators throughout the country. The professional body most immediately affected, the Western Philosophical Asso-

[28] For a review of the legal aspects, see Walton H. Hamilton, "Trial by Ordeal, New Style," and Morris R. Cohen, "A Scandalous Denial of Justice," in John Dewey and Horace M. Kallen, eds., *The Bertrand Russell Case* (New York, 1941).

[29] See Cohen, "A Scandalous Denial of Justice," *ibid.*

ciation,[30] unanimously passed a resolution adverse to the nullification by the judge of the appointment. The Chancellor of New York University, Harry Woodburn Chase, protested that the action of the judge was a blow "struck at the security and intellectual independence of every faculty member in every public college and university in the United States."

The action of the judge had even wider implications, inimical to the very being of a democratic constitution. The judge voided the decision of the properly constituted administrative authority, essentially not because that authority had exceeded the bounds of its competence but because he disapproved the course it took. It has been pointed out many times that this kind of judicial intervention is calculated to destroy the basis of all civil liberties, but nowhere more clearly has its character been exposed than in the words written by Thomas Jefferson into the Resolution of the Bill of Rights of Virginia.

To suffer the civil magistrate to intrude his power in the field of opinion, or to restrain the profession or propagation of principles on the supposition of their ill tendency, is a dangerous fallacy, which at once destroys all liberty, because he, being of course the judge of that tendency, will make his opinions the rule of judgment, and approve or condemn the sentiments of others only as they square with or differ from his own.

Not only did the judge do so in this case but he was grossly unjust to the moral position of the man he attacked—and then refused to allow him to be heard in his own defense. He gave a lurid picture of the foulness of his writings, ascribing evil and criminal motivations to their author. Actually in the books thus denounced Russell was dealing, forthrightly and sincerely, with the most problematic of all areas of social relationship. He was as much concerned for social well-being as was the judge, and his object was to formulate the ethics of sex relationships that in his judgment would best serve that end. It is a subject on which there is wide diversity of viewpoint. The judge had a different one from Bertrand Russell, but neither the principles of a democratic constitution nor the office entrusted to him entitled him to decide officially that a man who holds different doctrines from his own is not qualified to be a professor of philosophy.

It is accepted in accordance with our constitution that there shall be

[30] At the time of Russell's nomination he was teaching at the University of California.

no establishment of religion, but it is still believed by many that there is or should be an establishment of morals. In other words, while the religion of no group confers on that group any right of censorship or control of any kind over the religion of another group, there are many who have the will and believe they have the right to impose their particular moral tenets on other groups. Minority groups as well as majority groups reveal this attitude. It seems to be particularly characteristic of this country, most of all with respect to doctrines concerning sex. In no other area of human behavior is there so unbridgeable a gulf between the officially sanctioned ethics and the socially accepted ways. Here it is not a question of morals, it is a question of the relation of morals to laws. There is a dangerous and often quite false assumption that because we, or our group, disapprove of something as immoral therefore there ought to be a law against it. As Dean Richard McKeon, himself a distinguished philosopher, has put it, those who take this position do not face the question "whether morality and religion can be advanced by enforced acts of conformity and politically engineered acts of suppression and whether custodians of the spirit attain to things of the spirit by posting doctrines and condemning inquiry." [31]

When legal action is taken to suppress or penalize doctrines in the name of morality it is the more dangerous because those of us who share the same morality often fail to recognize the intolerance or to perceive its further consequences. The lesson is written in the history of civilization, from the time when the first great philosopher, Socrates, was condemned to die under the same charge which was brought against one of the most eminent of present-day philosophers, that of "corrupting the youth."

[31] Dewey and Kallen, eds., *The Bertrand Russell Case,* p. 97.

XI: COMMUNISM AND THE CAMPUS

There are no known adherents of the Communist Party on our staff, and I do not believe there are any disguised communists either. But even if there were, the damage that would be done to the spirit of the academic community by an investigation aimed at finding a crypto-communist would be far greater than any conceivable harm such a person might do.

JAMES B. CONANT

THE CONTROVERSY

WHILE VARIOUS STATES and municipalities have been making enactments and imposing oaths designed to oust communists from employment in public institutions, including colleges and universities, and while public opinion, influenced by current conditions and by politically motivated leaders, has been moving strongly in the same direction, a considerable controversy has been stirring over the question among educators themselves. Those who support the trend to debar communists rely mainly on the argument that a communist, at least a Party member, has renounced his own intellectual liberty and is no longer qualified to seek the truth wherever it may lead or to impart knowledge without bias. Thus Professor Arthur O. Lovejoy says that a Party communist should not be permitted to teach because he adheres to an organization that is against freedom of inquiry, of opinion, and of teaching and is himself committed to a movement to extinguish academic freedom.[1] And President Allen of the University of Washington summed up the matter in the words: "A member of the Communist Party should not be permitted to teach in an American college because he is not a free man." [2] On the other hand,

The quotation at the head of this chapter is from James B. Conant's final report addressed to the Board of Overseers of Harvard College.

[1] "Communism *Versus* Academic Freedom," *American Scholar,* XVIII (Summer, 1949), 333.

[2] "Statements by the President and the Dismissed Professors," *American Scholar,* XVIII, 327.

there are many educators who, while having no leaning toward communism, regard any such ban as needless and unwise, as a wrong approach to the problem, as opening the road to a perilous censorship, and altogether as a menace to the principle of academic freedom in the name of which it is imposed. And no less a champion of conservative republicanism than the late Senator Taft has gone on record to the effect that he would not dismiss a communist faculty member unless the evidence established that he was using his position to indoctrinate his students.

The issue here before us is perhaps the most difficult and many-angled of all those we have to face. Men of the highest integrity, scholarship, and regard for academic freedom take opposite sides on it. Must it not then, we may feel at the outset, remain a matter of judgment, an issue on which we may range the pros and the cons, frankly admit that there are powerful arguments advanced on each side, and recognize, if we give greater weight to one side than to the other, that we are merely adding another opinion where any verdict remains as open as before?

The risk must certainly be admitted, but there is one consideration that leads us to believe that the issue can be clarified and the difference between the two sides, at least within the scholarly world, reduced from a sheer opposition of viewpoint to a series of minor disputes within a fairly substantial consensus. May the answer not in large measure depend on how the question is framed? The practical problem is not whether a communist has any *right* to be permitted to teach in public or in private institutions of learning, nor is it even whether he can investigate with an "open mind" or teach without a tendency to bias. The concept of *right* is merely a source of confusion in this context, where it is a matter of weighing qualifications and disqualifications. And if we make the absence of bias the criterion, who is safe from judgment, if the righteous judge could be found? For us here there is one central issue, as well as a number of subsidiary ones. The question of communists as *school* teachers is not before us. We are dealing with the situation in colleges and universities, and an important part of the argument depends on the different situation of the college student in his pursuit of knowledge and particularly on his greater maturity. We shall have something to say on the question whether a communist is under any condition an eligible candidate for a faculty position, but we must in the first place draw a definite distinction between the problem of *appointment* and the problem of *dismissal*. And our central question is whether communists should as such be dismissed from positions in institutions of higher learning, account being taken of all the relevant consequences of such action and of the processes through which the result can or is likely to be achieved.

We are concerned with the total effect, so far as it can be ascertained, on the institutions themselves, on the morale of their faculties, on the attitude of their students, on the spirit of free inquiry, on the strength of the democracy we are seeking to defend. It may be hard to arrive at an assessment in these inclusive terms, but it is surely the only way in which we can properly determine our stand. Many of the reasons given in favor of dismissing communists, or in favor of letting them alone, confine themselves to particular effects without envisaging the whole impact of the policy recommended. Does the cause of higher education, do the standards of our democracy itself, gain or lose on balance by the dismissal of communists from teaching posts?

We must make the question more specific by limiting the denotation of communist here to anyone who is known to be a present member of the Communist Party or who gives convincing evidence that he subscribes to these communist policies which are exposed to the three charges presently to be set out. Throughout the discussion that follows we shall use the expression "Party communists" to include these two categories and these alone. We distinguish Party communists from former Party members who have abandoned this allegiance, from Marxists or near-Marxists—those who find themselves in sympathy, in whole or in part, with the doctrines of Marx himself but dissociate themselves from adhesion to the authoritative "Marxism-Leninism-Stalinism" of the Party—from socialists of any other category, and from those who may be dubbed "fellow travelers" either because they show "radical" tendencies or because they belong or have belonged to organizations regarded as communist fronts.

For reasons to be adduced later we repudiate any attempts to discipline or to dismiss any otherwise qualified educator because of objections merely to his ideological or philosophical viewpoint. Unfortunately the distinction we have here drawn is not admitted in the current agitation against "communist" faculty members. The term "communist" is used in the loosest sense and thus the real issue is thoroughly confused, so that the way is opened up to all kinds of insidious attacks on the university—and on the essential principles of education.

THE THREE CHARGES

Of the three charges brought against Party communists as educators, the first is that of intellectual subservience. The Party member, it is said, has committed himself to the rigid discipline of an authoritarian body. The decisions of the Party, which means the fiats of an autocracy, are not interpretations and applications logically derived from a philosophical doctrine called Marxism but policies swayed by the changing relations of the Soviet block to the rest of the world, by the demands of a monopolized propaganda machine, by the contest for power. Anyone who in a free country pledges himself to follow the Party line is abdicating his intellectual liberty and therefore Party membership is incompatible with the standards and goals of scholarship. The Party communist is betraying the first obligation of the seeker after knowledge, to reach his conclusions only by weighing the evidences and not to accept authority, above all a political authority, as the determinant of what is true and what is false.

The betrayal is all the more heinous because this particular authority makes pronouncements not merely on socio-political questions but on matters of every kind. The Central Committee of the Party delivers the word. It announces that modern biology is infected with damnable heresy. It proclaims that certain leading scientific theories are contrary to the sacred principle of dialectical materialism, and the Soviet Academy of Science bows the head. It lashes out at philosophers and at economists, at poets and dramatists, even at musicians who in some obscure way fail to strike the precise chords to which the ear of the dictatorship is attuned.

The indictment unquestionably has weight, but before accepting it let us in fairness hear the argument for the defense.

"The Party member is responsive to the dictation of an outside authority." In a broad sense everybody, including every scientist, accepts many things on authority. Nearly all of us—unless we happen to be astronomers—take on authority the doctrine that the earth moves round the sun. Everybody, except the physiologist, takes on faith the circulation of the blood. The most meticulous scientist accepts vastly more things on authority than he ever investigates for himself or learns by checking over the evidence. Any investigation anyone makes is predicated on a whole body of knowledge taken on authority.

The defense so far does not, however, fit the case. The authority accepted by scientists in their various fields is that of the experts in these fields; there is no useful analogy between authority of this kind and the politically minded authority whose dictates are the expression of expediency and the will to power.

The defense retreats to another ground. Communism is specifically concerned with the relation of the state to the economic order. It offers its answer to the question of how the two should be related, and in this respect it is the antithesis of capitalism, another doctrine of the way in which the two *should* be related. Science does not make any pronouncements on such questions. Science validates no *shoulds,* no value systems. A statement of value, in the moral sense, is a statement that something is good, worth while, to be preferred, to be achieved. It selects and rejects within the world of objective reality—and this world, or the science that reveals it, gives no warrant for such discrimination. It is the needs, the drives, the interests, the traditions of differently disposed men or groups that account for the variations of human valuations and of the "isms" in which they are formulated.

It is true that most "isms"—capitalism, socialism, totalitarianism, fascism, liberalism, republicanism, and so forth—adduce facts or evidences to support their claims, and such evidences can be verified or refuted. But the doctrine itself does not depend on any *particular* facts and can always resort to others if some are disproved. Such "isms" are not generalizations deduced from factual evidences but normative systems concerning the way in which society should be organized. Marxism, unlike most other "isms," did claim to be scientifically established, though that claim has little if any relation to the character of the system or to its acceptance by its devotees. Science no more validates or refutes the Marxist doctrine of how society *should* be organized than it validates or refutes any opposing theory. Scientists, like other human beings, have diverse and conflicting allegiances. Of six equally competent physicists one might be a Protestant, another a Roman Catholic, a third an agnostic, a fourth an Orthodox Jew, a fifth a Buddhist, and the sixth a Marxist. Their physics may lead them to reject the mere cosmologies traditionally associated with one or another of these faiths, but they will regard these aspects as irrelevant to the faith itself.

Such is the argument, but however valid it may be as applied to other "isms," it ignores the peculiar character of the "ism" known as communism. In the first place communism does claim to be scientific. Its system is the inevitable fulfillment of inexorable law: capitalism will fall not because it is evil but because it is doomed by the ineluctable processes of history. The key to history is the principle of dialectical materialism. Indeed, this dogma may be regarded as the root doctrine of communism, as expounded by Marx, of which the coming of the socialist society is merely a corollary.

The onus of the charge, however, is not that the communist interprets historical developments in the light of a dubious metaphysics. That fact renders him scientifically vulnerable, but the major accusation is directed not against the Marxist as such but against the Party communist, who has pledged his loyalty to an authoritarian structure that officially pronounces on all sorts of questions, including questions of fact. How can the scholar submit his own intelligence to this kind of authority?

The relation of authority and scholarship, it might be answered, is not so simple. The mind of man, even of the sincere scholar, is not exclusively focused on a single objective, not even on the quest for truth. An "ism" is not merely a theory; it is a dynamic theory, one that imperatively calls for behavior directed toward its realization. It can be brought to realization only by concerted action, by organization. If you are an earnest believer in the doctrine, you must join the organization that is best calculated to advance it. You may not agree with all its policies. A man belongs, say, to a political party or to a business organization, but he may not agree with all its commitments. For the sake of the cause he goes along with it, nevertheless. An educator, being also a citizen and a man, belongs, say, to the Republican or to the Democratic party, but it does not follow that he subscribes to all the policies or activities of the party organizations.

Whatever organizations he belongs to, it is the primary obligation of the scholar to avoid bias, that is, not to permit his other interests to distort the objectivity of his scholarship, or cloud his vision, or deflect his interpretation. To avoid bias is a permanent problem even for the scientist. Why is it, for example, that any great new theory, say the Copernican theory or the Newtonian theory, has at first been rejected by many of the older authorities in the subject it revolutionizes? It upsets their established ways of thought, their expectations and habits, even their prestige. They approach it in a sceptical manner, and they find reasons, plausible, perhaps even substantial reasons, to justify their scepticism. They thought they were unbiased, but they were unconsciously prone to seek reasons to discredit it and to ignore evidences in its favor. It is not alone the communist scholar who has a problem of bias. The capitalist scholar has the same problem. Everyone has.

Here the defense has a better case. But the prosecution is not through. It points to the peculiar character of the authoritarian control to which the Party member pledges allegiance. The Party is dictatorial. It demands "iron discipline" and unswerving obedience. Members cannot express disagreement with a particular policy without violating its principle and their own pledge. Stalin himself stressed the necessity for "the complete liquidation of factionalism and deviation in the [American Communist] Party." [3] How can a genuine scholar accept this kind of dictation? How can he, no matter what economic doctrine he cherishes, accept the authority of a party that notoriously treats all difference of viewpoint as damnable heresy?

The prosecution scores a point. It must surely be admitted that the attitude of the Party toward difference of opinion is one that cannot be reconciled with the spirit of free inquiry that is incumbent on the scholar. It may be replied that the Party member is not the only kind of person who subscribes to a creed that is interpreted by an authority that treats all deviation as heresy. Is it not true of the members of certain churches, and particularly of the Roman Catholic Church? Yet no one proposes their dismissal from institutions of higher learning. There are, of course, differences between the kind and the range of issues on which the Church makes pronouncements and those that the Party officially decides, and there is the further difference that the one represents a faith believed by the membership to be divinely inspired and the other can claim no authority except the wisdom of a group of powerholders. But if the objection is to the scholar who accepts an "outside authority," should it not apply to both cases alike?

It may be said that the Christian believer may take some latitude of interpretation concerning pronouncements made on authority—with respect to miracles, for example—and that if he is denied this freedom on explicit points, he can still remain loosely associated with the structure

[3] In his speech to the American Commission of the Presidium of the Executive Committee of the Communist International, May 6, 1929.

and in the last resort can, if his convictions lead him so to do, renounce his allegiance to his Church.[4] But is the same not true of the Party member, in this country at least? There are many instances, some of them in our universities, of men who have abandoned the Party. The evidence suggests that some members retain a certain independence of judgment and end by rejecting the "outside authority" when it seriously conflicts with the integrity of their own convictions.

Reviewing the first charge in the light of the arguments for and against we find no sufficient ground to justify decisive action. It is indeed hard to reconcile the function of the scholar, as a seeker after truth, with membership in a Party which operates in so ruthlessly authoritarian a style. But it is impossible to draw any clear line beyond which the acceptance of authority, so long as the member who accepts it is still free to reject it at will, is incompatible with the obligations of scholarship.

The second charge is that the Party communist is committed to the destruction of fundamental liberties, and particularly of the liberty of thought and its expression. So long as he remains a member, he manifests his acceptance of the principles and major policies of the Party. He may have reservations on particular pronouncements—though that is contrary to Party discipline—but he must surely, since he is free to leave it, be at least in broad sympathy with its operations. He must presumably be equally sympathetic to the parent Communist Party in Soviet Russia, for the American Party has throughout maintained this attitude and has on several important occasions reversed its viewpoint to conform with a new line of Soviet policy. On numerous occasions, moreover, the American Party has supported the Soviet side when it was in conflict with the position of the United States, for example in its interpretation of the Korean War.

It would then seem incomprehensible that an American educator would subscribe to the Party unless he were prepared to defend or at least to condone the methods persistently followed by the Soviet dictatorship. Here, then, is the gravamen of the second charge.

The Communist Party, wherever it is in control, habitually employs methods of intimidation and terrorism against those who in any way

[4] The problem of authority and intellectual freedom obviously cuts more deeply than is suggested by our remarks above. We seek to face the problem, so far as it concerns us, in Appendix A.

disagree with or refuse to cooperate with its activities. The Party demands unswerving automatic obedience within its own ranks. It has, everywhere within the ambit of its power, a grim record of purgation and persecution and liquidation. It monopolizes all propaganda, and its leaders have officially advocated the resort to any wiles or falsehoods that will mislead the "bourgeois" world and aid their own cause.

How can any educator enlist himself under this banner? How can anyone who believes in the free mind and the search for truth espouse a system that perverts all institutions of learning into mere mechanisms of propaganda and thought control?

There is no effective rebuttal of this charge. At best there are dubious and evasive attempts to minimize its gravity. A scholar might feel so deeply sympathetic to the major tenets of communism that he adheres to the Party while rejecting the Party attitude toward the liberty of thought. It is a difficult position to hold, but he may summon to his aid the Marxist myth that suppression is a temporary necessity by way of preparation for the coming reign of freedom when communism is fulfilled. The meaning of terms such as "liberty," "truth," and "democracy" are twisted round into their opposites—a favorite resort of all modern tyrannies—and the iron rule of the Soviet system is explained as a political necessity, as the only way, given the conditions, in which the revolutionary Soviet order could be imposed and maintained. But to represent a necessity as the very virtue it destroys is another matter.

The fact, then, that the Party member belongs to and actively fights for a system that habitually suppresses the fundamental liberties, indeed mocks at these liberties and pretends that its own tyranny is a greater liberation, casts a grave doubt on the eligibility of the member for the role of educator. There may indeed still be a case for an aberrant member here and there who lives in a curiously compartmented universe of his own, in which his right hand does not know what his left hand is doing. He may be driven by some strong conviction to accept communism and therewith the Party, while in another area of his existence he is devoted to the search for truth. Human beings have at times shown they are capable of this inconsistency, but certainly the doubt we have dwelt on can be dispelled only by a careful scrutiny of the individual case. The doubt is reasonable, but here, as always, the judicious course, that which alone can assure against unfair conclusions, is to test its application to the individual himself.

As to the third charge, that the Party is prepared to use violent and suppressive means to overthrow the government should the opportunity occur, the evidence in its support is conclusive. It is no doubt entirely possible for a person to be a member of the American Communist Party and yet to repudiate the resort to revolutionary devices. After all, the platform of this Party explicitly denies that it believes in or advocates the forcible overthrow of government. Nor do we doubt that the official Party in this as in some other statements is just as ready to dupe its own less "advanced" members as it is to present an innocent face to the world. But any scholar who is a Party communist and accepts this disclaimer in spite of the whole recent history of the communist movement must surely be so naive or so emotionally overwrought that his scholarly fitness may again be called in question.

A review of the evidence in support of the charge would be out of place here, since it would necessitate a review of recent world history as well as of communist doctrine and literature. What is required here is qualification and clarification rather than an accumulation of evidence.

First of all, the charge goes beyond a mere question of loyalty or disloyalty. Disloyalty is an accusation that the citizens of a democracy should be extremely wary of applying. A democracy assures its members the right to choose not merely any particular administration rather than another but any kind of government that seems good in their eyes, *provided they do so through constitutional means*. Through constitutional means, they can amend the constitution and by a process of amendment completely change its character. Back of this right lies necessarily the right of every citizen to advocate any kind of government, including a dictatorship. It is not unconstitutional to advocate Marxism, communism, or any other form of socialism. It is the citizen's right in a true democracy to condemn democracy and urge its abolition. If he does so, he is not properly convicted of being subversive, or disloyal, if disloyalty means the willful violation of any fundamental law.

While it is important to clear away this misunderstanding, the third charge against the Party communist is not thereby removed. It is one thing to advocate communism, it is quite another to advocate the forcible overthrow of the existing form of government. Anyone who does the latter is *ipso facto* disloyal to the constitution. Nay more, he is guilty not only of a serious legal offense but also of a grave moral offense, in that he would substitute the suppressive force of his own minority to destroy the rights of the majority.

Every government must endeavor to suppress the use of violence by private persons or by groups of any kind. To incite to violence is a crime, to take joint action with others for the purpose of forcibly overthrowing the government is conspiracy. It is the first business of every government to ensure that law shall prevail over violence. Unless it does so, its authority is undermined, its right to govern is forfeited. This is equally true whether the government is democratic or dictatorial. No government, whether it rests itself on force or on the will of the people, can take any other stand.

The answer is made—and it wins support from not a few good liberals —that a clear line should be drawn between advocating the resort to force and actually resorting to force. A man, they say, should be free to speak his mind on all things. The only way to deal with what we may regard as error is to confute it with truth, to let reason have free play. If we curb the liberty of thought at any point, we open the way to thought control. If we begin to be afraid of ideas, we are losing our faith in democracy. The first amendment of the Constitution expressed this faith. It made this faith the basis of a fundamental law. "Congress shall make no law abridging the freedom of speech."

The charge we are here concerned with refers not to opinions but to actions. The charge is that the Communist Party in this and other noncommunist countries is inherently conspiratorial, that it resorts to any deceit or falsehood that serves its objectives, and that it is committed to the *policy* of seizing power by violence whenever and wherever it deems the opportunity to be present.

The charge before us at the moment is one of disloyalty. Under the Smith Act it is a crime to advocate the overthrow of the government by force. The constitutionality of this act has been upheld by the Supreme Court. It is therefore the law of the land, even if there are champions of free speech who, with the American Civil Liberties Union and with Justices Black and Douglas, reject the grounds on which its constitutionality has been decided. That is, however, another issue. Nor are we concerned at this point with either the wisdom or the expediency of the act. But here again we need to remember that to establish guilt, the courts have required proof that the individual member was personally linked with the advocacy of force for the overthrow of government.

It may still be claimed, even if the admission is made that the Party approves the violent overthrow of democratic governments, that it is for the state and not for the college to take action in such cases and that if the state refrains from so doing in a particular case, the college might well follow the example. But the question for the college is not whether a teacher is prosecuted under a criminal charge but whether he is guilty of an offense that, even if he is not indicted or subject to legal indictment, is nevertheless of a kind that gravely militates against his fitness to be a member of the faculty. The offense in question is of that kind. To establish the offense from this point of view we need not examine the distinction between advocacy of the overthrow of government and incitement to it, or between advocacy and overt action. The offense stands apart from such distinctions. The Party is guilty of that offense. The Party communist incurs the liability of pledging himself to a body guilty of this charge.

Reviewing our comment on the three charges raised against the Party communist, we find that on the first charge the most favorable verdict that can be delivered against the individual defendant is the Scottish verdict of "not proven"—i.e., that the evidence is strongly adverse but not so completely conclusive that the defendant can be denied the benefit of the doubt; that he must be convicted on the second count, although he may plead extenuating circumstances; and that no acquittal is possible on the third charge except on the ground of mental incompetence.

It is well to observe that the indictment of the communist as educator depends not on any one of these charges taken by itself but on the weight of all three together. The Party itself is open to these charges. The fitness of the Party communist is properly subject to serious doubt because he deliberately identifies himself with a body so notoriously amenable to them. When he is challenged on that account, all he can decently ask is the right to exonerate himself, if he can.

The question at issue is whether the Party communist should be suffered to teach in a college or university. The evidence showed convincingly that *anyone who accepted without important reservations the methods and policies characteristic of the Party was not a fit and proper person for an academic position.* Whereas, if he did make such reservations while still remaining in the Party, his attitude was equivocal and engendered a reasonable doubt concerning his qualifications.

Does this then mean that all communists should be excluded from the academic profession and that any communists who now hold academic positions should forthwith be dismissed?

Let us ask first: to secure what end? Broadly, the policy before us must be justified on the ground that it would be for the benefit of our institutions of learning, for the sake of the integrity of their teaching and research, to advance the objectives for which these institutions exist. We have therefore to look at the question in the light not merely of the particular qualifications and disqualifications of the communist educator but also of the total chain of consequences that would follow from the implementation of the policy.

These latter considerations scarcely arise when the question is only whether avowed communists should be acceptable as candidates for academic positions. A number of factors relevantly enter into the choice between candidates. The practice in this country is to make inquiry concerning potential candidates and follow it up by an invitation to one of them. If any such potential candidate has a Party affiliation, or acts as if he had, that is quite properly a matter to be taken into account. No principle of academic freedom is directly violated when a college decides that a communist is a less desirable candidate or even, in view of the analysis we have already made, that no Party communist is to be regarded as an eligible candidate. But, for reasons later to be developed, this should be a matter for the discretion of the college departments and the college administration, not a rule imposed on the college by some political authority. Even so, the bearing of the argument that follows is to the effect that the only judicious way is to examine each individual case on its own merits and that any general rule of exclusion, even if it is set up by the college itself, may, because of the procedures it inaugurates, become a threat to academic freedom, and that the far better course is to regard the matter as one to be determined in each instance by the judgment of the faculty concerned.

The more serious question, however, concerns the policy not of hiring but of "firing." It is important to repeat that we are limiting our attention here to institutions of higher learning, recognizing that in certain respects the problem faced by the schools is different.

It is sometimes contended that no proper distinction can be drawn between the criteria of unacceptability for appointment and those that justify dismissal. Interestingly enough, this contention comes, with reversed emphasis, alike from those who advocate the more drastic policy and from those who do not agree that communist affiliation as such should be a bar to academic employment. The contention either way is unrealistic. In making an appointment, you assess the respective qualifications of different candidates. An unfavorable factor may make all the difference when it is a matter of preference. The same factor might not be at all decisive if the issue were one of dismissal. Indeed it happens not so very infrequently that a person chosen for a position later reveals, or develops, some attributes that had they been known in advance would have turned the scales against him—but he is not dismissed on that account. Moreover, appointment is done privately, it has no public repercussions for the rejected candidates. It carries no implication concerning the unfitness of the latter, whereas dismissal has very serious consequences for the reputation and the future of the person who is subjected to it. Finally, if a member of the staff does exhibit some undesirable attribute, in this instance a communistic affiliation, he is at least already known to his colleagues, and thus they are able to judge whether or not he permits his affiliation to influence his teaching, say in a field remote from the social sciences, or whether at any rate he is a trouble maker. On the other hand, a candidate who has the same disqualification is an unknown quantity and presents an unassessable risk that any institution would be most anxious to avoid.

We have acknowledged that there is a significant case to be made against the fitness of Party members to be instructors of our youth. We go further and assert that those noncommunists who plead their cause and denounce their exclusion, without admitting that there are two sides to the question and that the case against them has substantial weight, are not displaying the impartiality, the fairness of presentation, that so vexed an issue demands.

There are, however, other considerations that must be brought to bear before we can properly decide whether or not a policy of total exclusion is desirable. What matters in the last resort is not that a handful of communists should find lodgment somewhere within the vast confines of the academic domain. What matters is that no procedures be instituted, for the purpose of their exclusion, that will seriously affect the integrity of our institutions of learning, the intellectual independence of the faculty, or the professional status of the educator. No one who has any knowledge of the history of academic freedom in this country or who has followed certain recent cases can fail to see that any program of mandatory exclusion is likely to entail such consequences.

The impact of the processes through which a policy of exclusion is carried out is so far-reaching that it will require more extended treatment.

THE PERILS OF THE PURGE

You cannot purge our colleges and universities of communists by simply issuing an order to that effect. Somebody, some committee or board, must do the investigating and make the decisions. The records of faculty members must be checked. Suspicions are aroused and charges made. Elaborate hearings are called for.

Someone must conduct these hearings. It is the faculty that is under investigation. The final decision, when any of its members is impugned, is not in its hands but under the authority of its governing board. Inevitably, the faculty feels that an outside body, with which it has practically no contact and which may know little of its problems, is sitting in judgment over it.

The situation is rendered more hazardous by the looseness frequently associated with the definition of the term "communist" and by the fact that, in situations where communism is taboo, some Party members go "underground," disguising their affiliation. The chairman of the governing board of a large university informed the writer, at a time when this university was inaugurating an elaborate screening process, that the minimum the board would insist upon was the elimination of "all communists and fellow travelers." The additional disqualification is ominous, opening the road toward the establishment of a compulsive economic orthodoxy. On the other hand, if only Party members are to be eliminated, it is virtually impossible to *prove* membership, since the use of pseudonyms on Party cards has been common practice. The evidence of ex-communist informers is not always trustworthy, as certain cases have shown. So we have a curious anomaly. When investigations of the kind we are now considering are in process and faculty members are asked whether they adhere to the Party, some sturdy champions of academic freedom, standing at the opposite pole from the communist position in this matter, will refuse to answer and are likely to suffer dismissal—as happened in the course of the protracted and confused controversy over the regents' oath at the University of California [5]—whereas a Party communist who has kept his connections so hidden that he does not fear being convicted on a perjury charge is not unlikely to answer with an emphatic "No!"

There is a further problem associated with this type of investigation. The suspect is never asked merely if he is *now* a Party member. If he answers in the negative, the question that almost invariably follows is whether he has ever been a member. When an investigation takes place it is proper enough, and indeed inevitable, that this further question be raised. But it puts the person who was once a member and has now abjured the Party in an unhappy predicament. To confess his previous adherence may very well put his career in jeopardy. It is generally regarded as a black mark against him. And if he is honest enough to admit the fact, he may well hesitate about doing so for another reason. He is most likely, especially if he comes before an official committee, to be quizzed respecting his associates at that time. We have had some indications that the apprehension of the one-time communist lest he be under judicial compulsion or at least very strong pressure to bring trouble on his former friends has been in some instances a powerful incentive to evasion.

Under such conditions any thoroughgoing attempt to discover the presence of communists on a faculty—whether or not any may actually be there—is bound to become a vexatious scrutiny that causes, in all probability, more disturbance to the lovers of democratic liberty than to its opponents. There are no simple test questions the answers to which will infallibly unearth a communist. Nor is the case any better if, having found our communist and, being willing to give him the benefit of any doubt, we ask him the test question proposed by Professor Arthur A. Lovejoy: "Do you reject the teaching of Lenin (still to be found in current Party publications) that a Party member should, when it will serve the interest of the movement, resort to 'any ruse, cunning, unlawful method, evasion, and concealment of the truth?' " [6] Alas, the question merely highlights the dilemma of the investigator. If the Party member does accept the teaching of Lenin, would he not therefore answer, "Yes"? *If* he happened to be some kind of innocent idealist who accepted the doctrine of communism and disliked its tactics, would he not equally answer, "Yes"?

[5] See, e.g., George R. Stewart, *The Year of the Oath* (New York, 1950), Part I.
[6] *American Scholar,* XVIII (Summer, 1949), 337.

These preliminary considerations already raise questions respecting the efficacy and the desirability of investigatory procedures for rooting out communists in institutions of learning. They suggest that only some rather serious peril to the institutions themselves, or to the students whom they educate, can justify intervention of so inquisitorial a character. There may be the rare case, say in some college in a great metropolitan center, where a communist cell is or has been strong enough to exercise in some degree a subversive influence, but in the great majority of cases where investigations are conducted no ground has been discovered for any such conclusion. So that we can look more fully into the matter let us consider the various ways in which, at the present time, our faculties are subjected to tests or checks designed to assure that no "disloyal" or communist educators shall exercise a subversive influence on the students.

First, and very prevalent, are state-imposed oaths to be taken by faculty members. This requirement is one form of the numerous measures adopted by states throughout the Union, from New York to California, in order to curb "subversive" activities. The innocuous form of the oath simply requires a pledge of loyalty to the Constitution of the United States and that of the particular state in which the institution is located. In the case of state universities, the oath taken by faculty members is that which is required of all public employees. Where nonstate universities are involved, the oath is specifically directed to ensure the loyalty of the teaching profession. Municipal educational institutions are subject often to locally imposed rules directed against communists.

The simple form of oath above referred to raises no serious objections from faculty members. Many of them have a dislike to this wholesale imposition of oaths. They dislike the fact that teachers are often enough selected out for this treatment. Some of them feel that the oath, especially the part referring to the constitution of the particular state, has subtle implications making in the direction of political conformism. But no one can protest against the mere requirement that the teacher be a loyal citizen. There is, however, a widespread belief that actually the oath itself accomplishes nothing and that, so far as it may be used as a weapon against communism, "it is," in the language of one college president, "less effective than a toy pistol." [7]

[7] James P. Baxter, "Freedom in Education," in Clair Wilcox, ed., *Civil Liberties Under Attack* (University of Pennsylvania Press, 1951), p. 139.

There is, it is true, a quite defensible ground on which the educator might be treated as having a special responsibility, greater than that of the average citizen. For this reason as well as for more practical ones, it is bad strategy to oppose loyalty oaths on the ground that they discriminate against the profession. This faulty strategy, we venture to suggest, was adopted by the faculty group at the University of California at an early stage of their opposition to the regents' oath requirement.

The futility of such oaths is another matter. Nor is there any reason to think that much is gained by expanding the oath to include words to the effect that the teacher is not a member of the Party, does not belong to any association that advocates the overthrow of the government by violence, has no commitment that is in conflict with his obligations under the oath, and so forth. The endeavors of our lawmakers in this respect, seeking to pin down the offender as they more elaborately, but also more loosely, define the offense, are indeed becoming dubiously constitutional and certainly ominous in their encroaching preoccupation with anything deemed to be subversive.

A favorable sign is the resistance manifested in some states to this elaboration of the loyalty oath. In Nebraska, for example, an amendment to the oath was introduced in 1953, requiring the signers to engage themselves in the endeavor "to promote Americanism at every opportunity." It was subsequently withdrawn. In Oregon, in 1952, opposition to suggested additions to the law was led by the Oregon Education Association, the Oregon State Grange, and the leading verterans organizations.

A good illustration of the futility of such oaths, and of the fuss and furore they create, is afforded by the proceedings under the Pennsylvania Loyalty Act fathered by State Senator Pechan. This act was upheld by the Common Pleas Court of the state because of a ruling of the United States Supreme Court, but in so doing the judges declared that its application to "nonsensitive" positions rendered "the entire loyalty system not only absurd but oppressive." The act is an elaborate one and includes a provision requiring that the head of each state-aided university submit annually a report setting forth the steps his institution has taken to discover and dismiss subversives. Some institutions took the simple method of certifying they had no reason to believe they employed any subversives. Penn State College, however, felt under obligation to issue a questionnaire to all in its employ in which they were asked whether they advocated the overthrow of the constitution by force or violence and whether they knowingly belonged to any organization that so advocated. One member, Wendell Scott MacRae, of the Department of Public Information, refused to answer, protesting in the name of the American tradition and that of Pennsylvania, which calls on men "to resist oppressive and tyrannical legislation."

The Loyalty Review Board took up the case, and although Mr. Mac-Rae gave them most convincing testimony of his nonsubversiveness, it concluded that it lacked sufficient evidence that he was not subversive. President Milton Eisenhower felt he had then no alternative but to discharge him. A special committee of college members urged President Eisenhower to reopen the case. A former dean of the Pennsylvania Law School was asked to investigate. He cleared Mr. MacRae "unqualifiedly," and the President was able to reinstate him. As Professor Clark Byse remarked in an excellent "Report on the Pennsylvania Loyalty Act," "almost invariably the person hurt by a loyalty program is not the disloyal or the subversive, but the idealist and the nonconformist." [8]

From the legislative type of oath we pass to the special oath set up by governing boards, of which the best-known example is that which so long agitated the University of California. Again we admit that the requirement made by the oath was such that any decent citizen could fully approve it. Why then, it has repeatedly been asked, should the faculty have objected to it?

In the first place men of independent minds have always an objection to being compelled by any authority to repudiate a *belief,* no matter how alien to their values the belief may be. If, for example, they had been bidden instead to repudiate a belief in polygamy or, say, in witchcraft, they would probably have felt no less disturbed. In a truly democratic country belief remains unbound, and laws and regulations are designed to restrain men's actions, not to put a curb on their opinions. This is the implication of the First Amendment. And any attempt to discipline belief itself appears an intrusion and a precedent ominous of a new resort to the ancient ways of tyranny.

This argument was implicit and was not as such advanced in the faculty resistance to the oath. We observe in passing that in the earlier stages of the dispute the intrinsic grounds of objection to the oath required by the Regents were not presented with adequate clarity, though later they became sufficiently apparent.

[8] *University of Pennsylvania Law Review,* CI (January, 1953), 480–508.

Moreover, this new exercise of authority by a board over a faculty contained implicit threats against the status of the educator, against the two most vital interests of the profession. The protesting faculty members saw in the new requirement on the one hand a threat to academic freedom, on the other a threat to security of tenure. The pro-oath regents denied that any such threats were involved. They no doubt meant it quite sincerely, but this lack of understanding is one of the too frequent consequences of the lack of *rapport* that exists in this country between faculties and governing boards.

As for the tenure issue, it must be remembered that subscription to the oath was made in the first instance an annual requirement. This in itself was vexatious and suggested a lack of confidence in the integrity of the faculty. To an important group of faculty members it conveyed a further danger. With the prevalent tendency to label as communistic any "leftish" opinions, faculty members might be exposed to charges and subjected to investigation on the ground that they did not live up to their pledges under the oath. Any unconventional viewpoint might be adduced as an indication of communistic leanings, an occurrence by no means without precedent in the academic field. Certain happenings at the University of Texas, to mention only one of many instances, highlighted the danger. The faculties of American universities had on the whole accepted without demur the right of governing bodies, on which they had no representation, to administer the affairs of their institutions, but they understood in so doing that the specific qualifications of fitness to teach and to conduct research should be primarily their own prerogative. Their professional status depended essentially on this claim. Now it was endangered. A body of educators, specialists in their respective fields, among them scholars of world-wide reputation, must annually give anew a pledge to a governing board not composed of scholars, a board on which they were in effect without representation. The continuation of their employment depended on the giving of this pledge. The tenure on which they relied, their only safeguard, was jeopardized by a new ruling. In due course it appeared that scholars of repute who objected to the form of the new ruling, although the condition which it stipulated was one they fully met, were summarily dismissed from their positions.

These men stood for a principle. It was their interpretation of the principle of academic freedom, and that alone, which brought about their dismissal. Very many of their colleagues, who for a variety of reasons could not follow the same course, were in thorough accord with them. Scholars throughout the country were overwhelmingly on their side, as is shown by the number of the associations of scholars which went on record to that effect.[9] These men objected not only to the mode of dictation adopted by the board, they saw in it also a wedge of domination, an arrogation of authority by boards over faculties that, unless resisted, would imperil the free mind. They knew how easily the campaign for the suppression of communism was converted into a device for the establishment of economic orthodoxy. The record showed how often alumni or donors or newspapers or members of governing boards had demanded the dismissal or "disciplining" of scholars as being "reds" when they were simply liberals or radicals or "new dealers" or socialists or something else uncongenial to conservative minds. There were evidences that in departments or faculties, here or there, disguised or subtle pressures had been applied to prevent the advancement of such nonconforming members or against the renewal of their appointments if they lacked tenure. It was not that the scholars who protested against the oath requirement were themselves "nonconformists"—there were many good conservatives among them—but, whatever their economic viewpoints, alike they apprehended a growing peril to academic freedom.

Attacks on academic freedom can come from various fronts, but none seems to be more disruptive than that which emanates from governing boards. With the ostensible aim of "rooting out the last communist," as one board member expressed it, they rock the institution over which they preside. Governing boards are seldom prescient of the effect such edicts produce. They are too remote from their faculties to know how they feel and react to such measures. Often the disturbance that ensues comes to the governing boards as a complete surprise, as in the case of the rigorous screening measures adopted with a minimum of discussion at Ohio State University. Such censorship, or the imposition of special oaths, apart from their futility in operation, imply that the faculties are not fit to govern themselves in their own special field. Censorial and inquisitorial action on the part of those who themselves are not devoted to the scholar's search for truth is for the true scholar a vital threat. Nor is it less serious when it comes in the guise of a campaign to counteract

9 "The Consequences of the Abrogation of Tenure: An Accounting of Costs" (Interim Report of the Committee on Academic Freedom to the Academic Senate, Northern Section of the University of California, February 1, 1951).

communist or "subversive" activities.[10] It is indeed then the more dangerous, since practically all loyal citizens, including educators, are opposed to the ways of the Communist Party.

The danger to academic freedom from this campaign, or rather from the manner in which it is conducted, is seen even more clearly in the records of the various state legislative commissions or un-American activities committees. We have already discussed the mode of operation of these bodies and so will limit ourselves here to illustrating the impact on the faculty of their procedures. In the first place, it is worthy of notice that several universities that have imposed oaths or otherwise taken some kind of drastic action to oust communists are situated in states where these investigatory bodies were active. In California the Tenney Committee had by 1949, the date of the regents' oath, already published five rather alarmist reports, with much attendant newspaper publicity. As if that were not enough, another group of state senators, in the form of the Senate Investigating Committee on Education, were conducting public hearings and issuing reports, fulminating against "disloyalty" in the schools. It seems utterly improbable that President Sproul would have introduced the oath proposal before the regents but for the recommendations of new controls over teachers, including university professors, made in the 1947 and 1949 reports of the Tenney Committee. Whether President Sproul's action, designed to fend off a regular inquisition over the faculty, was wise strategy is another matter. What concerns us here is that the Tenney warnings and threats and proposals created the most serious apprehensions among leading educators.

A not dissimilar situation developed in the State of Washington. There the source of concern was the Canwell Committee (Joint Legislative Fact-finding Committee on Un-American Activities). The committee named ten members of the faculty of the University of Washington as present or past members of the Communist Party. This university was in one respect better equipped to deal with such charges, since they went in the first instance to the Faculty Committee on Tenure and Academic Freedom in accordance with the Administrative Code of the institution. The faculty thus had a definite role, a rallying point, and some degree of authority—conditions that were lacking at the University of California. Consequently the amount of disturbance caused

---

[10] A good illustration is afforded by the results of the so-called "self-investigation" that took place at the University of Colorado. See Appendix B.

by the affair was much less than it otherwise might have been. Indeed, while any charges of this order, fanned by the agitation of a very unacademic political committee,[11] were bound to cause some uneasiness in the faculty, this would have been dispelled if the president and the governing board of the university had been able to accept the judgment of the competent faculty committee. University professors, like other men, differ in their opinions concerning the proper way of treating communist members on the staff, but the decision of the faculty committee was respected by them all, and its acceptance would have been a signal precedent in the history of the struggle for academic freedom.

Complaints had been filed by the Dean of the College of Arts and Sciences against six of the faculty, centering around their alleged communist affiliations, and referred to the committee in question. The committee held thirty-three sessions and issued its report. It unanimously agreed that there was no ground for discharge of three out of the six. These three had testified to the cessation of membership in the Communist Party, to which they alike acknowledged they had once belonged. The committee said with respect to them: "We strongly feel that intellectual Marxism, unaccompanied by Party membership or activities, does not justify removal under the Administrative Code." A majority of the committee recommended the discharge of one of the six, on the ground that his responses to questions regarding his communist affiliations were evasive and that his relations with the university administration were uncooperative and unsatisfactory. As for the two remaining cases, there was considerable difference of opinion. Some felt that their freely admitted membership in the Communist Party was a sufficient ground for dismissal. Some felt that it was a reasonable ground but that it was not specified as such under the Administrative Code, and that unless that code were amended in this respect they could not recommend such action. Others felt that membership in the Party was not enough to justify dismissal, since the evidences before them were to the effect that the two members concerned had not allowed their communist leanings to affect their instruction—their fields were respectively English and Philosophy. The upshot was that a majority of the committee voted against their discharge under the terms of their jurisdiction.

[11] We offer as a minor exhibit of its attitude and style a facsimile of a letter received by the American Academic Freedom Project in reply to our request for a copy of the reports of the Committee.

REPRESENTATIVES
F. CANWELL. CHAIRMAN
RANT C. SISSON
DNEY A. STEVENS

SENATORS
THOS. H BIENZ. SECRETARY
HAROLD G. KIMBALL
R. L. RUTTER, JR.

UN-AMERICAN ACTIVITIES COMMITTEE

ROOM 116
146TH FIELD ARTILLERY ARMORY
SEATTLE 9, WASH.

NATOR THOS. H BIENZ. SECRETARY
BIENZ BUILDING
DISHMAN. WASH.

June 12 , 1951
Dishman , Washington

Mr. Leo Koutouzos
American Academic Freedom Project
515 Fayerweather Hall
Columbia University
New York 27 , N.Y.

Dear Mr. Koutouzos :

Your request of May 24 th has been
received .

I have hesitated to send you material
pertaining to the subject you have under advisement
because of the extreemly questionable character of many
of the Professors and students of Columbia University .
You cannot be unfamiliar with this situation .

There is no way of my knowing whether
or not you and your committee is just another semi
commie front organazation . Understand I am not accusing
you but I just do not know .

Nothing would please me more than to
have definate proof that your committee is really making
a study of Academic Freedom in Colleges from an
AMERICAN point of view . Heretofor nearly all investigations
of such nature ulitmately gave our mortal enemies a pat
on the back .

I am interested in hearing from you
again .

May I buy a copy of the transcript
of your findings ?

Very truly yours ,

Thomas H. Bienz
Bienz Bldg.,
Dishman , Washington

The President of the University, Raymond B. Allen, submitted the faculty report to the Board of Regents, accompanied by his own analysis which disagreed at significant points from that of the faculty. He accepted the favorable recommendation of the committee with respect to two of the three who had cut their Party connection. His comments with respect to the third were adverse, and he laid stress on a charge brought against him that the faculty committee did not regard as a sufficient ground for dismissal.[12] He also asked that the two who were still acknowledged members of the Party should be discharged. The Board acted accordingly.

There were, naturally, some repercussions. The overriding of the faculty committee's verdict created a sense of uneasiness in many members of the university. One faculty member sent in his resignation. A hundred others expressed their feelings in a statement of protest, in which they said: "We believe, finally, that the action taken has already done serious damage to the University and to the cause of education. The reputation of the University as a center of free inquiry has declined; the *esprit de corps* that gives confidence and character to any institution has deteriorated; and the University of Washington has invited education to join in a retreat from freedom which, if it continues, will weaken the morale which is democracy's best defense against totalitarian communism." [13]

Wherever a state investigating committee, on the hunt for communists, has made a successful inroad on colleges or universities, the result, according to the testimony of the vast majority of educators who have expressed their views, has been harmful to the free pursuit of knowledge and to the general welfare of the institutions affected. Dean Joel H. Hildebrand of the University of California has said: "No conceivable damage to the University at the hands of the hypothetical communists among us could have equaled the damage resulting from the unrest, ill-will and suspicion engendered by this series of events." The statement is well documented in a brochure on the subject prepared by members of the University of California, showing the number of teachers dropped and courses suspended, the frequent refusal by scholars to accept positions at the University, the protests of professional organizations in

[12] This defendant had, "on advice of counsel," denied in the first instance his former communist association but was troubled about it, consulted another attorney, and went and told Allen the truth, in advance of the Canwell Committee's hearings.

[13] University of Washington *Daily,* April 7, 1949.

various fields, several of which went on record against accepting its invitations, but even more serious was the bitterness of many faculty members, the uneasiness or sense of helplessness of others, and the utter impasse existing between the faculty and the pro-oath regents.[14] These scholars felt that they had been reduced to a state of educational subordination to a body of nonscholars. They could not forget, for example, that one of their number had signed the oath and had testified that he had never been a member of the Communist Party (though he had been associated with a communist movement in earlier years) and that he was dismissed on the ground that he did not meet "the minimum requirements for membership on the faculty." [15] What these requirements were, the faculty was not informed. They dreaded, with good reason, the approach of state-established educational orthodoxy. Had not Senator Tenney wanted to make it a misdemeanor "to teach any system or plan of government except the American system or to inculcate preference in the mind of any pupil for any such system?"

The University of California case is particularly significant for a number of reasons, and not least because it reveals so clearly the unwisdom of a policy of "appeasement." There can be little doubt that the original oath requirement was intended to stave off more drastic measures that seemed to be portended by the sound and fury of the Tenney Committee. To this end the oath was presented to the Board of Regents by President Sproul—it had not been demanded in the first instance by the regents themselves. Thus was set off the series of disturbances that has shaken this major university. The oath was at length rescinded, when the balance of power on the board was changed with the accession of new members appointed to fill vacancies by Governor Warren. But the hurt done to the university could not be healed so quickly—its prestige was injured, and it still suffered from the loss of the men who had left it and those who had not been reinstated. The

[14] Report of the Committee on Academic Freedom and Tenure to the Executive Committee, July, 1951, *Association of American Law Schools,* pp. 4–5 (mimeographed).

[15] Stewart, *The Year of the Oath,* pp. 42–46. We should note, however, that the assistant here referred to was employed at the University Radiation Laboratory and that special security considerations would thus be involved. Whether these latter considerations justified the dismissal of this faculty member is a matter that has been disputed, but our knowledge is inadequate to pass any judgment. We do point out that the broad formula used, considering especially that the investigation into academic fitness was made by the board and not by a faculty committee, set a precedent that might well seem ominous to the faculty.

Levering Act, with its more general application, came in as a kind of substitute for the regents' oath, so far as the university was concerned.

There was comparative peace, for a short time. In 1949, after the publication of a particularly flagrant report issued by the Tenney Committee under the editorship of a highly alarmist gentleman named Ed. Gibbons, the Senate Rules Committee voted to appoint Senator Hugh M. Burns to succeed Senator Tenney as the chairman of the State Senate Un-American Committee. Senator Burns was regarded as being more judicious than Tenney—he himself declared: "I would never use the hammer-and-tongs, dog-eat-dog methods Tenney used." But it soon began to appear that the quieter methods of the new chairman might be no less formidable than the noisy ways of his predecessor. The report of the "Burns Committee" for 1951 contained an ominous attack on Professor George R. Stewart's *The Year of the Oath* as being an example of "the naive academic attitude toward communism," and the Committee complained that the University had been permitting "subversive infiltration." Then on March 25, 1952, the administrative representatives of ten Southern California institutions, including President Sproul, met by invitation with the Committee.

A plan was unfolded. The proposal was that each institution appoint a "contact man" to watch out for subversive tendencies and report to the Committee. The ten officials agreed to the proposal. President Sproul explained that the Committee agreed there would be "no interference with the normal processes of faculty selection" and that the arrangement could be ended by either party at any time.[16] With these provisos he and other executives had accepted the offer of "friendly cooperation" made by the Committee.[17]

Here we have the unhappy picture of how the guardians of a number

[16] Statement of President Sproul to the Academic Senate of the University of California. The account of the whole affair is taken from reports in *The Daily Californian*, March 27–28, March 31, and May 5–6, 1952.

[17] So far as we know, this is the first instance in which a program for a regular system of "contact men" has been officially set up. We have heard reports of the operation of an unofficial or clandestine contact man in more than one institution, without being able to check the evidence. The writer has, however, an interesting testimony from one of his former students. While holding a religious office at a Southern university during the winter of 1951–1952 this gentleman became acquainted with a special agent attached to Military Intelligence. They became friendly and the agent in question made a proposal to him: would he undertake to watch out for "radical activities, such as the distribution of leaflets" at the University and report the same to the office of the agent? My former student was shocked by the proposal, especially since it was so incompatible with his function as a clergyman.

of institutions of learning have bowed to the will of a legislative committee that has shown scant respect for or understanding of the goals and principles of education. We may feel some sympathy for officials who have been so long battered by the constant harassments to which they and their institutions have been subjected, but there is little in this record that reflects any particular credit on their leadership. The chief counsel for the Committee has stated that the establishment of the contact man is the "first phase of an overall program." Three months thereafter the presidents of the colleges and universities of the northern part of the state accepted a similar plan. The chief counsel explained as follows the duties of the contact man: "If we have information about a communist front organization moving to campus we'll contact the contact man. Or if a notorious front-joiner is seeking a position on the campus we'll inform the college on that account." He has since testified that "hundreds" of persons have been prevented from obtaining jobs in educational institutions as a result of the new system.

On the credit side of this dismal reckoning there is one important item, the ruling of the State Supreme Court invalidating the special loyalty oath, a ruling delivered a year after the oath itself had been rescinded by the Regents. This decision, aside from its general significance, prepared the way for the reinstatement, so far as they were not already committed to other institutions, of the group of seventeen non-signers who had refused to accept a compromise and in whose name the case had been carried before the high court of the state.

In some cases, fortunately for the institutions under consideration, the demands on the colleges and universities made by these investigating bodies have been stoutly resisted. A salient case is that of the Illinois "Broyles Commission," which among its other activities conducted an "Investigation of the University of Chicago and Roosevelt College" and published a report to which was appended a series of drastic recommendations designed to purge these two institutions.[18] These recommendations include the rejection of any teachers who are members of any "communist front" organization on the Attorney-General's list, the dismissal of any student from any tax-supported educational institution who states he is a communist or refuses to say he will fight for the United States in the event of war with Russia, the ban of the sale of

[18] *Special Report,* Seditious Activities Investigation Commission, State of Illinois, 1949.

any communist literature within colleges and universities, the thorough scrutiny of textbooks and of all "questionable organizations," and the withdrawal of tax exemption from any school or university that does not comply with these recommendations.

The hearings of the commission were in the form of questioning by an "interrogator," J. B. Matthews, with members of the commission chipping in. The interrogator took the role of a prosecuting attorney, with no defense attorney provided for cross examination. Some leading members of the University of Chicago were "investigated." Statements were also made by Chancellor Hutchins, by the Chairman of the Board of the University of Chicago, and by President Sparling of Roosevelt College. The statement and subsequent responses of (then) Chancellor Hutchins constitute perhaps the most signal deliverance on the principles of academic freedom that any political investigating body has ever heard —but it obviously had no influence on the commission.

In passing we cannot resist quoting a few of his utterances:

The University of Chicago does not believe in the Un-American doctrine of guilt by association. The fact that some communists belong to, believe in, or even dominate some of the organizations to which some of the professors belong does not show that these professors are engaged in subversive activities.

It would not be in the public interest to exclude students of communist leanings. If we did, how would they ever learn better?

· · · ·

The danger to our institutions is not from the tiny minority who do not believe in them. It is from those who would mistakenly repress the free spirit upon which those institutions are built.

The policy of repression of ideas cannot work and never has worked. The alternative to it is the long and difficult road of education. To this the American people have been committed.

· · · ·

The university believes if a man is to be punished that he is to be punished for what he does, and not for what he belongs to. If I may venture to do so, I should like to remind you of the words found in our scripture: "He consorted with publicans and sinners." Therefore, he is guilty.[19]

Senator Broyles and his associates did not unearth any hidden communists, but they sponsored a whole series of bills embodying their recommendations. Eight of ten proposed measures failed to get sufficient

[19] *Ibid.*, pp. 19, 21, 49.

support in the Illinois legislature, and a ninth, Broyles's major Senate bill, was vetoed by Governor Stevenson. The University of Chicago and Roosevelt College were thus saved from what would certainly have been a most disintegrating blow to all their standards. Even so, the threat may have had some insidious effects in nursing a spirit of illiberality in the less educated sections of the public. And in certain quarters it sowed suspicion against distinguished educators whose loyalty the commission sought to discredit.

The evidences we have given, which could be greatly multiplied, may suffice to show that the type of legislative committee with which we have been dealing is ill-adapted to conduct watch-dog investigations of our institutions of learning. The various studies of these investigatory bodies made by men with scholarly qualifications reveal beyond question that for the most part they have been grossly careless of the rules of evidence, have spread their inquiries beyond the range of matters that fall with any propriety within the area of legislative control, have refused to give decent opportunities for rebuttal of charges or cross examination of witnesses making them, have acted as prosecuting and not as judicial organs, have freely accepted the principle of "guilt by association," have loosely applied the epithet "subversive" to innocent activities, and in addition have tended to regard as subversive any witnesses who disputed their contentions.[20]

In sum, legislative inquisitions directed at colleges or universities or special oaths imposed on educators by states, municipalities, or by governing boards, have a disturbing effect on faculty morale and threaten the spirit of free inquiry which is the peculiar enterprise of our institutions of learning and the primary devotion of the scholar. The historical record shows how pernicious and wasteful have been the efforts of possibly well-meaning but always misguided power holders of the past to suppress the explorations of the free inquiring mind. The new resurgence of these controls carries the same threat to our own age, and in no democratic country is the threat so clamorous as in our own.

[20] The reader is referred particularly to the Cornell University Press series dealing with this subject, including: E. L. Barrett, Jr., *The Tenney Committee* (1951); Vern Countryman, *Un-American Activities in the State of Washington* (1951); L. H. Chamberlain, *Loyalty and Legislative Action* (1951). The whole subject is reviewed in the volume edited by Walter Gellhorn in the same series, entitled, *The States and Subversion* (1952).

THE IMPACT ON THE STUDENT

Both in Europe and America, most academic circles attached high importance to academic freedom for the teacher long before they recognized the importance of academic freedom for the student. It was for the student to learn what the teacher was minded to teach. His not to reason why. He must sit at the feet of the master. He was free to learn what the teacher must be free to teach. This passive *Lernfreiheit* was enough; the real issue was *Lehrfreiheit,* the privilege of the teacher.

While *Lehrfreiheit,* so understood, was associated with the dignity of the scholar, with a high respect for his function that is now mostly lacking in this country, it had also a less happy aspect. Academic freedom was thought of as a kind of professional prerogative. Its social significance was underestimated, its value was narrowed. Academic freedom, in its proper significance, is not primarily for the benefit of the scholar but for the benefit of society. This point is well made in an essay by Dr. John W. Caughey, a distinguished historian of the University of California, Los Angeles, who was himself dismissed from that university for his uncompromising attitude toward the regents' oath. He explains that freedom to teach is really freedom to learn, that it is for the sake of the learners there must be freedom to teach.[21] Here we add another point. When the educator's freedom to teach is controlled, the freedom of the student to learn is challenged. It is done, they say, for his good, to protect the student against "insidious influences" and "false indoctrinations." That indeed may be the intention, but let us see how it works out.

In a later part of this work we deal more fully with the interest of the student in academic freedom. One aspect of that theme is the way in which the student is affected by the atmosphere of freedom or of restriction that pervades the faculty. Another aspect, and the more neglected one, concerns the freedom to think, to hear, and to organize and express his views that is accorded to the student himself. We can therefore the more briefly touch at this point on the impact on the student of the present flurry of control imposed alike on teachers and taught as a presumptive safeguard against the inroads of communism.

Some testimony has been adduced tending to show that on a number

[21] "The Inquiring Mind, Bulwark of Democracy." Unpublished Article.

of campuses students were becoming less inclined to speak their minds freely, or even to engage in argument, on controversial issues. Where this is so, it is surely an undesirable state of affairs, since it means the loss of one of the most stimulating intellectual experiences of student days, the broadening awareness of the problems of the world we live in as young minds meet in lively debate concerning them.

While some groups of students react in this manner, others are considerably agitated over the danger of paternalism that would deny to them access to any doctrine and by the threats of external controls that reduce the liberty of their teachers. Some student organizations, such as Students for Democratic Action, have expressed their resentment of such procedures. The writer attended a forum of students drawn from many women's colleges, at which a strong volume of protest was raised against this kind of "protection." [22] The students gave clear approval when the words of President Conant were cited: "I do not believe that we should exclude any ideas, no matter how antagonistic they may seem to our present mode of thought."

The policy of sheltering students from exposure to communist ideas is unwise on several counts. It is, in the first place, based on a false idea of the educational process. It says to the student, in effect: "You must not be allowed to hear certain ideas of which we disapprove, because you might be influenced by them." The way of education is to have the student wrestle with ideas, to teach him to *reason,* to exercise an intelligent choice, and to give him the opportunity to do so. "The scanning of error," said Milton in his *Areopagitica,* is necessary "to the confirmation of truth." And a later thinker added the point that the truth itself, if imposed by the power of law, loses its quality and becomes superstition: "the meaning of the doctrine itself will be in danger of being lost, or enfeebled, and deprived of its vital effect on the character and conduct." [23] If these arguments apply to the coercive withholding of "obnoxious" ideas from the public in general, they apply far more cogently when the students of our universities and colleges are subject to such treatment. Aside from that, however, it is ridiculously shortsighted to attempt to keep them from direct acquaintance with a philosophy that has nearly half the world under its sway, or from hearing that philosophy

[22] S. Parkoff, "Freedom and Security" (Sixth College Forum), *Mademoiselle* (August, 1949), pp. 194–97 ff.

[23] John Stuart Mill, *On Liberty,* Chapter 3.

explained by an occasional advocate of it, instead of only from those who oppose it.

Where the subject lies within his field of interest, the student should have the same opportunity to study the ideas of Marx as those of any other historical figure. He should be as free to assess the ideas of Marx as those of any other thinker. The critique of Marx's ideas which the teacher offers should be just as careful and as open to free discussion as the critique of any other system. Here as in all other teaching the exposition of ideas should be presented as fairly as possible and should not be framed from the outset in terms of denunciation. In other words, Marx and his followers should be presented in their historical setting and the exposure of the weaknesses and errors of the doctrine should be offered with the appropriate scholarly detachment. The student can and should be treated as capable of drawing his own conclusions. It is important, for practical ends as well, that communism should be understood as it is, in its various aspects, including an explanation of the reasons why it has captivated—or taken captive—so large a portion of the earth, and especially the East. We cannot meet its challenge unless we know that, too.

Moreover, if students feel that in any respect their teachers are under constraint from outside, they no longer will have the same assurance in the full integrity of their teaching. And since in the appropriate courses the teacher must deal with Marxism, communism, the Soviet state, and so on, his utterances will no longer sound to his students like the free comments of a free man and will be discounted accordingly.

Are we then afraid to let the student judge for himself? Such a fear can surely be entertained only by those who have no trust in the virtues of our own system, no faith in democracy. Such people doubly deny their professed faith. On the one hand, they reject the open forum for ideas that is the inherent condition of democracy in operation; on the other hand, they seem to fear that the ideas of one communist are more potent than the ideas of a thousand noncommunists. The Broyles Commission and other groups of that ilk have asked for laws to expel any student who is discovered to have communist leanings, lest he contaminate the whole flock. They are afraid that the presence of one communist, or maybe two, on a whole faculty will contrive in some damnable way to ruin the institution. What could such a lone dissentient do?

Supposing he did influence one or two students, against the whole tide of opinion—such students also must learn for themselves. Students are not so easily led away by any Pied Piper. All worth-while students want to think for themselves.

Let us also remember that college students no longer live in a cloister. The doctrines that are banned upon the campus they will certainly hear spoken outside the gates. For some, the mere fact that the doctrines are taboo will be an added interest. They become intrigued to hear more about what their preceptors are forbidden to mention except by way of condemnation. Would it not be more sensible to let the student hear them, if he wants to, where the issues can be more intelligently discussed—in the academic forum of ideas? How otherwise can his own ideas gain vigor and grow to maturity? How can he even be fitted to meet squarely the communist case?

It would seem then that those who would purge out communists from the campus by banning their books, by excluding their speeches, by inquisitional procedures to assure that no communist lurks among the members of the faculty, do not realize the consequences of the methods they adopt. They are not educators, for the great majority of educators are totally opposed to such measures. They do not understand either the needs or the reactions of the students they seek to protect. They are most often well-meaning people—except for some politicians who exploit the fear of communism—but good intentions without enlightenment often work great harm. They want to impose on the student a "fugitive and cloistered virtue," which happily the student himself rejects. They do not understand the processes of democracy, for they adopt the suppressive devices of its worst enemies. They do not understand that democracy is founded on the free man's choice between principles, between programs and platforms and philosophies. They do not understand that if democracy is to flourish, the habits of free choice between ideas must be fostered nowhere so much as on the campus, whence so many of the leaders of democracy emerge.

THE LARGER PERSPECTIVE

In the light of the preceding review we can now offer our answer to the question: should communists be permitted to teach in our institutions of higher learning? As we have seen, the question must be broken up into several distinct questions. Let us state them again briefly, together with our conclusions so far.

1. *Do Party communists, as the designation is here understood, possess the requisite professional qualifications for appointment to teaching positions?*

The academic disqualifications of the Party communist are so serious that no injustice is committed if he is excluded from nomination or appointment. In taking this position we again insist that our argument has no application whatever beyond the particular group here specified, and that the exclusion on ideological grounds of other qualified candidates, such as ex-communists or collectivists, is unwarranted and violates the principle of academic freedom. Furthermore, we regard as undesirable the imposition of any general regulation that would take the decision of *individual* cases of appointment where a Party communist is concerned out of the hands of the faculty and the administration. Any such regulation would remove the discretion and flexibility of action that can surely be entrusted to the institution of learning.

2. *Should there be laws requiring that no communist be employed as a teacher?*

Any attempt of the state to prescribe particular rules controlling the *educational* policies of the local and regional boards which are the constituted educational authorities is contrary to the American tradition and is regarded by leading educationalists as an ominous threat to fundamental liberties. In this country each community chooses the members of its own board, and each board has a large autonomy within the school system. The local boards are vested with responsibility, and it is surely better to retain the trust in them than subject them to an act of the legislature that threatens them with punishment if they fail to meet its conditions. The country has never felt that the public control of primary and secondary education was dangerous, precisely because this control was left in local hands and supported by local taxes. This happy condition is threatened by the new laws against the employment of communists in schools.[24]

[24] For a succinct presentation of the issue see President Conant's statement before the Massachusetts Joint Committee on Education, made in opposition to a bill of the type referred to—available in reprint by the American Civil Liberties Union (1949).

Our argument here is relevant to the public schools. When we come to our colleges and universities, whether they be state or nonstate institutions, the argument is reinforced by the consideration that their faculties and boards are in a far better position to know their needs and to safeguard their objectives than is any legislature.

3. *To assure that communists are excluded from teaching positions, is it appropriate or desirable that special politically organized bodies, whether set up ad* hoc *or for any more inclusive purpose, should investigate our colleges and universities and make recommendations and pronouncements concerning them?*

Here again the answer is unequivocally: "No." We are not, of course, disputing the right of politically constituted or politically appointed bodies to survey certain aspects of institutions of learning. Since these institutions are normally tax-exempt, the federal government or state governments may properly inquire, should any doubts arise, as to whether some particular institution meets the conditions. They may properly inquire into such questions as to whether they are discriminating, in the selection of students or staff, against particular groups of citizens. Nor would any serious objections be raised against an inquiry to ascertain whether, in view of rising costs or other conditions, they need subventions in order to maintain their standards and services to the community.

The Report of the Senate Internal Security Subcommittee, entitled "Subversive Influence in the Educational Process," justifies its investigations of colleges and universities on grounds we find wholly untenable.[25] "Our purpose," said Senator Jenner, "is to protect and safeguard academic freedom." Almost in the next breath he declares "there can be no academic freedom until this Soviet conspiracy hidden in our schools and colleges is exposed to the light." We hold this statement to be a total misrepresentation of the facts. We specifically deny that the situation in our colleges and universities constitutes a "national danger." We specifically deny that in these institutions "academic freedom is under attack by a monstrous growth no individual or community of scholars can fight alone." There is no scintilla of evidence that the policies or programs of any of our institutions of higher learning have been influenced or are in danger of being influenced by communist educators.

[25] Report of July 17, 1953, U.S. Government Printing Office, Washington, D.C.

The ex-communist informer Bella Dodd, formerly legislative representative of the New York Teachers' Union, testified that she knew of "cells of one or more" having existed in some eighteen colleges. How does a "cell" of one educator "conspire" against hundreds or thousands of colleagues? What sort of espionage by one or more communists has been unmasked within any of the colleges she mentions? If not espionage, where does the "national danger" come in? The body of university educators is, we repeat, thoroughly and invincibly loyal, and perfectly capable of maintaining the integrity of their institutions without any aid from Senator Jenner.

In sum, the whole character of the campaign ostensibly directed against communists in teaching positions and conducted by Congressional committees and state committees has been thoroughly misguided. It is the business of the legislators to make new laws and change old ones, and also to study conditions that suggest the need for new laws. It is not the business of the legislator, and emphatically not the business of a small legislative committee, to make pronouncements on the way in which universities should conduct their educational affairs.

4. *What then, as a device for excluding communists, of the policy of requiring a specific anticommunist oath, whether by legislative measures or by regulations of governing boards, from the members of faculties?*

Here it remains only to sum up. The device is futile, vexatious, and likely to bring about conditions of disturbance and even demoralization in the institutions where it is applied. It is futile. Never was there a better illustration of the saying: "The mountains were in labor and brought forth a mouse." How many communists has it unearthed at the University of California or at the University of Oklahoma or anywhere else? Indeed, it is so obviously ineffective and so obviously disturbing that those who still insist upon it are either woefully ignorant of the facts or else are animated by some ulterior motive. The demoralizing consequences are more serious when a governing board is responsible for the requirement, but, remote as some boards may be from any understanding of faculty reactions, the case of the University of California has made the consequences so manifest that surely no board can any longer have any misapprehension on the matter. If, therefore, a board still insists on this device, it is hard to avoid the conclusion that it is animated by the desire to deter nonconformity, to discourage "deviationism" from the economic orthodoxy its members approve. The term "communist" is easily extended to include "fellow travelers," and that vague term in turn can be interpreted as including anyone who "does not meet the [unspecified] minimum requirements for membership on the faculty," as it was put at the University of California, or who is not in accord with the "traditions" of the institution, as it was put at Ohio State University. Anyone whose orthodoxy is dubious is *ipso facto,* to such minds, "subversive," and after all, what difference is there between a subversive and a communist?

The "current American swearing epidemic," as one law journal has expressed it, has aroused great concern among those who prize academic freedom and, more broadly, the fundamental freedom of the mind. From many fine statements we select, to conclude this argument, one from an individual scholar and one from an organization of scholars. Professor Henry Steele Commager sums up the case as follows:

Finally, disloyalty tests are not only futile in application, they are pernicious in their consequences. They distract attention from activities that are really disloyal, and silence criticism inspired by true loyalty. . . . From the beginning Americans have known that there were new worlds to conquer, new truths to be discovered. Every effort to confine Americanism to a single pattern, to constrain it to a single formula, is disloyalty to everything that is valid in Americanism.[26]

The statement adopted by the Association of American Law Schools is a highly significant one, not least because it takes a position contrary to that of the American Bar Association. Its Committee on Academic Freedom and Tenure had previously made a report which, among other interesting points, noted "the ambiguous character of these negative disclaimers," remarking that not one of the test oaths under review was limited to a disclaimer of membership in the Communist Party and that many of them reached out to membership in or support of "subversive" organizations, "variously and vaguely defined." We quote from the Association's statement:

There are grave objections to any requirement that compels a teacher to disclaim particular beliefs or associations before being permitted to take up or continue his office. It is deeply distasteful to the loyal citizen to be asked to clear himself by a process of forswearing. The offensive quality of the procedure is not offset by any tangible gain, for it can hardly be supposed

[26] Henry Steele Commager, "Who Is Loyal to America?" *Harper's Magazine,* CXCV (September, 1947), 198–99.

that a traitor would obligingly reveal himself by refusing to make the required disclaimers. Finally and most importantly, experience, both recent and ancient, shows that tests of this sort once instituted are likely to be extended to everwidening areas of conduct and belief. . . . What began as an attempt to ferret out traitors is likely to end as a device for determining whether a man's opinions, and the opinions of those with whom he associates, conform to some standard pattern. When this occurs freedom of scholarship is at an end.[27]

We have thus far examined three expedients which have been employed for banning communism, or rather communists, from the campus. We shall refer to two others—briefly, since they involve to an aggravated extent the mischief inherent in those already reviewed. One is the resort to *ad hoc* investigations of the faculty by governing boards. No method is better calculated to disrupt the institution and demoralize the faculty. Action along this line is not infrequently demanded by irate alumni, sometimes accompanied by refusal to make contributions to the institution should the demand be rejected. This, for example, was the import of a letter to President Conant by Frank B. Ober, chairman of the Maryland Commission that drafted the antisubversive legislation of that state. He requested Harvard University authorities to pass under review the loyalty of its faculty members, citing the cases of two professors, one of whom had been active at a "progressive" rally opposing anticommunist legislation and the other of whom had acted as chairman of the communist-backed Peace Meeting in New York. Mr. Ober was protesting entirely against extracurricular activities of these professors and proposing that "the University" keep watch and ward over any such doings of its faculty members. President Conant briefly rejected, in a reply to Mr. Ober, the proposal of the latter, and left it to a senior member of the Harvard Corporation, Mr. Grenville Clark, himself also a lawyer, to state more fully the position of Harvard. Grenville Clark's rejoinder is a fine exposition of the Harvard tradition. To take the course Mr. Ober recommended, said he, "would be to repudiate the very essence of what Harvard stands for—the search for truth by a free and uncoerced body of students and teachers." If Harvard accepted Mr. Ober's philosophy of censorship, he asks, "what sort of place would Harvard be? . . . It would, I think, not require six months to destroy

[27] Statement on "Loyalty Oaths and Related Matters" adopted at the Association's Denver meeting, December 28–30, 1951.

the morale of both our teachers and our students, and thereby our use-fulness to the country." [28]

The considerations we have so far adduced apply even more forcibly against methods for preventing an occasional communist speaker from appearing at campus meetings when properly invited by an organization of students or by faculty members. With the prevalent fear of com-munism and lack of trust in our democracy, it is only a rare college or university that does not bring authoritative pressures to bear against such happenings. If we had any confidence whatever in the merits of our case, we would at least permit, under appropriate auspices—in-deed, we would gladly welcome and provide for—opportunities through which the students would hear discussions between communist and anti-communist speakers. Instead of which, we think we safeguard democracy by adopting the alien methods of its worst adversaries.

The screening of communist or near-communist speakers is easily ex-tended into a general censorship of all meetings on the campus. The most notable case is that of Ohio State University, where as the sequel to a controversy whipped up by two local newspapers the governing board passed a most drastic ruling. All speakers were made subject to the president's veto, and not even a questionnaire could be sent out by any faculty member without the president's "O.K." The volume of protest from the faculty, the official representative of the alumni organization, the students, local leaders of both the Methodist and the Roman Catholic Church, various public bodies, and important elements of the Ohio press was so great that the board soon began to retreat from its position. Unquestionably the University would have been completely disrupted if the "gag ruling" had been insisted upon. What concerns us here, how-ever, is that under the guise of excluding communists the Ohio State University authorities were setting up a censorship that would at once curb the freedom of the faculty and prevent the students from hearing any views deemed "undesirable" by the powers that be. It is significant that the board ruling was in the first instance evoked by some news-paper clamors about the campus appearance of a noncommunist, a re-tired professor of education who in a textbook written many years ago

[28] See the full text of the exchange in "Freedom at Harvard: An Exchange of Letters by Frank B. Ober of Baltimore, President Conant, and Grenville Clark, Fellow of Harvard College," reprinted from the *Harvard Alumni Bulletin* of June 25, 1949.

had made some sharp criticisms of the operations of free enterprise, and that the axe fell first not on a communist but on a Quaker. The President of the University, who fully approved the new ruling, explained that though it was primarily directed against communists, that could not be given as the sole ground for exclusion. There were others than communists, he said, who would do harm to the university if they were permitted to speak on its territory. He himself, or the board, had a greater responsibility for the interests of the university than had the faculty. Moreover, it would never do to say to any excluded speaker, "We do not want you because you are a communist"—since the charge of communism, however justified, could not be proved in a court of law and the university might find itself exposed to expensive legal suits. The grounds for the exclusion of speakers must therefore be left to the discretion of the authorities.[29]

We have now examined all the methods by resort to which attempts may be made to carry into operation a total ban on the presence of communists, whether acknowledged ones or secret ones, in our colleges and universities. In every case we have found these methods hazardous, mostly futile, vexatious and burdensome, entailing moral and intellectual costs that grossly outweigh any conceivable benefits. When therefore we are asked the question whether there should be rules or laws excluding communists from teaching in these institutions, our answer must be framed in the light of the knowledge already available respecting the procedures by which any such ruling must be administered and applied. The answer is accordingly: "No." In this matter the general rule must rather be to trust the faculties themselves to maintain proper standards.

All the tension and all the damage and most of the problem, so far as colleges and universities are concerned, would disappear if only the dangers and costs of these coercive methods, imposed on faculties from above or from without, were realized. Then, instead of general rulings or inclusive taboos, the matter would be left to each institution, and in the first instance to the faculties concerned. Then each case would be examined squarely on its academic merits and only when sufficient occasion arose. No university would be turned upside down because some professor of old English or some instructor in mathematics had

---

[29] These points were made by the president in discussions with faculty members and also in a conversation with the writer.

communist leanings. No controls would be set up by the administrative staff to teach the teacher his business, to lower his standards, and to break his morale. Freedom of inquiry would be unimpaired, and in this healthful intellectual atmosphere the spirit of democracy, the fierce foe of all totalitarianisms, from the left or from the right, would prevail.

This is the principle that after considerable discussion and study has been accepted by important groups that themselves are invincibly anti-communist, including the American Association of University Professors, the Association of American Law Schools, and the American Federation of Labor. It is a principle that, in times of popular excitement, some state universities and some municipal colleges may have very great difficulty in maintaining. But it should be asserted on every campus, without concession or equivocation. And for the most part its successful application can be assured by a proper understanding between governing boards and their faculties, itself a requirement that, as we show elsewhere, is of the greatest importance alike for the maintenance of academic freedom and for the general well-being of our whole system of education.

SUMMATION

We have treated the communist issue at considerable length. The length is disproportionate to the importance of the communist in the university: he is a rare enough phenomenon in our halls of learning and nowhere more than a minute percentage of the members of the faculty. On the other hand, the volume of agitation created by this issue and the numerous ways in which it has been made the ground or the excuse for attacks on the autonomy and the integrity of our institutions of learning have made it necessary to deal thus fully with the whole matter. Since it has many complications we now set out in conspectus the principles which we submit should guide us in dealing with communism on the campus.

1. The Party communist, as above defined, is exposed to serious charges directly affecting his qualifications as an educator. The Party to which he subscribes or adheres authoritatively rules on many matters concerning which the educator should be guided solely by the weight of objective evidences; it advocates the resort to illegal methods and foments conspiratorial and revolutionary designs; and, wherever it has

gained control, it has totally suppressed academic freedom and the right of free inquiry. However, the case against the Party communist as educator is primarily based on his relation to political *activities* of a suppressive or conspiratorial character, and not at all on his economic *theories*. It is the essence of the democratic liberty of opinion that no one is restrained or penalized merely because the majority disapproves of his opinions. No competent educator should therefore be dismissed or disciplined merely on that account.

2. No college or university educator should be dismissed or disciplined on the ground that he is an ex-communist, a theoretical Marxist (without Party connections), a socialist or "radical," or a political nonconformist.

Our conclusion is addressed specifically to the treatment of persons who already occupy faculty positions. Within a very important range it should be extended also to new appointments to the faculty. The principle of academic freedom is violated when a faculty nomination to a position on the staff is vetoed by administrative or other authority on any of the grounds referred to above.

3. In view of the charges to which the Communist Party is open, a communist, whether he carries a Party card or not, may properly be dismissed or disciplined if he injects communist propaganda into his teaching or into his relationships with students.

Conversely, the communist, even the Party member, who teaches a subject such as mathematics or geology, who keeps communism as his private faith, who in all his academic relations refrains from any tendencious statements concerning it, and who, moreover, says nothing to suggest that he personally is amenable to the three charges we make against the Party, could in accordance with the democratic tradition be suffered to hold his job. A democracy that has confidence in itself and in its cause would let him alone.

4. When questions arise concerning the presence of a communist on the faculty, the proper body to undertake an investigation of whatever charges are made is the faculty itself, through an appropriate committee. While the final authority is the governing board, that body should pay high respect to faculty judgment on the matter.

5. Any general investigation designed to uncover possible communists on the faculty is wholly undesirable.

6. The imposition of special loyalty oaths on faculty members—that

is, oaths requiring a denial of communist affiliations—is a derogatory, injudicious, and futile expedient.

7. If an organization of college or university students invites a communist to address them, they should be permitted to hear what he has to say.

8. No student should be debarred or dismissed from any institution of learning because he professes communist ideas.

Part Four

THE STUDENT AND THE TEACHER

XII: THE ACADEMIC FREEDOM
OF THE STUDENT

*Without a spirit of trust in our colleges and faith in our young people,
without a belief that we can settle our affairs with positive, bold, democratic action, we will move from one timid mistake to the next into
ultimate failure.*

HAROLD D. TAYLOR

THE FREEDOM THE STUDENT NEEDS

ACADEMIC FREEDOM is formally a freedom pertaining to a special
group, though actually it is no more than the special application to this
group of the first of all freedoms, the freedom of the mind. This group
has a special professional need for a freedom properly claimed by man
as man. However, in the history of Western civilization the struggle for
this freedom was fought on other battlegrounds. The great issue was
religious freedom, for the most part interpreted in a rather limited way.
The issue of academic freedom came much later. The group to which
it was regarded as applicable was that of the teachers, the academicians.
After it became established in the universities of Western Europe there was
still little recognition that a certain intellectual freedom of the student
was a corollary of the intellectual freedom of the teacher. The distinguished former president of Columbia, Nicholas Murray Butler, was
forthright in his assertion that the intellectual freedom the teacher
claimed—the freedom to question the established ways, to think inde-
pendently without academic penalization—did not belong to the student.[1]

This attitude may be a carry-over from the old days when colleges
were hardly more than high schools, and students were still pupils. But

The quotation at the head of this chapter is from Harold D. Taylor in the *Harvard
Educational Review*, XIX (Spring, 1949), 73.

[1] "Columbia University in This World Crisis," an address by Nicholas Murray
Butler, October 3, 1940.

it is incongruous with modern conditions when large numbers of college students are old enough to vote—and to marry—and when the more advanced students in the universities are already becoming competent scholars in their own right.

The idea of the student as a mere pupil, which still is evidenced in many institutions by the elaborate network of organized controls to which he is subjected, is harmful not only to the evocation of the student's capacities and thus to the progress of knowledge but also to the intellectual vitality of the institution. In West European universities the student is much less supervised and much less controlled, particularly in his extracurricular activities, than generally in American institutions, but at the same time he manifests more respect for his teachers. It is true that professorial lectures are more formal and rarely provide any opportunity for student questioning. But this is compensated for by tutorial and seminar discussions, at least for the more advanced students.

Whatever the system may be, the breath of life dies within it unless the student is freely permitted, indeed encouraged, to think for himself, to question, to discuss, and to differ. This statement covers the essential freedom the student needs. In the phrase of President Harold Taylor of Sarah Lawrence College, he should be thought of as the subject rather than the object of education.[2] In the common enterprise of learning he should be the junior partner of the teacher. The process of free inquiry in which the teacher advances his own knowledge is also that in which the student most effectively acquires his. The teacher learns as he teaches, and in a measure the student teaches as he learns. For his questions and his difficulties challenge his teacher to greater clarity of exposition and thus of comprehension, while the problems and the suggestions of the more advanced students may well lead him to new inquiries and new discoveries. And if in the fullness of years and of repute the teacher should be inclined to lapse into a "dogmatic slumber" there is nothing so likely to check that tendency as the keen questioning of his students.

The intellectual atmosphere of the classroom and the laboratory is enlivened and enriched when the student has a free opportunity to express his doubts and his ideas. If this initiative is not encouraged, if he is expected merely to accept and to reproduce the arguments and conclusions of the instructor, then the latter is imposing in degree the same kind

[2] Harold D. Taylor, "The Student as a Responsible Person," *Harvard Educational Review,* Vol. XIX (Spring, 1949).

of academic orthodoxy on his student that he would repudiate if imposed on himself. This mode of inculcation has a way of reacting on the instructor and fostering in him a more authoritarian and intolerant attitude. The student is only a beginner, his opinions are sometimes brash. But there is a better way of treating him than the mere exercise of authority. And there is a better way of gaining from him the respect he owes than the mere assertion of the teacher's superior knowledge.

The spirit of inquiry in the student may be suppressed in various ways. One of them is the practice of giving him a continuous succession of assignments to be duly learned, so many pages of text per day, and then expecting nothing from him except to recite them back or summarize them without variation or free discussion. It is a worse offense when the instructor grades the work of the student by the degree in which it echoes his own deliverances. In his *Education for Modern Man,* Professor Sydney Hook tells the incident of a teacher who used to give the lowest ratings to those of his students who leaned toward the doctrine of dialectical materialism. Some years later he underwent a change of mind and thereafter he consistently gave the higher grades to those who favored that doctrine.[3] It is hard for us to recognize scholarly ability in those who present a case for doctrines we dislike, but the duty of the genuine teacher is to recognize and to stimulate whatever intellectual capacities the student possesses. He can then with more hope of success point out to the student the flaws, false inferences, unsound generalizations, or other defects he may find in a doctrine advanced by the student. But if the student has some reason to think the teacher is unfair in his grading how likely is he thereafter to be convinced by *ex cathedra* arguments?

This, then, the freedom to express and to defend his views or his beliefs, the freedom to question and to differ, without authoritative repression and without scholastic penalization, is the academic freedom the student particularly needs.

At the present time it is particularly important that the campus should evoke and sustain this freedom. Outside the campus the pressures making for conformism impinge strongly on him. Some of them are directed especially toward him. Moreover, he soon learns that conformism pays. It is likely to make things easier for him when he seeks to secure a job in some industrial corporation or to pass the scrutiny of loyalty investiga-

[3] *Education for Modern Man* (New York, 1948), p. 182.

tions when applying for a governmental position or to be accepted by some bar admission committee.

The academic freedom of the student fits admirably into the academic freedom of the teacher, and a brief review of the relation of the two will strengthen the case for the student's share. In this relationship the teacher has properly the initiative. It is not for him to preach a cause or to expect the student to take his mere say-so on any matter concerning which men dispute. But it is for him to state his reasoned conclusions on matters within the area of his instruction. Here he is appealing to the student's own reasoning powers, and how can he do so effectively unless the student is at liberty to question the findings of the teacher? The latter should do so with proper respect for the teacher's greater experience but nonetheless with the readiness to follow his own reason wherever it leads.

The congeniality between the intellectual freedom of the teacher and that of the student appears also in the fact that any curtailing of the teacher's freedom of thought or of expression reacts on the attitude of the students. The more thoughtful among them, the better students in other words, become uneasily aware that the teacher is not a free man and lose their respect for him and their trust in the honesty of his teaching. They become more sceptical, even cynical, and are often inclined to believe that the suppressed doctrine must have virtue in it. Students have on several occasions been more vehement in their resentment against violations of the teacher's freedom than have many of the teacher's own colleagues. Certain present-day student organizations, including the National Student Association and, on the political front, Students for Democratic Action, have as a major objective the promotion of academic freedom. And some student organs, most notably the *Harvard Crimson,* have been persistently active in the fight on its behalf.

A distinction should, however, be drawn at this point. The manifestoes of some student groups couple academic freedom with "democratic government." If by that expression we mean the participation of the student body in the control of the educational policies of the institution, that is a separate issue which we would not here prejudge. If, however, it means the relative autonomy of student groups and student organizations in the conduct of their own extracurricular and extramural activities, then it certainly stands for another aspect of the freedom the student needs.

To develop his intellectual capacities and to be truly enlisted in the honest search for the truth of things, the student must be free to exercise his own reasoning powers in the processes of instruction. This primary requirement receives further impetus if outside the classroom he is not enmeshed in an elaborate system of institutional controls.

Like most other areas of American society, the campus is the scene of a great proliferation of organized activities. A large part of this organization is itself of student origin. It takes the form of athletic systems, fraternities, sororities, social clubs of every description, debating societies, political clubs, student's councils, and student press organizations. Reaching down into these activities there is an array of administrative controls, faculty supervisory committees, and so forth. While the everyday operation of the network of student organization is for the most part left to the students themselves, so that they arrange and carry out athletic and social events, club meeting, elections, dormitory regulations, campus publications, honor systems, and so forth, these activities are subject to overall regulation and supervision that in many institutions appear to go beyond the limits necessary to assure a proper respect for decency and order.

It is true that student self-government in some sense of the word has been widely adopted in American colleges. A survey conducted in 1943, in which 122 institutions were canvassed, showed that 88 percent of them had some arrangement of this kind.[4] This information may, however, be somewhat misleading, since the autonomy of students over their own affairs is subject usually to overall codes for the regulation of these activities, and there is usually in addition an element of administrative discretion to check such activities when they meet with official disapproval.[5] The institution must, of course, safeguard itself against any direct association of its name with any student behavior that is out of accord with its honor or its dignity and may properly intervene when any activity conducted under its aegis is seriously offensive on moral grounds. But students are not pupils and should not be treated as though they needed the watch and ward methods of a jealous foster parent. Not with this in mind do they think of their college as *alma mater*.

A good teacher understands that the interests and the enthusiasms

[4] B. H. Peterson, "Student Government in Collegiate Institutions," *Journal of Higher Education,* XIV (April, 1943), 205.

[5] See, e.g., Alonzo F. Myers, "Communication, Participation, and Democracy on the Campus," *Harvard Educational Review,* XX (Spring, 1950), 103–11.

of the young are not to be corraled into the habit grooves of their elders. Students need a wide range of liberty for the development of their capacities. They should certainly be allowed, encouraged rather, to think for themselves, even if there be a certain "wildness" in their thinking. It is the more sensitive among them, the more perceptive, the more idealistic, who suffer most or react most strongly from paternalism.

The other side of the picture is that the American student is well cared for, that his various needs are looked after through medical services, hygiene training, personnel work, voluntary religious ministrations, advisory services of various kinds, and in some institutions psychiatric treatment. These advantages, however, can equally well be provided under a system that avoids any paternalistic control of the students' own affairs, as some of our best institutions demonstrate.

The same type of excessive regulation exercised on many a campus over student activities may extend into the learning process itself. Our interest here, however, is limited to those interventions from above into student activities which may reasonably be held to infringe the needed academic freedom of the student by suppressing in some way his desire to express his own ideas or to listen to the ideas of others. Such controls have two main directions—over the campus organizations he forms and the meetings he plans in order to hear outside speakers, and over the campus publications that are run by the student body or by student groups.

THE STUDENT PLATFORM AND
THE STUDENT PRESS

Like all other groups united by common activities and common interests, the student body forms its own distinctive society, and since many of its members share the same residences on or around the same campus, there is created an interesting type of near-community. Its members are of the same age group; in some cases they are all of the same sex. It is a stratified group that loses a portion of its membership, usually a fourth or more, every year, and gains the same proportion of new members. It is a group regulated by an authority outside itself, an authority that gives and can withdraw the privileges of the campus. It is a select body whose members have passed a series of tests for intelligence and educational proficiency and have met other admission standards. Inevitably so distinctive a body has its own media of expression. Inevitably it sets up a variety of organizations for the purpose, some short-lived, some enduring through many generations of students.

The question of the student's academic freedom arises when institutional authorities limit his right to carry on these group activities as he thinks proper. The question reaches the heart of the matter when permission is refused to student groups to organize meetings of one kind or another, or to invite certain speakers to their meetings, or to express freely in their own papers certain views and comments. We must therefore center our interest on the degree of freedom accorded the student to run his own forum and to edit his own press. While the subject has received very scant treatment, anyone who examines the numerous cases in which the student has protested against what he regards as unwarranted interferences of authority must recognize that it has considerable importance. Within our limits we can give it only summary treatment.

We assume at the outset that no board and no administrative office and no faculty committee can be justified in censoring or otherwise curbing the expression of student opinion simply on the ground that it is distasteful to authority, and that such action should be taken only on clear evidence that the group or organization subjected to it is transgressing the bounds of order or common decency, or sailing under false colors, or breaking the law, or flagrantly violating the standards or regulations of the academic community.

The principle just enunciated is widely disregarded. To begin with, some institutions bar altogether student organizations for the discussion of religious or political questions. A very large percentage of colleges and universities refuse campus facilities for political campaign speakers invited by student organizations.[6] "Surely," as Monroe E. Deutsch has remarked, "political activity is as worthy as writing sports columns or concocting jokes for the college papers." [7] Some authorities are so fearful of the false association of their institution with the activities of particular student groups that they seek to ban everything controversial from the pure—or stagnant—air of the campus. In many instances the permission of a faculty adviser or of an administrative officer is neces-

[6] Robert F. Fay and Richard H. Plock, *Partisan Politics on the Campus* (Institute of Public Affairs, State University of Iowa, Iowa City, 1950), p. 8.

[7] Monroe E. Deutsch, *The College from Within* (University of California Press, 1952), p. 198.

sary before an outside speaker can be invited, and rejections of the unorthodox or the "radical" as campus speakers have been frequent in some areas, and particularly in state institutions. An extreme example was the case of Ohio State University, where a "gag rule" was issued—short-lived because of the widespread protests it met—enacting that no speaker could be invited to the campus without the express permission of the president. The regulations that still control student meetings in this university remain, in our judgment, unwisely restrictive. Not only must invitations to outside speakers be approved in every instance by a faculty adviser but, if the adviser has any doubts, the application is to be referred by him for the decision of the president. Under such a ruling there is a strong temptation for the adviser to play safe.

To treat students thus would seem to imply a strange conception of the preparation for life careers that the college offers. The campus is neither a schoolroom nor a barracks. Authority has its place on the campus as everywhere else, but it should not for extraneous purposes suppress the proper initiative of those subject to it. As an early advocate of a freer campus expressed it, "The idea that authority arbitrarily superimposed from above is good character discipline for young men would be a joke if this country did not suffer so much from it." [8]

It is a proper exercise of authority to check the *bona fides* of any student organizations that claim a place on the campus. But this scrutiny should go no further than is necessary to assure the administration that any such body maintains proper standards of decency and honor. It should not attempt to curb the expression of doctrine beyond that point. Every form and variety of student opinion should be equally free to express itself.

Here we come directly to the question, should authorities suffer student groups to organize associations of a communist character? We recognize that in states that outlaw the Communist Party it is their official duty to refuse permission to any such organization. But where this is not so, there is a good case for letting them exist. There is usually a handful of students who entertain a youthful obsession for communism, and not infrequently they are students of considerable ability with a touch of romantic imagination in their make-up. If the organization is banned, they feel a resentment against authority and are likely to foregather in

[8] Statement by Richard Welling, as reported in the *New York Times,* June 16, 1912.

clandestine ways. This situation tends to deepen their obsession. We must never forget, in dealing with this difficult subject, that banning does not ban ideas nor do expulsions expel them—rather, in situations such as this, they have the contrary effect. It would seem therefore more strategic, as well as more in conformity with the ideals of a free society, to allow such organizations to carry on.

Institutions that accept this principle may quite properly inform their students about the true character of organizations the names of which are misleading. This is the policy, for example, of Hunter College, which refused to ban American Youth for Democracy but publicly announced to the students what kind of organization it was. The University of Wisconsin took a similar position. Referring to the Labor Youth League, the only campus organization that appears on the Attorney General's list, it made the point (November, 1953) that this body "may operate legally with no more hindrance than pertains to an artistic or social organization, and its members now face no immediate consequences because of membership." But it warned students that their affiliation to it might entail consequences for them in the future—they might find themselves barred from federal employment or may be unable to obtain passports.[9]

Student organizations should be given official recognition when they comply with the ordinary rules of registration, when their *bona fides* is established, and so long as they conduct themselves in a manner that brings no deserved disrepute on an institution of learning. Some general stipulation such as that just mentioned is a necessary safeguard of official recognition. The stipulation, however, should be as simple as possible and such loosely defined disqualifications as "conducive to immorality' or "contrary to the best interests of the university" are objectionable, since they allow the widest latitude of interpretation and therefore of control. When a student organization is officially recognized it should, for reasons already suggested, be free to invite speakers of its own choosing without prior screening by administration or faculty. Columbia University successfully ended a situation in which controversies between students and administration were not infrequent by adopting a new policy under which any recognized student organization is free from any

[9] The information concerning Hunter College policy is contained in a letter to us from President George N. Shuster, dated November 19, 1953. The attitude of the University of Wisconsin is set forth in the "Report by the Committee on Student Life and Interests to the Student Body" (November 12, 1953).

censorship in inviting speakers of their own choice—though there has been some criticism by students of the phrasing of the stipulation for recognition. At Harvard University, any student organization is free to hold a meeting in a Harvard building (if a room is available) and to listen to any speaker it can persuade to come. We are informed by the associate dean of Harvard College that the only exception applies to persons under indictment, who cannot be invited without a ruling by the Corporation. A similar situation obtains at the University of New Hampshire, where, however, persons under indictment are definitely ineligible. This university in a Statement of Policy issued in 1950 points out that "both freedom of speech and assembly ought to be encouraged as the fundamental prerequisite of free inquiry and free discussion." Unfortunately a considerable number of institutions have still to learn that lesson.

The frequent restraints on the right of students to invite speakers are not, we believe, due so much to administrative belief in the educational desirability of such measures as to the fear of adverse public reactions if "controversial" speakers are admitted to the campus. The case against restriction is well stated by R. S. K. Seeley, as follows:

Not infrequently there is danger of student activities drawing toward the university—undesirable notoriety either by some radical pronouncement or by offending the canons of good taste. Since the public mind is quick to attribute to an institution the behavior and attitude of some of its members, it may be claimed that unrestricted freedom may be detrimental to the total value of the university. In general, however, the danger is a small one. Public memory is short and the universities can afford to set an example in showing an indifference to uninformed public opinion. There is far greater danger lest the university in its efforts to remain in good graces of influential friends may impose upon its students a standard of deadly mediocrity.[10]

We must acknowledge, however, that the administrators of state universities are often confronted with far more serious difficulties in seeking to follow this policy and need not only courage but also much persuasive ability in endeavoring to convince the public, or at least the legislature, that it is educationally a wise one. In this regard we venture to quote a comment from a letter written to us by J. Edward Gerald, the President of the Association for Education in Journalism—the national organization of the teachers, administrators, and schools of journalism: "There is no disposition or activity evident among the universities to persuade the general public to accept student discussion of critical issues as a neces-

---

[10] *The Function of the University* (New York, 1948), p. 64.

sary part of the process of growth toward maturity and as a valid link in the universal quest for truth."

The writer of this comment was thinking primarily of undergraduate journalism, a field of student activity that has witnessed even more agitation and trouble than the speakers' forum. Here we meet more acutely the issue whether the intent of the First Amendment should apply to the student body.

Some special features of undergraduate journalism should first be mentioned. For one thing, the college paper is seldom self-supporting. In the great majority of cases it relies on institutional subsidies. Frequently it is distributed freely over the campus, though in some cases it is sold instead, and in some it is sustained by a compulsory annual student fee.

Second, the undergraduate journal enjoys a kind of monopoly position. There may be other sheets or bulletins issued by student groups, but there is nearly always a single officially recognized campus newspaper, with some institutional privileges. However, it is not the monopoly element itself that is significant—it is only the same kind of monopoly that practically every local journal possesses—but the institutional support it receives. This, for example, enables it to appear as a daily, unlike the country newspaper, in the larger institutions. In a number of state universities the student paper is organized under a separate corporation, a system that is supposed to confer on it a greater amount of freedom; but cases that have arisen in some of these institutions make the claim rather doubtful.

Third, the official recognition and support bestowed on it involves at the same time certain obligations. The student press is a medium of information appraising its readers concerning all matters of college interest. It does a particularly important service by stimulating the sense of community in the student body, the sense of the college as a whole. It is useful also to the faculty and to the administration as a source of information regarding student attitudes.

Because of its official recognition and its semi-official status as the organ of the undergraduates as a whole the question arises whether alike in its editorial columns and in its news reporting it has the obligation to be properly representative of student opinion. The charge of a lack of representativeness is one that has at times called down administrative discipline upon it, as in the case of *The Chicago Maroon.*

If we take literally the demand for representativeness, we do not see how any newspaper can editorially voice the views of the whole community it serves. We have never seen such an organ, nor do we know how an editor can express a consensus that does not exist. If it be claimed that the paper should strictly follow majority opinion, it would have to conduct polls on various themes before it said anything about them and to change editors every time the poll went contrary to the opinions of the incumbent. What, however, might reasonably be expected is that the paper give adequate opportunity for the expression of all shades of student opinion. In this sense the student paper must show a sense of responsibility to the group it primarily serves.

It is on this count that there was a genuine case against an editor of the *Maroon,* weekly undergraduate paper of the University of Chicago. This editor had for quite some time been giving a strong play to the Party line, a viewpoint obviously not held by any except a very small minority of the students. The actual occasion of his dismissal was, however, his sponsorship of and attendance at the East Berlin Youth Festival in August, 1951. The University, through its dean of students, Dr. Robert M. Strozier, claimed that he had gone there as representing the student newspaper and without the permission of the University in so doing. The paper was accordingly suspended until the election of a new editor. The *Maroon* had earlier in the same year been a center of controversy. A faculty-student committee had recommended that it be investigated by a board of experts. The Dean was at first adverse to any such intervention but soon afterwards introduced a series of proposals intended to ensure that editors would be elected by and responsible to the student body as a whole. The action of the Dean and the proposals he made aroused considerable controversy. No doubt if a system had previously been established under which the student body as a whole had been in a position both to elect and to dismiss editors presumably representing them, it would have been well to have put the question of dismissal up to them for decision in the first instance. The National Student Association protested the action of the Dean, while admitting that the editor had abused his responsibility, and recommended a broad study of the relations of the campus press to the student government and to the institution as a whole.

While the University of Chicago is itself one of the institutions that have shown a high respect for the freedom of students and teachers alike, the recommendation of the NSA arising out of the *Maroon* case is one that is fully called for. The censorship and close supervision of undergraduate journals is an old story, and there is some evidence that these controls are tending to increase rather than diminish. A survey in 1952 showed that out of 141 institutions 91 exercised supervision over editorial policy, and in 64 of these the control "predicated prior censorship of the editorial content." [11]

If a college administration looked only to its own comfort and freedom from vexation, it would certainly take steps to control and to censor the undergraduate journal. For quite frequently it is a thorn in the side of the president and his staff. As President John S. Dickey of Dartmouth College said in a very revealing letter dated May 9, 1951, "few things are more trying to the man on the job than living day in and day out with the problems of undergraduate journalism. For every occasion on which someone beyond the campus is annoyed, there are probably fifty occasions when the official college is manhandled with all the zeal of which a certain type of undergraduate is capable when confronted with an adult target." But he goes on to give two major reasons why the price of this freedom ought to be paid. He puts first the educational value accruing to a community of scholars that has "its own experience with the raw material of freedom." Next he speaks of the practical effects of control and censorship. If the free student press gives trouble to the college, the attempt to control it is also a source of trouble. The college is then made responsible for whatever the paper prints—and "a little censorship leads quickly to more."

The most distinguished nonstate colleges and universities adopt the principle of giving practically complete freedom to the student press; the state institutions have greater problems so far as they attempt to follow the same line, though some have notably succeeded in doing so. Testimony to the educational value of this freedom has come from a number of presidents and administrators, including President Colgate W. Darden, Jr., of the University of Virginia, Chancellor R. B. House of the University of North Carolina, Chancellor William P. Tolley of Syracuse University, President Robert Gordon Sproul of the University of California, and President Deane W. Malott of Cornell University.[12] The leading women's colleges also set a very good example in this respect. A particularly interesting case of a free paper is that of the *Harvard Crimson,* which itself

[11] Russell E. Bert, "Trend Is toward Supervision of Student Newspapers," *Journalism Quarterly,* XXIX (Winter, 1952), 62–65.
[12] "Presidents Tell Policy for Student Papers," *Editor and Publisher,* Vol. LXXXV, Part I (September 27, 1952), p. 48; (October 4, 1952), p. 56.

has taken a distinguished part in the battle for academic freedom. It is managed by a separate corporation, made up of alumni, among them former editors, over which Harvard University claims no control.

In many institutions, however, an entirely different spirit prevails. Some go so far as to insist that all editorial copy be read and approved by a supervisor before it is set in type—this policy was announced recently by the University of Oklahoma. A large number hold that "the freedom of the student press should be commensurate with its responsibility"—as that responsibility is interpreted by the administration. Some take the position that they do not really exercise any censorship, but when a student paper goes off the track they discuss the matter with the students involved, in order to give them an opportunity to "correct the mistake." We should like, however, to know what happens should some editor persist in his deviant way, refusing to admit that he is "mistaken." We are unable to take at face value the announcements of certain institutions that they exercise no censorship over their undergraduate journals, when we find, for example, that a faculty committee "works with the editor," or that the dean of students "helps" the editor to interpret college policies, or that certain faculty members and administrators "act as advisers and counselors to the newspaper staff."

Various grounds are adduced as justifying the deposition of the undergraduate editor. He has transgressed the limits the administrator has laid down respecting the permissible area of editorial discussion. He has been unfairly critical of administrative policy and has unduly harped on institutional shortcomings. He has shown bias or partiality and distorted the facts. He has misrepresented the opinion of the student body. He has shown poor judgment or bad taste. His writing has been sloppy or careless. He has paid too much attention to sex and published vulgar jokes.

On one or another or several together of these counts quite a number of editorial heads have fallen. We shall limit our illustrations to a few cases that have a particular bearing on the academic freedom the student needs and on the consequences of the denial of it. Nowhere is the violation of this freedom less warranted and more contrary to the whole spirit of the institution of higher learning than in the curtailment and curbing of the expression of student opinion on important problems of the times. We shall present some instances in which, in our judgment, this kind of arbitrary and unwise control has been applied.

There was, for example, the case of the student *Daily* at the University of Washington. It happened during the heyday of the Canwell Committee's investigation of subversive activities in the state and particularly at the University of Washington. The editor of that paper, Leonard Saari, vigorously and in our opinion very intelligently exposed in a series of issues the methods of this committee and the state antisubversive bills it fostered. Saari printed at the same time student opinions on both sides of the question.

Ostensibly, at least, he was not dismissed because of this campaign. The faculty adviser of the *Daily* took exception about this time to other items proposed for publication by Saari. One was a news story concerning a former student who while in Alaska on military service made a wager with an acquaintance that he could mail a letter to Joseph Stalin and that it would be delivered. He was promptly taken in custody by security officers, sent to the neuro-psychiatric ward of a naval hospital, and listed as a "simple schizophrenic." This story was not published, because of the objections of the faculty adviser. The same person also objected to an article by a senior in journalism analyzing the situation behind a recent scandal in college basketball. It was also dropped accordingly. These incidents led to considerable disagreement between the faculty member and the editor.

A little later Saari spoke before the student organization in support of a resolution condemning the subversive activities bills as "invasions of the civil liberties of the people of the State of Washington." The same day the faculty adviser asked for Saari's dismissal. He was charged with various editorial offenses, such as harping too long on a single theme and "promoting the interests of a special segment of the campus." The faculty of journalism, which possessed this authority, accordingly dismissed him.

We have studied the available evidences in this case, including a carefully prepared thirty-three page report submitted to President Allen by an "independent students' committee," and conclude that the dismissal of Saari was ill-advised and unwarranted. We have no means of knowing how far the motivation was simply the fear of what the Canwell Committee would say or do about it, and how far other considerations entered in, but the charges brought against Saari were devious and misleading and suggest that other factors were at work. Was the impact on the university of the rough-riding Canwell Committee not one of the most important issues that the institution faced? Was it unreasonable of a student editor to devote so much space to it and freely to speak his mind? Was it only "a special segment of the campus" that had an interest in the affair? We may be permitted in passing to surmise that if Saari had defended the ways of the Canwell Committee, such charges would not have been preferred officially against him.

Quite frequently it is outside pressures, especially when these find a sympathetic response within the governing board, that induce the administration to curb the academic freedom of the student. A clear case of this type was the dismissal in 1945 of the student editor of the *High Hat,* undergraduate journal of William and Mary College. The editor, Mary Kaemmarle, presented social and biological arguments against racial discrimination. She did not advocate the violation of the state segregation laws, as was charged against her, but certainly favored their repeal. At once there were fulminations against her from all over the state, and she made the opposition the more furious by looking forward to a time when the Negro would be free to attend the same classrooms and even to intermarry with whites. Nevertheless a significant member of Southern newspaper editors, while disapproving of the editorial, came out in favor of free speech for the editor, and some expressed general sympathy with the objectives, though deprecating the direct approach, of the editorial.

The college board instructed the president to take corrective and disciplinary measures and to see to it that the contents of student publications were properly controlled. President John R. Pomfret, a man who was held in high regard, found himself in a very difficult position. He appeared before a student meeting and stated that if student publications were to continue, Miss Kaemmerle would have to resign and the contents of all future issues must be subject to faculty approval.

The students strongly protested and passed a resolution invoking the principles of their "honored alumnus, Thomas Jefferson," and asking for "free and uncensored student publications." Finally a compromise agreement was accepted, setting up a student review board, composed of the editor and six junior editors, which would refer all controversial matters to the faculty. The faculty itself, conscious of the difficulties President Pomfret faced, passed a vote of confidence in him, though there was some questioning of the handling of the problem and a considerable minority were against the control to be exercised over the student press. Miss Kaemmerle resigned her post, and the new order was established.[13]

[13] This account is based on various press reports, and particularly on those of the

Our next, and last, case has certain distinctive features. It illustrates some consequences of administrative prescriptions concerning the character and contents of the student paper. The President of Brooklyn College, Harry D. Gideonse, disliking the orientation of the *Vanguard,* which had a "remarkable similarity" to that of a "variety of ideological groups," expressed the desire that it confine itself to matters of local academic interest. Some time later, in June, 1950, the faculty-student Committee on Publications ruled that there be multiple editorials on every controversial issue. The *Vanguard* was regarded by the President as a troublemaker and on one occasion was suspended after the resignation of its faculty adviser. A few months after the new ruling came into effect, two students who had written opposition editorials complained that their contributions had been cut. The Committee on Publications proceeded to revoke the charter of the *Vanguard.* The four faculty members and one of the four students on the committee formed the majority for revocation. The other three students opposed it. Incidentally, the fourth student had written one of the cut editorials. A committee of the American Civil Liberties Union conducted an investigation and concluded that while the two editorials in question had been themselves edited, there was no evidence of intent to censor or to distort them. In its judgment, the Committee on Publications had acted hastily and unfairly. The President declared, however, that the affair was "a closed chapter" and that the *Vanguard* had exhausted the patience of a committee "which had over the years been exceedingly patient with the errors of undergraduate journalism." [14]

We could cite a number of interesting cases in some respects similar to those already mentioned, but to discuss them, with the various complications they contain, would take us beyond our limits of space. However, we take occasion here to remark that it must not be inferred that the institutions we cite are particularly bad offenders. On the contrary, a case is more significant if it occurs at an institution that generally maintains high standards. It is also well to remember, when we are dealing with the freedom of students, that no cases occur at colleges where there is complete censorship, open or disguised. We are not overly impressed when the head of a Midwestern state college informs us that the adminis-

_____

New York Herald Tribune, February 12–15, 1945. The editorial in question was reprinted in the issue of February 14, 1945.

[14] Our evidences in this case come from members of the student body and faculty at Brooklyn College, from the SDA investigator, and from the memorandum of the Academic Freedom Committee of the American Civil Liberties Union.

tration feels free to discuss with the students involved and with the faculty adviser any situation in which the college paper violated "the generally accepted principles of good newspaper conduct," a policy which "has invariably been successful." [15] We are still less impressed with the record of another academy, which reports that "the student publications never seem even to consider criticizing any faculty or administrative policy." [16] Being not unacquainted with the ways of students, we feel that something is awry.

It is well that students should realize the responsibilities involved in the editing of the college paper. But genuine responsibility is the child of freedom to act. True, that freedom needs to be fenced against serious abuse. An undergraduate journal should in the first instance be responsible to the student body. It is their journal, not the journal of the administration. Among other things, it should be free to criticize the administration. The administration should claim no right to censor it, for that is to treat students like school boys. There should be a clear understanding that the student body, acting through a student council, has the duty and the right to regulate their own paper. A faculty adviser can serve a useful purpose by bringing to the attention of the staff what he regards as faults or errors, but he should have no power of censorship. There should be no advance censorship by *any* controlling body, whether administrative, faculty, or student. If the faults appear flagrant and are persisted in, the faculty representative should advise the student council to that effect. It is for this body to assure the responsibility of editorship and to elect and to dismiss its own editors. The administration should step in only under the rarest conditions. If it reposes trust in the student body, it will protect itself as well. For then it has a proper answer to those who put pressure on it, holding that the institution itself is implicated in everything its students think and say. On the other hand, if the administration regards the control of the student press as a normal exercise of authority, it will not only be proclaiming the bankruptcy of its educational processes but will also, in the words of President Dickey, be "taking the first firm step toward altering the best in the character of America and thereby really opening the way for enthroning here the errors and evils which we abhor in so many other parts of the world."

[15] *Editor and Publisher*, Vol. LXXXV, Part I (October 11, 1952), p. 32.

[16] Taken from a series of reports in answer to a questionnaire sent out by the Student Guidance Center at the University of Utah.

XIII: THE RIGHTS AND RESPONSIBILITIES
OF THE EDUCATOR

What then are the limitations on the freedom of the faculty? They are the limitations on independent thought. They could be nothing more than the laws of logic and the laws of the country.

ROBERT M. HUTCHINS

This institution will be based on the illimitable freedom of the human mind. For here we are not afraid to follow truth wherever it may lead, nor to tolerate any error so long as reason is free to combat it.

THOMAS JEFFERSON

ACCENT ON OBLIGATION

IN NO DEMOCRATIC SOCIETY are there rights without obligations or obligations without rights. Every man who has a trust bestowed on him receives a corresponding obligation. The greater the trust the more imperative the obligation; the greater the freedom the greater also the responsibility. The proper distinction between liberty and license—a distinction so often misused—is that liberty passes over into license when the responsibility attached to it is rejected.

To the educator is entrusted a mission of primary importance to society. His special rights and obligations are those inherent in the nature of his mission—the communication and enlargement of knowledge. This assignment requires for its accomplishment academic freedom. Knowledge is of many kinds and has different degrees of certainty, but whether it concerns the physical universe or the mind of man or the history of his organizations or of the arts and the lores he has devised, the same

The quotations at the head of this chapter are from Robert M. Hutchins in the *Bulletin of the American Association of University Professors,* XXXVII (Summer, 1951), 243, and from a letter from Jefferson to William Roscoe, dated December 27, 1820.

necessity requires that it be sincerely sought and honestly imparted and that the educator be free sincerely to seek and honestly to impart. His freedom and his responsibility are wholly inseparable. They are the two aspects of the same trust. If here we lay stress on obligation, it is only for convenience of exposition that we set aside for the moment its correlative of right.

No elaborate code is needed to define the particular obligation of the educator—to seek knowledge sincerely and to impart it honestly. This simple obligation, however, fulfills itself in a series of relationships in each of which certain conditions have to be met and certain temptations overcome. If we spell these out, the full character of the educator's obligation becomes manifest. These relationships of the educator are (1) to his subject; (2) to his students; (3) to his colleagues; (4) to his institution; (5) to the public.

1. We set down first the scholar's relation to his field of knowledge, for his obligation here is basic to all the ensuing relationships. The right of academic freedom is anchored more deeply in the learning process than in the teaching one. The educator must first be a learner, an inquirer, and if he ceases to inquire and to learn his teaching loses its vitality. Moreover, it is new learning, new inquiring, that is most exposed to the attacks of the enemies of academic freedom and therefore most needs to be vindicated. Finally, the greatest service the educator can render, alike to his students and to the whole society, centers in the spirit of open-minded inquiry.

The educator's obligation to his field is a moral as well as a professional one. He must be scrupulous in his respect for all relevant evidences. He must not draw hasty conclusions. He must be fair-minded. The subject an educator professes is sometimes spoken of as a "discipline." Its first demand on him is intellectual honesty. He is called on to exhibit that honesty not only in his learning and in his teaching but also in all his public relations. An educator who does not reasonably present the pros and cons of a highly debatable issue, who does not first examine both with decent care, who treats unverified hypotheses as though they were invincible verities, who plays some favorite doctrine and drags it in where it is irrelevant or wholly out of place, is betraying his discipline and rejecting the primary ground on which he is entitled to professional status or respect.

2. It is the teacher's first duty to aid and sustain his students on the

road to knowledge. He should seek to inculcate in them the spirit of inquiry and to stimulate them to think things through for themselves. For him this should be an enterprise of the highest worth. He is disloyal to his trust if he regards his teaching as a routine performance, as merely a means to earn a living, or if he gets by with as little expenditure of effort as possible, or if he assesses the work of his students in terms of their ability to reproduce his own deliverances, or if he is superior or sarcastic when they venture to differ from him. The teacher should be free to teach his subject in whatever manner he finds best calculated to evoke a genuine interest in it in his students, but he should not resort to meretricious methods to display his own virtuosity. As it is put in the 1940 Statement of Principle on Academic Freedom and Tenure: "the teacher is entitled to freedom in the classroom in discussing his subject, but he should be careful not to introduce into his teaching controversial matter which has no relation to his subject." [1]

We might include here also the obligation of the educator to uphold, or at the least to refrain from curbing, those extracurricular activities of students that bring them together for discussion or inquiry.

3. The obligation faculty members owe to one another, to the whole body of their colleagues, deserves particular attention in an age of increasing specialization, when departments divide and each division becomes a nearly separate enclave, when individual scholars make highly delimited areas of knowledge their provinces. Under these conditions the *esprit de corps* of the faculty is easily dissipated. Their common interest, their common objective, the common faith that makes them truly scholars, has no rallying ground.

An important sign of this lack of *esprit de corps* in some institutions is the fact that more than a few faculty members may display a considerable indifference to violations of academic freedom that affect colleagues or departments remote from their own. If there is no immediate threat to their own academic interests, they remain complacent, disregarding the injury to the greater cause that unites them all. Sometimes, too, the faculty of a college that is under fire must fight a lone battle, with little aid or comfort from other institutions. There are happily, on the other hand, encouraging instances in which an important institution suffering grievous harm has been greatly sustained by the strong volume of effective

[1] *Bulletin of the American Association of University Professors,* XXXIV (Spring, 1948), 243.

support offered to its faculty by numerous other institutions. The most notable instance was that in which so many universities and various learned societies, alike by public protest and by practical contributions, came to the aid of the University of California in its time of trouble during the controversy over the invidious "oath" requirement.

It is incumbent on faculty members to eschew unfounded allegations or misrepresentations, and not least when they directly or indirectly involve their colleagues. To make flagrant charges without adequate evidence is peculiarly reprehensible in a scholar, since it betrays the very basis of scholarliness. Yet sometimes faculty men feel free to behave in other respects with a laxity and intemperateness that would wholly disqualify them if practiced in the study, the laboratory, or the classroom.

Occasionally the faculty member transgresses by making public propaganda for his side in an essentially intramural controversy. A situation of this sort occurred at the University of Illinois, in which gross insinuations were made against their colleagues by a small group of faculty men. It was during the controversy over the reorganization of the College of Commerce, a case already cited in another connection.[2] During this controversy a professor who had resigned to take a position elsewhere used improper tactics to cast doubt on former colleagues with whom he was in disagreement. Speaking before a businessmen's club he remarked that it was "barely possible there might be a few 'pale pinks'" among them, adding that "great Reds from little pinkos grow." Another member of the same faculty group gave interviews to the press that were likely to have a prejudicial effect. Since the local press, backed by certain interests, was already conducting a by no means scrupulous campaign against the reorganization, this action was all the more deplorable. Moreover, false and ugly rumors were being assiduously disseminated against the administration, and specifically against the new dean of the College of Commerce, Howard R. Bowen, and against President Stoddard. It would have been far more judicious if members of the university had refrained from public controversy and had sought instead, in a dignified manner, to reach some adjustment in consultation with their colleagues. To circulate prejudicial charges against their colleagues, to disseminate hints about their "unsoundness" before business clubs and other outside audiences, is unworthy behavior on the part of the scholar.

4. Every member of the association of scholars has not only his par-

[2] Chapter 10, pp. 132–33.

ticular field but also his particular viewpoint. The institution that brings them together has no particular field and no particular viewpoint. The university as an institution does not stand for any particular doctrine. If it is a true institution of higher learning it stands for no doctrines beyond the prescription of intellectual integrity. It has no dogmas, it prescribes no formulas, it bars no hypotheses, in the quest for knowledge. It makes one major demand on its members, sincere devotion to the cause of knowledge. It has one major goal, the facilitation of the pursuit of knowledge and of the spread of knowledge, so that society may receive in greater measure the inestimable benefits that accrue from the revelation of the nature of things and of the experience of mankind. So noble a goal stands in its own right. Whatever else man needs, whatever else he seeks, alike it calls for the guidance, the correction, and the equipment that comes from the increase of knowledge.

It is the obligation of the scholar-educator to uphold the honor of his institution and not to discredit it by conduct that is discordant with its goal. In matters that lie outside his professional field he should not display a cocksureness or a partisanship that would properly discredit him if carried over to the area of scholarship. He should always remember that he holds his institutional position not as a universal authority but as, presumably, a qualified practitioner in a particular field. He takes undue advantage of his position if he makes his classroom a forum for deliverances on the world at large.

Only in flagrant cases can offenses against this obligation be controlled by disciplinary action. There was, for example, the case of a teacher at Hunter College against whom the complaint was made that he spent half his teaching time on matters that lay outside the syllabus of his course (hygiene); that he continually preached his own social, political, moral, and religious views, dogmatically sweeping aside the beliefs held by large and well-respected groups in the community; and that in the process he made loose and indiscriminate accusations against some of his colleagues. The complaint was generally sustained by college investigation. Such evidence as we have read appears to confirm the charge, and if we may broadly assume that it was justified, then there was certainly no violation of academic rights in the action officially taken—which was to transfer the offender to a nonteaching post.

The requirement that the scholar uphold the honor of his institution and that he do not, either in his professional or in his public relations, act so as to discredit what it stands for, is sometimes stated in a misleading way. For example, a college president, while speaking of the value of academic freedom, went on to define it as "freedom with responsibility and restraint which, in its relation to the institution, must not injure or embarrass that institution." When we should speak of an "institution" as "embarrassed" is perhaps a difficult question to answer, but probably most administrators would regard their institutions as embarrassed when one of its members takes a position that arouses the resentment of a dominant group, or when a large proportion of the faculty protest against a ruling of the governing board, as in the famous University of California case, or when the faculty as a whole takes such a position, as at Ohio State University. Yet it is only by such "embarrassing" procedures that academic freedom can be preserved. If the institution is true to its own principle, or rather to the very ground of its existence as an institution of learning, it will not be embarrassed when educators seek to vindicate this principle. Sometimes it may suffer, because the public may not be educated to understand what is involved. It would indeed seem as if our educational institutions must do more to educate the public in this respect. If in the process they suffer somewhat, is it not true that all freedom entails some risk of loss in the very act of defending it? There is no freedom, any more than there is any achievement, without risk.

Let us frankly admit that the defense of academic freedom may have its costs, sometimes serious costs, that it may embarrass the institution financially and otherwise. In these times some administrators must have perplexedly put the question to themselves: is it worth the price? They are the custodians of the institution; can they afford, have they even the right, to endanger it? Since, however, the alternatives are simply the assumption of the risk or the betrayal of the cause, we hold that the answer must be, in the words of a distinguished administrator: "Yes, it is worth the price, any price." [3] Nor should we forget that the willingness to take the risk becomes the finest lesson to the people of the worthiness of the cause for which the risk is taken.

It is the obligation of the educator to act so as not to embarrass the institution in fulfilling the mission to which it is or should be dedicated, so as not to injure the reputation of his institution as one dedicated to this mission. But the institution, so understood, is not to be identified with

[3] Chancellor Emeritus of the University of Buffalo, Samuel P. Capen, *The Management of Universities* (Buffalo, New York, 1953), p. 28.

its governing board or with its administration, and if the president or the trustees should pursue a policy that in his judgment is detrimental to its cause, the scholar is not under obligation to hold his peace. On the contrary, it is his right and, according to the conditions, it may be his obligation to protest. He should of course do so in the proper place and in a seemly manner. In earlier times it was a commonplace for presidents to dismiss offhand educators who objected to their procedures. Happily that spirit no longer prevails, but there are still some institutions where the old autocracy lingers on.

A recent case offers a good illustration. In the fall of 1952 Dr. Minard W. Stout assumed office as president of the University of Nevada, having previously been principal of the University High School of the University of Minnesota. In his first appearance before a general faculty meeting he stated some of his ideas about university organization. One statement he made raised some doubts in members of the staff. It suggested a "chain of command," reaching down through the administration to the faculty, in which faculty committees would play a purely advisory role. In effect he did remove some of the influence and authority of these committees; a special state investigating committee reported in April of the following year that he had "discontinued that portion of the faculty committee in which university policies were formulated." [4] Presently he promoted a policy that made all high school graduates in the state, no matter what subjects they had taken or what grades they had made, eligible for university admission as "unclassified students." This policy was regarded by various faculty members as lowering university standards. A group of five, including Professor Frank J. Richardson, head of the department of biology, were outspoken in their objections. Professor Richardson, a quiet, scholarly man who was chairman of the local branch of the AAUP, led the opposition, and in the process he distributed among a number of faculty members copies of an article by Professor Arthur E. Bestor, Jr., of the University of Illinois, entitled "Aimlessness in Education." [5] In this article the charge was made that professional educationalists had arrogated to themselves the right "to speak for the

[4] As reported in the *Reno Evening Gazette,* April 27, 1953. A detailed account of this dispute may be found in the pages of the *Nevada State Journal* during April, May, and June, 1953. See also "Nevada Fracas," *Newsweek,* XLI (January 22, 1953), 86.

[5] The article was published in the *Scientific Monthly,* LXXV (August, 1952), 109–16.

universities in matters of public policy" to the exclusion of other faculty members. Richardson also sent a copy to the president, "with a conciliatory note."

President Stout was indignant. He told Richardson to mind his own business. What did a professor of biology know about educational standards? Had he read the latest research on the subject? Throughout the proceedings Stout made much play on this point. He drew a bill of particulars against the offending faculty members—containing such items as the attempt to develop friction between the University and the public schools of the state; the spreading of false information to infer (*sic*) the lowering of academic standards at the University; the alarming of faculty, townspeople, and legislators, etc.—and on such grounds summoned the faculty members in question to show cause why they should be allowed to retain their positions.

After this kind of harassment four of the five members signed letters expressing their desire to "cooperate" with the president and were pardoned. Richardson refused to "cooperate." Stout moved for his dismissal, and the Board of Regents, after long deliberation, unanimously voted accordingly.

The matter at issue here was clearly one of educational policy. The standards of admission are properly within the competence of the faculty. No scholar who is really concerned with the standing of his institution can be indifferent to proposals that in his judgment would degrade these standards. Whether the policy of President Stout was for better or worse, his attitude toward the faculty members who criticized it was deplorable; and his behavior, accusing these critics of "insubordination," advising them to stay in their own bailiwicks, threatening their peremptory dismissal, and actually causing the discharge of a leading faculty opponent, was a gross violation of academic rights.

5. The obligation of the educator to his institution is so closely bound with his obligation to the public that in dealing with the former we have already indicated the latter. There are, however, some aspects of this relationship that call for further consideration.

Like any other citizen, the scholar owes and gives services to the public outside of his official duties within his institution. These are voluntary services and there is no determinate obligation assigning their extent. The scholar is in demand to address groups on subjects that fall within his field of interest and to contribute to the spread of knowledge by giving popular expression to new scientific developments. This is aside from the more technical services he contributes to special organizations. The days when the scholar lived in the ivory tower are long gone by. For the average faculty member the sum of his extramural services is considerable, and much of it is cheerfully done without remuneration.

Again, like any other citizen, many a scholar takes an active part in local public affairs. Who can deny that this is desirable or that it tends to raise the level of discussion and of policy-making? We are personally acquainted with two communities in which the civic activities and responsibilities undertaken by educators has markedly benefited not only the local school situation but also various other community affairs. Nor is there any proper reason why in his citizen role the scholar should not take a stand in political controversies. The point is clearly stated in a pronouncement of the AAUP: "This Association regards any attempt to subject teachers to civic limitations not imposed on other citizens as a threat against the academic profession and against the society which the profession serves."

A more legitimate doubt may arise when scholars actively participate in state or national politics. Such activity not only diverts interest and energy from scholarly pursuits but also may promote habits of mind and approaches to problems that are uncongenial to the methods and principles of scholarship. On the other hand, the scholar has here an opportunity to gain direct knowledge and an insight into public affairs otherwise hardly available to him. Much depends on the motives of the individual who thus engages himself—whether, in particular, personal ambition or the desire to render a genuine public service is more impelling. We have known educators who after entering public life kept their scholarly values. We have known others of whom the same could scarcely be said. No hard-and-fast line can be drawn. By way of summation of the issue we may quote from the 1915 Declaration of Principles of the AAUP, formulated at the outset of its career:

It is manifestly desirable that . . . teachers have minds untrammeled by party loyalties, unexcited by party enthusiasms, and unbiased by their personal political ambitions; and that universities should remain uninvolved in party antagonisms. On the other hand, it is equally manifest that the material available for the service of the State would be restricted in a highly undesirable way, if it were understood that no member of the academic profession should ever be called upon to resume the responsibilities of public office.[6]

One clause in the above citation may be misinterpreted. It must not be inferred that a university is in any sense involved in party controversies because some of its members, in their role of citizens, take sides on political issues. While in general this principle meets with no opposition, there are ways in which it is whittled down. We have already commented on this subject but there is so much confusion about it that it deserves further examination. Here is a typical situation. A number of like-minded members of a particular institution get together to issue a public statement on some matter of national importance. They identify themselves as members of the same faculty—even if they didn't, the identification would be made for them if their pronouncement received any publicity—but specifically point out that they are acting as a group of citizens and that the institution is in no sense committed to their particular views. Some administrators frown on such action, declaring that faculty members should not "compromise" their institution. Authorities of state universities are more apt to dislike it, for obvious reasons, but the objection comes also from other quarters. For example, the president of the University of Notre Dame publicly deplored the behavior of some sixty-five members of the staff who during the Eisenhower-Stevenson campaign ran a paid advertisement in favor of Stevenson.[7] This behavior, he said, "jeopardized" the school's nonpartisan position—this in spite of the fact that the group statement carefully pointed out that the signers were acting as individual citizens and in no way representing their institution.

Clearly, if the people at large associate the institution with whatever any group of faculty members may choose to proclaim, even when these members expressly disavow the inference, it is time that steps were taken to explain to the public the nature of a university. To attempt to curb the civic liberties of the profession because of the presumptive failure of some of the public to understand that a university is not dedicated to conformism is surely a poor expedient.

In passing we note that a few universities impose particular conditions on their members who seek to run for public office. Thus Indiana University requires that any full-time employee who is a candidate for a full-

[6] *Bulletin of the American Association of University Professors,* XXXV (1949), 57.

[7] The president's statement was carried in the daily press under date of October 30, 1952.

time political position—except for minor municipal offices—shall from the day of nomination be placed on leave of absence without pay, until the date of election; and any staff or faculty member who accepts the chairmanship or vice-chairmanship of any segment of any party organization is put on "compulsory leave of absence." [8] Purdue University requires that no employee of the university shall engage in any political activity while on duty for the university, that any employee must obtain leave of absence who wishes to campaign for or to hold any political office requiring full-time service over a period exceeding two weeks—aside from nonpaying local offices—and that this leave of absence is conditional on agreement that the person involved shall neither represent himself nor knowingly allow himself to be represented as an employee of the university. [9]

The scholar is under obligation to show the same regard for evidence on the platform that he does in the classroom and not to resort to cheap and prejudicial methods of persuasion. He should not be intemperate in his proposals or abusive in his language. If he acts thus, he cannot blame the public for thinking that his behavior in the classroom may also be unworthy of the scholar. Thus he brings disrepute on the institution to which he is attached. The scholar should show a decent respect toward the honest convictions of others, no matter how they differ from his own. Nor should he feel surprised or outraged, when he ignores this injunction, if those whose convictions he makes light of turn round and denounce him. As was said by John Dewey, "lack of reverence for the things that mean much to humanity, joined with a craving for public notoriety, may induce a man to pose as a martyr to truth when in reality he is a victim of his own lack of mental and moral poise." [10] It is the very exceptional scholar who seriously violates this rule and in the better institutions he thereby loses the esteem of his colleagues and usually does damage to his academic career. But this obligation emphatically does not imply that the educator should, in his public statements, refrain from expressing his own convictions on questions of general interest or should in any way modify them lest his views incur the disapprobation of other-minded men.

There is another point to be considered here. We must remember that knowledge, the best knowledge we can attain, does not by itself resolve

[8] Letter to the American Academic Freedom Project from Herman B. Wells, November 28, 1953.

[9] Executive Memorandum No. A-58, Purdue University, May 15, 1952.

[10] "Academic Freedom," *Educational Review*, XXIII (January, 1902), 8.

questions that involve decisions pertaining to human values, as all questions of policy, or even of strategy, do. It merely clears the ground for the intelligent examination of them, without the confusions and misunderstandings that cluster about them. In short, knowledge enables us to see the problem more clearly, instead of "through a glass, darkly." Scholars will still differ as to how the issues should be evaluated. Nevertheless, they have something of significance to contribute here also; indeed, the clarification they can offer, imperfect as it is, would not only avert vain wranglings and foolish disputes but would also take some of the bitterness and misdirected hostility out of the issues on which men of different minds and different interests must honestly differ.

In the review above we have not dealt with all the professional or functional obligations that properly fall on the educator. We have not, for example, been concerned with his obligations as an examiner, as a writer of textbooks or other works, as a member of committees, as an adviser of students, as a writer of testimonials—where he is so frequently a sinner—and so forth. Our view has been limited to those responsibilities that stem directly from his rightful claim to academic freedom.

Here several questions arise: What is there to assure that the educator will live up to his responsibilities? What penalty does he face if he flouts them? Who are the guardians of the obligation that is the counterpart of the scholar's freedom? These questions come up with particular cogency at the present time, when some of our congressional investigators claim that their investigations are necessary because faculties are unwilling to expose communists and others who grossly abuse their academic freedom. And there are even a few educators who assert that if institutions of learning would only "police" their own membership, outside intervention would be "unnecessary" and might be avoided.

We hold that this latter position is based on mistaken conceptions. In the first place the behavior of the congressional committees that have been operating in this field is not such as to encourage the idea that they are animated by any regard for academic freedom or have any clear sense of its implications. No academic group would conduct that kind of inquiry, or think it proper to harass faculty members who had innocently given their names to organizations that later on were put on the Attorney-General's expanding list, or insist that scholars who had at one time been attracted to the Party and later abjured it expose the names of their former associates, or give publicity to unproven charges of "redness" or "pinkness." The congressional investigators who have made a Roman holiday out of every opportunity for "investigation" would surely have called any faculty inquiry on the subject a "white-wash."

In any event it is not, we submit, the business of the faculty to conduct general inquiries into the present or past doctrines of its own members. Such proceedings are hardly conceivable and would be destructive of morale. It is, however, entirely proper that the faculty should take cognizance of any of its members who grossly violate the obligations attached to academic freedom, particularly by slanting their teaching so as to propagate or to insinuate any kind of totalitarian doctrine, whether communist, fascist, or nazi in type. For these doctrines are alike deadly enemies of the open-minded search for knowledge.

The threat is sometimes made, usually by outsiders who themselves have an inadequate conception of academic freedom, that unless educators live up to their responsibilities their rights may be taken away from them. This is, however, rather loose speaking. Who defines those "responsibilities"? Who guards them and penalizes those who violate them? No other body has the particular responsibilities that pertain to the academic profession. No other body, as a whole, has more respect for these particular responsibilities of theirs than the academic profession has. What then does the threat mean? Significantly, it is made at a time when academic freedom is gravely imperiled, and by groups who seek not to vindicate but to destroy the responsibility that attaches to the search for truth. It is reasonable enough that such scholars as reject their responsibility should lose their status. But to propose that any non-educational body, particularly any political body, should as it were police our universities in order to assure that they live up to their *educational* responsibilities is mere foolishness.

We do not deny there are colleges and even so-called universities quite unworthy of the name, some that are more devoted to the propagation of particular interests or beliefs than to the advancement of knowledge, others that have the shoddiest standards of admission and of grading and seem more concerned about receipts than about qualifications. In a country of this size, with so wide an interest in the prestige and career values of higher education, some such institutions are always likely to spring up. Occasionally too, a once reputable college may fall into incapable or unworthy hands. Educational authorities such as the Association of American Universities and the various accrediting agencies have a competent knowledge of the situation. They are in an excellent position to make recommendations, were the matter entrusted to them, in all doubtful cases. Our major point is that, wherever questions or complaints arise respecting the failure of any institution to live up to the educational responsibilities it has assumed, it is the appropriate educational authorities, and not some outside noneducational group, who should be called upon to propose remedies.

We have no reason to doubt that the members of the academic profession respect their obligations as well as do the members of any other profession. No one lives up all the time to the full sum of his obligations, nor does the professor succeed in doing so any more than the doctor or the lawyer. But when we hear it said that the academic profession, because of its shortcomings and disregard of responsibilities, is itself primarily to blame for the onslaught of investigations, regulations, and censorial controls to which it is being subjected we must emphatically demur. Much of the brunt of the attack has fallen on men who were singled out because of their independence of mind and their honest courage in maintaining it. We have cited not a few cases where this has happened, and throughout this work we have explored a total situation that cannot be explained away by a simple resort to the derelictions of professors.

The proposal is occasionally made that a code of professional ethics should be drawn up by educators, to which new entrants into the profession would be called on to subscribe and which would be made the basis of academic discipline.[11] We are not convinced that the device of a standard professional code would be particularly serviceable. It is, however, true that within the ranks of educators there are those who seem to have, or to act as though they had, inadequate conceptions of the obligations their calling imposes on them, and any way in which these obligations could be more fully impressed on them would be worthwhile. But what is needed, perhaps, is not so much the formal structure of a code as the fuller development of an *ethos* that is already well established in the finest institutions of learning. The history of other professional codes shows that they do not produce nor are they any substitute for that genuine dedication to a noble cause which turns mere obligation into wholehearted service.

[11] See Sidney Hook, *Heresy, Yes—Conspiracy, No* (New York, 1953).

The essential thing is a stronger conviction among educators them-selves—and here we include administrators as well as teachers—of the priceless worth of academic freedom. Then they will more jealously guard it against assaults from without and against infringements from within their own ranks. This is the only sure way in which serious violations of the scholar's responsibilities can be prevented or properly dealt with if they occur. Educators should not ignore or condone infringements, especially if they are persisted in. Often if the academic violator is made aware of the disapproval of his colleagues, he will be sufficiently re-strained. He will know that his scholastic standing and also his chances of advancement are at stake. In the more serious cases official action may be called for. In most institutions, and potentially in all, there is some committee that has the function of reviewing academic offenses and rec-ommending action. In a word, every reputable institution of learning is fully competent to guard the integrity of its discipline, and if it occasion-ally fails to do so against an individual offender, what is desirable is not the intervention of some political authority but a livelier sense within it of the need to protect its own values.

ACCENT ON RIGHTS

No professional service can be properly rendered unless the practitioner is granted the conditions under which he is free to obey the inherent demands of his art or craft or skill. Without these conditions the lawyer cannot plead aright, the judge cannot pronounce just judgments, the physician cannot effectively apply the healing art. Each profession needs its own kind of freedom, and these professional freedoms, it should be noted, differ in this respect from the other freedoms men want or need in that the primary consideration is not the benefit of the group that enjoys them but the benefit of the society they serve. The mission of the scholar determines his particular obligations and in consequence his particular rights.

When we speak here of the scholar's rights we do not refer to legally established guarantees, for the law provides few of the particular safe-guards he needs, and in the nature of the case it must probably remain so. Nor do we mean simply institutionally assured rights, although the academic institution, when wisely governed, becomes a great bulwark of the educator's rights. We mean more broadly those conditions of academic service that have *ethical* validity, that therefore should be institutionally affirmed and supported and, where feasible, sustained by law.

For the assurance of these rights, even more important than any such sanctions is the education of the people in the meaning and value of academic freedom. This, however, may be a slow process in view of the important forces opposed to it. But some of the grosser misconceptions ought to be more easily dispelled—for example, the notion that the educator is a hired man who can and should be told by his employer how to do his job, a notion that is still entertained by some of the more unregenerate governing boards. Where it prevails, academic rights are non-existent.

Deriving these rights from a consideration of the scholar's function and consequent service to society, we may broadly classify them as follows.

1. The right professionally to decide matters calling for professional competence—a subject we have already discussed in considering the role of the faculty in the institution of learning.
2. The right to a status adequate to his responsibility and consonant with the high service he renders to society and to civilization.
3. Specifically, the right to conditions of tenure that will assure him against dismissal or professional penalization on grounds other than professional incompetence or conduct that in the judgment of his colleagues renders him unfit to be a faculty member.
4. The right to a private life free from controls that are not imposed on other citizens.
5. The right to exercise the same political and civil liberties that are enjoyed by other citizens.

The first three of these rights express the intramural conditions, the last two the extramural ones, on which depend the evocation of the most capable and high-minded body of scholars the country can provide and of the greater service they can render to society through the advancement of learning and the spread of enlightenment.

The need for all these rights has already been sufficiently revealed in the course of this work. A few additional comments will therefore suffice, except for the third-mentioned, the right of tenure, which has important aspects that have not so far been considered.

The first two rights in our list are closely conjoined. Where either is fully acknowledged, the other accompanies it; where either is diminished, the other is also diminished. If the educator is not entrusted with the determination of intrinsically educational decisions, if noneducators arrogate over him the exclusive right to make policies that by their very nature call for expert judgment concerning their educational consequences, then the training, skill, and experience of the scholar are made of no account. Suppose for a moment that the medical or the legal profession were accorded treatment of the character just mentioned, what would it do to the status of these professions or to the quality of the services they render? But we cannot conceive the development of a situation in which either of those professions would tamely accept so subservient a role.

We are aware that the professor occupies a high rank in the rating scales employed in various surveys of occupational status.[12] Why there should be a discrepancy between this ranking and the substantive indications of status has been a puzzle to some commentators, as it is to the present writer.[13] It may be the sampling, it may be that there are considerable disparities in estimation between different parts of the country, or possibly the verbal responses may express an abstract estimate or even some conception of how the profession *should* rank that has little relation to actuality. Such evidences as the readiness of some legislatures to vote enthusiastic sums for new university buildings and comparatively little for higher professional salaries; or, more generally, the lowly income level and poor economic prospects enjoyed by the profession as a whole; or, for example, the fact that at a time when the national budget runs to astounding billions the appropriation for the Office of Education is cut by the House and the Senate Appropriations Committee from nearly three millions to two and a half; or, more directly, the prevalence of the doctrine that the governing boards of institutions of higher learning need not, or rather should not, contain any practicing educators—such evidences are hard to reconcile with the higher status assigned by the men with the rating scales. We are ourselves inclined to associate the disparity with the observation made in our discussion of public opinion, that the American public places a very high value on education as a means to utilitarian ends but has much less perception of its intrinsic worth.

[12] See, e.g., W. H. Fox *et al.,* "Prestige Ranks of Teaching," *Occupations,* XXX (October, 1951), 33–36.

[13] See Richard H. Shryrock, "The Academic Profession in the United States," *Bulletin of the American Association of University Professors,* XXXVIII (Spring, 1952), 52–54.

No further comment is necessary for the interpretation of the last two rights in our list, which have been amply dealt with in earlier chapters. Let us turn, then, to the right that is the main safeguard of all the other rights of the scholar—that of tenure. It is a right especially associated with the academic profession and one that receives the widest recognition. It gives the educator a charter assurance of the continuance of his position. It presumptively protects him against any kind of arbitrary dismissal. We might therefore ask: why does he have, or why does he need, this special right—or privilege?

There is certainly a case to be made against it. It assumes the continued efficiency and devoted service of the tenure holder. But in the chances and changes of life, even assuming the initial tenure appointment was carefully made, there will occasionally be a faculty member who loses his zeal, or allows outside attractions to divert or dull his interest in his academic work, or develops eccentricities that make him quite unsatisfactory as a teacher, a colleague, or a seeker after knowledge. Tenure is not without its costs. It protects not only the thinker, the intellectual pioneer, the social critic but also the inert, the barely competent, the perfunctory reciter of ancient lessons, and the one-time scholar who now devotes his best energies to more lucrative pursuits.

Such considerations have prompted proposals so to limit or define tenure that it will protect only those who deserve its protection. Thus the former head of a women's college writes: "There should be a clear-cut demarcation between the protection of a teacher's right to proclaim the truth as he sees it and the protection of his job whether or not he does the job well. . . . Whenever the non-cooperative, irascible person hides behind his rights to academic freedom to protect himself from the consequences of his non-cooperation or irascibility, he strikes a blow at academic freedom." [14]

Unfortunately, in a world where the motives of men are complex and frequently rationalized or concealed behind more worthy ones, this desirable demarcation does not seem possible. How easy it would be to get rid of the independent spirit because he is perhaps irascible or subject to some other temperamental flaw! And as for being "uncooperative," we may recall that this was precisely the charge brought against Professor Richardson in the University of Nevada case. He did not "cooperate"

---

[14] Mildred McAfee Horton, "Academic Freedom," in Amos N. Wilder, ed., *Liberal Learning and Religion* (New York, 1951), p. 249.

with the president of that institution when he was bold enough to protest against what he believed to be the lowering of academic standards.

Safeguards against gross abuses of tenure must be sought along other lines. In the first place there is the probationary period for the younger teacher. The consensus of administrative and faculty opinion is that this period should not exceed seven years after the first appointment to the rank of full-time instructor, with the proviso that this total term may be somewhat extended to allow for not more than four years in the institution to which he has transferred after his initial appointment.[15] It is important that his department and his faculty be thoroughly assured of the merits of any candidate for promotion to tenure. This is by no means always the case. The recommendation should be backed thoroughly by the members of his department, and if there is any doubt or division on the matter the decision should require a clear majority of an appropriate faculty group.

Occasionally a junior member protests the failure to appoint him to tenure as a violation of academic rights, claiming that he has been passed over on account of his doctrines and in spite of his qualifications. Such claims call for highly judicious treatment. Tenure is, or should be, so important a right that if the nominating faculty members have any serious doubts regarding the merits of a tenure candidate, they should refrain from making the recommendation. To refuse to recommend for tenure is not an accusation but simply an admission that the faculty members concerned are not convinced that the case for permanent appointment is adequate. To take an example, two members of City College in New York made protests in 1949 that tenure was being withheld from them because of their activities against racial discrimination. The departmental vote and that of the appropriate faculty committee had been adverse. We have no opinion on the scholarly merits of the candidates, but after reading the reports and discussing the matter with faculty members we believe that these members sought fairly to weigh the claims of the candidates and themselves cherished no racial prejudices that would have inclined them to an unfavorable verdict.

On the other hand, the fact that a scholar lacks tenure is sometimes taken to imply that the failure to renew his appointment is not under any circumstances a violation of academic freedom. This position is untenable. Tenure is indeed some safeguard against unjust or arbitrary

[15] American Association of University Professors, "1940 Statement of Principles."

dismissal, but the lack of tenure does not make any dismissal unarbitrary or just. The fact that a man lacks tenure makes no genuine difference in the seriousness of the offense against the proper liberty of the qualified educator when he is dismissed because his doctrines are not palatable to someone in authority over him. This is all the more so because quite a few institutions have a very inadequate tenure system, so that a man may go on over many years as a successful teacher without being given this security.

We have no accurate information regarding the tenure policies of a considerable number of American institutions of higher learning, but the available statistics show a wide range of difference between the best and the worst, with many colleges falling toward the lower end of the scale. In a survey conducted by The Reverend Wilfred M. Mallon, S.J., Dean of the College of Arts and Sciences at St. Louis University, 246 out of 358 institutions from which information was requested sent in replies.[16] We may conjecture that the 31 percent that failed to answer are rather less likely than the others to have had a satisfactory system, where they had any at all. One hundred and ninety-one non-Catholic institutions and 55 Catholic ones, out of 270 and 88 respectively, responded. Of these respondents, 106 had no written contracts with *any* faculty members, and of the 106 there were 64 listed as institutions "approved by the Association of American Universities." The author of the survey notes that many of the institutions having written contracts provided them against their will, under the requirements of state laws. One hundred and sixty-one non-Catholic colleges and 48 Catholic ones answered the question whether they had "permanent tenure." Of the Catholic group, 65 percent had none. In the case of the others there was a marked difference between institutions which were members of or approved by the AAU and nonapproved colleges, only 2 percent of the former as compared with 29 percent of the latter having no members on permanent tenure. Some of the institutions that give permanent tenure limit it to full professors, and most of the others do not give it below the grade of associate professor.

Lack of tenure can be made a convenient cover under which a department head or an administrative officer or a board can quietly sift out the unorthodox. It is particularly easy for a department head or a

---

[16] "Faculty Ranks, Tenure and Academic Freedom," *Bulletin of the National Catholic Education Association,* XXXIX (1942), 177–94.

departmental group to do so. Sometimes a dominant senior scholar, as chairman of his department or otherwise, yields to the human weakness of preferring yea-men above more independent candidates of higher merit, selecting the former alike for department membership and for promotion to tenure. This may not be directly a violation of academic freedom, but it displays an attitude that has an unhappy resemblance to that of the outright violator.

To return to our main theme, the careful scrutiny of candidates for tenure, especially when the faculty is enlisted as well as the department, together with reasonable care in the making of recommendations for further advancement, can reduce to a minimum the debit side of this great institutional safeguard of academic freedom. Without tenure the scholar could become the mere hireling of a governing board, bereft of intrinsic dignity and at the mercy of its predilections. Without tenure he would lack any assurance that he can freely express conclusions that may be contrary to the interests, convictions, or prejudices of minority or majority groups. The independence of judgment that is of primary importance both in the search for knowledge and in the interpretation of what is already known would be jeopardized.

The teacher, whether he belongs to the school or to the university, does not possess either the means of defense or the bargaining power that many other groups enjoy. He is not an employer on the one hand nor is he, typically, a unionized worker on the other. He has not the kind of defensive apparatus or the social and political power that is characteristic of the medical or the legal profession. He is not in business by himself or for himself, receiving direct payment for services rendered, as are the members of these and most other professions. He does not have the economic opportunities—save very rarely—or the economic rewards available to these other groups. The scholar is technically "employed" by boards whose members for the most part grossly outrank him in worldly goods. His tenure, offering him a degree of assurance that he can make his scholarly interests his life work, is his necessary mainstay.

It is the more necessary because the powers that rule him often understand so little the nature of the work, or of the service, to which the genuine scholar is devoted. We have already made some passing comments on this point. Even some high administrators fail to present aright the kind of intellectual independence the advance of knowledge requires. They speak as though the duty of the scholar were simply to wait until he had attained demonstrable certainty before he makes a pronouncement on any subject. Meantime he goes on testing, weighing, examining doctrines, sifting the false from the true, until in the clear light of knowledge he at length announces which proved to be true and which false. Were that the whole picture, academic freedom would be much safer than it is. But, for all the testing and examining the scholar can do, there are great areas of the realm of knowledge within which infallible conclusions are not and probably cannot be attained, where all we can hope to reach is a higher degree of probability or predictability, and there are other great areas within which logical proof or disproof has a minor role. Within the latter domain lie the major doctrines that preside over the ways of men. Alleged facts may be proved or disproved, alleged evidences may be established or refuted, alleged connections between things or events may be confirmed or shown to be erroneous. But major systems of thought are not disposed of this way. Yet they deserve from the scholar careful study and interpretation. Within this same domain lies the more important part of the work done by the historian, the student of literature, the anthropologist, the economist, the philosopher, the sociologist, and generally all scholars who work in the humanities and in the social sciences. They interpret and they form hypotheses and they draw conclusions. But they are not like mathematicians who can write Q.E.D. at the end of the argument.

When the scholar is occupied in any of these fields, he particularly needs the protection of tenure. It is his right and his duty to throw whatever light he can on the complex and practically important problems that dogma and group interest short-cut by their own convenient ready-made formulas. It is his right and even his duty not to take the safe course of presenting an arid array of facts and figures, expecting some mythical reader to give them form and meaning, but to interpret them and to state, with scholarly discretion and circumspection but also with whatever scholarly imagination he possesses, the conclusions to which they may point.

We have spoken thus far as though his tenure did protect the educator against arbitrary or unjust dismissal. Unfortunately tenure, as it exists in a considerable number of institutions, fails to accomplish this end. There are two main reasons for this failure. One is the lax definition of tenure itself, the other is the disregard that in certain institutions is shown for its provisions. Moreover, various smaller colleges and a considerable number of teachers colleges have no tenure system of any kind.[17]

The specification of the conditions of tenure is of first importance. Obviously no tenure rule can guarantee the instructor his position, safeguarding him no matter what happens and no matter what he does. But how should the proper line be drawn? The Statement of Principles of 1940 says the appointment should be terminated "only for adequate cause." But who is to decide what is "adequate cause?" To the authority responsible for a dismissal, it is always "for adequate cause." Without stipulation of the causes that justify dismissal, tenure may prove of little avail.

If we turn to the rules and regulations of institutions that provide tenure we find again a frequent lack of clarity. The Research Director of the American Civil Liberties Union, Dr. Louis Joughin, obtained in 1952 information on the subject from twenty-six colleges and universities. Eight of these drew the line at "adequate cause" without further explanation. Nearly all the others had "loophole" provisions, when the matter was not left simply to the "discretion" of the board. These provisions are expressed in such phrases as "necessary for the good of the College," "when the interests of the University require it," "serious interference with a teacher's usefulness," and so forth. In Dr. Joughin's judgment, only one institution, Vassar College, stated proper grounds for dismissal without adding additional categories of the vaguer kind.

Where the tradition of academic freedom is well established there is less need to spell out the meaning of "adequate cause." Where this freedom is well defended there is perhaps an advantage in leaving the rubric broad and discretionary, since the specific categories we must otherwise set down may be both too inclusive and too narrow to compass the particularities of circumstance within which an offense may or may not exceed the bounds of academic toleration. But the flagrant abuse of the power to dismiss so often witnessed in this country shows the importance of specific charter limitations to this power.

As an aid to the safeguarding of the more independent educator we submit that the charter of academic tenure should run somewhat as follows:

[17] National Education Association, *Tenure Policies and Procedures in Teachers Colleges* (Washington, D. C., 1943).

1. Tenure shall be understood as guaranteeing the continuance of appointment, after a reasonable probation period, up to the official age of retirement, except for adequate cause.

2. Adequate cause shall mean any one of the following grounds:

a. professional incompetence due to either physical or mental disability or manifested in gross negligence or grave disregard of scholarly standards or professional responsibilities;

b. serious criminal offense (such as the commission of a felony) or gross immorality;

c. emergency institutional conditions, particularly financial stringency.[18]

3. Any charge brought under either of the first two main heads against a faculty member possessed of tenure shall be referred to an appropriate faculty committee for report and only thereafter shall go before the governing board. Any teacher so charged shall have the right to be heard in his own defense at a trial conducted with due regard for judicial procedures. If the charge falls under 2.a above, the reputation of the scholar, as testified to by his colleagues and his students, should be the main and sufficient ground for a decision.[19]

These stipulations are in general accord with the statements of the AAUP. The third main head provides some assurance that the grounds assigned under the first two will not be abused. It is in line with the practice of the best institutions, and it is the more necessary in the others.

We would add that in setting down these stipulations we have in mind only state and municipal institutions and nondenominational voluntary institutions. We recognize that in accordance with their premises denominational systems may logically add further requirements for continuance of faculty membership. But these also should be specific and should not go beyond such stipulations as are needed to assure that the faculty member remains loyal to the institutional creed.

---

[18] It is important to observe here that real or alleged financial stringency has too often been the pretext for the dismissal of professors whom the administration or the board wanted to get rid of on other grounds. This matter has received considerable discussion in Committee A of the AAUP, which insisted that the nature of the stringency be demonstrated and proposed that the president of the institution explore, preferably with a committee of his faculty, ways of avoiding such dismissals.

[19] On this subject, see the 1953 Report of the Committee on Academic Freedom and Tenure of the Association of American Law Schools.

Part Five

THE UNIVERSITY
AND THE SOCIAL ORDER

XIV: THE GREATER MISSION
OF THE UNIVERSITY

The assertion of truth, the unveiling of illusion, the dissipation of hate, the enlargement and instruction of men's hearts and minds.

JOHN MAYNARD KEYNES

THROUGHOUT THE DISCUSSIONS that occupy this volume we have for the most part taken for granted the paramountcy of the value of academic freedom over any objectives that may be attained by its suppression or obstruction. We have mostly been content to speak of the quest for knowledge as declaratory of its own worth. Our whole case stands or falls with acceptance or rejection of its primary claim. This is the major premise of our argument. If it wins conviction, only minor differences of emphasis or of interpretation can be brought against our position.

For anyone who believes in democracy and understands what it means, the grounds for acceptance of the major premise are overwhelmingly strong. Yet in this country large numbers of people who subscribe or think they subscribe to the democratic faith ally themselves with the enemies of academic freedom. The view taken so long ago by the acute De Tocqueville is still entertained by some foreign observers of the American scene. De Tocqueville maintained that there is "no country in which there is so little independence of mind and freedom of discussion as in America," and there are many today who would agree, though of course they would omit dictatorial countries as outside the range of comparison. The viewpoint may be in certain respects unfair, but no one can deny that there are plausible evidences to sustain it.

How can this be when Americans take such pride in their democracy? We cannot pursue the subject very far within these limits, but certainly a major consideration is the extent of confusion concerning the nature of democracy that has been peculiarly persistent in this country. It is associated with a kind of loose egalitarianism, a leveling of standards to the measure of the "common man." If every man is as good as his fellow, the scholar is entitled to no more respect, even in his own field, than his untutored neighbor. But this attitude alone would not account for the situation, for this kind of "equality" would surely entitle the scholar to hold his own "opinion" against that of his neighbor. There is implicit a greater misunderstanding than the false assumption that democracy levels all differences when it levels differences before the law or in the polling booth, or that democracy gives everyone equality in everything (including admission to the universities) when it gives equality of citizenship. The greater misunderstanding is the assumption that democracy means the rule of the many over all the affairs of men. This conception, though widely entertained in America, is wholly erroneous and illogical. Since the many never rule, and since any form of government—monarchy, dictatorship, or any sort of oligarchy—may be in accord with the will of the majority, and even of their suffrage, democracy cannot be identified along this line. The distinctive feature of democracy is not the rule of the majority but the fundamental rights it assures to the minority.[1] The constitution of the United States did not create a democracy until the Bill of Rights was added.

The unreadiness to accept the application to minority groups of the democratic principle it proclaims has wrought much harm to the well-being and to the prestige of the United States. It is doing very serious damage in our times, when the United States has taken on the status of a world power. And just as our habits of racial and ethnic discrimination are defeating our international interests, so the tendency to discriminate against educational nonconformists is hurting, far more than most people conceive, our national well-being. Both forms of discrimination are parts of the same complex, and both are wholly inconsistent with the ethos of democracy.

When people attack academic freedom, they are defending something else to which they are committed, something else with which they think, rightly or wrongly, clearly or confusedly, that academic freedom interferes. Often it is their prejudice, sometimes their interests, and for some of the worst enemies of freedom it is simply the profit or power that comes from appealing to these interests and prejudices. Where prejudice is the motive, people not only believe they already possess the truth but also are afraid of the "heresies" of those who come to different conclusions

[1] For an analysis of the nature of democracy, see the author's *The Web of Government* (New York, 1947), Part III, Chapter 8.

—afraid lest these heretics mislead or corrupt others. They are un-willing to trust their own untested "truth" not only in the market place of opinions but also in the enclaves where men are peculiarly engaged in the search for knowledge. This attitude is the essence and the gravamen of prejudice.

Why then is the search for knowledge so worth while? Why must it be defended, wherever it may lead, against the interests and prejudices that would curb or limit it? What is its significance for all of us, for those who are remote from academies no less than for those who live in them?

The more obviously demonstrable fruits of intellectual freedom are its utilitarian achievements, the new powers and resources it brings to mankind. Marvelous and increasing as these are, our concern here is more directly with the social and cultural advances of which it is the primary condition. To these incalculably important values every area of the quest for knowledge has contributions to make—the wide range of the humanities, the sociopsychological sciences, the physicochemical sciences in all their forms and applications. Always it is the trust in the free quest for knowledge, wherever it may lead, that brings these gains, whether they be material or spiritual. It is the well-established practice of the great corporations that maintain expensive research laboratories to give their scientists a free hand, so that they can explore far and wide in directions that may yield no returns. These corporations do not merely assign to their research laboratories specific tasks or problems arising out of the processes of industrial operation. They know that a discovery, a new trail anywhere in the field may lead to new and utterly unanticipated applications. They know that advances in theory herald advances in utility. They have learned that the true scientist is a man of imagination as well as of knowledge and that only from this combi-nation do important discoveries come. They allow him to give play to his imagination. Many false trails must be pursued in the search for the secrets of nature. At the present time there is a general complaint among physicists and chemists because there is so much pressure for their services in the fulfillment of specific research assignments required by a network of governmental agencies that free fundamental research, the source of all the greater advances, suffers comparative neglect.

This freedom of exploration, this pursuit of trails that may end in the wilderness, this readiness to seek beyond data to hypotheses, how-ever contrary to accepted views, and to test hypotheses by the search for further evidence, this liberation of the self-disciplined imagination of the scholar, is as necessary in the social sciences as it is in the natural sciences. But in the former it encounters social obstacles that no longer seriously impede the latter.

The attitude we have just described is an integral part of the great liberating tradition that has developed through recent centuries in the West and has given impulse to the whole creative culture of the modern world. An essential quality of this culture is its refusal to take on authority any conclusion respecting the nature of things that is susceptible to the test of investigation.

The inveterate principle of all nonresponsible authority—that other doctrines than its own are dangerous, destructive, immoral, and wholly abominable and therefore ought to be suppressed—is no doubt as old as human society. Over the greater part of history it held total sway. Who was to challenge authority invested with power? Who was to resist the strong, when the strong armed themselves with righteousness? The great emancipation of humanity came with the vindication of man's right to hold opinions contrary to those of authority, man's right to freedom of thought. Most of the resistance to ecclesiastical power has not been resistance to religion but to the imposition of a religion by force.

Man wants an answer to everything, a key to every mystery. When it is beyond his little knowledge, he invents an answer, and the answer grows into a lore, and the lore becomes sacred and authoritative. Within the lore there might be important values and insights, but it is framed in a system of error that makes gross superstition the rule of life. The superstition becomes the vested interest of power. So the world would have remained in the worse ignorance that is petrified false knowing were it not for the daring spirits who at length were able to defy the taboo, though sometimes paying the price with their lives. Through them has come man's emancipation.

The university is the focal embodiment of this spirit of free inquiry. Charles Malik, of Lebanon, addressing the American Philosophical Society, named first among the four main components of the Western tradition "the existence of free and independent centers of learning and research." [2] This component is the expression of the belief in the power of man's intelligence to explore the laws of nature, to discover through

[2] "The Relations of East and West," in American Philosophical Society, *Proceedings,* XCVII (1953), 1.

patient, devoted, and adventurous search more and more of the truth concerning the ways of things, including also the ways of man. With the aid of this liberation of the mind the West has achieved its triumphs in the conquest of poverty, the control of disease, the annihilation of distance, and the opening up of far perspectives and undreamed-of powers. It has done so by putting its trust in reason and defying the superstitions that barred the way to understanding.

The Western acceptance of the principle of academic freedom was itself a somewhat late development of a much larger movement, rooted in a vast system of change which included the ending of theocratic overlordship, the establishment of the territorial state, the successful challenge of monarchical absolutism, the crumbling of the oligarchical class system, the growth of the consciousness of nationality, the accelerating advancement of science, scientific theory, and the scientific method, and the whole process of socioeconomic change that is summed up in the expression "Industrial Revolution." Inherent in these developments was a new tradition, a new order of habits and of thought forms that rejected the usurpations of authority based only on birth or predetermined status and proclaimed the right of man as man to cherish his own doctrines, to worship in his own way, and to compete for power or place on equal terms with his fellow men. Democracy vindicated the right of opinion and the consequent right of majority opinion to elect the government of the whole.

Now if the democratic claim is accepted, that opinion should be free from suppression or control, there is a yet stronger claim for the freedom of the scholar. While for the purposes of democracy his opinion on anything carries and should carry no more political weight than any other opinion, nevertheless his judgment on matters that fall within his proper field is something more strongly grounded than mere opinion. It may of course be mistaken, but it is the expression of a serious and sustained effort to reach the truth. He has qualified himself to search for it in a way in which the average man never or rarely does. Whatever his shortcomings, he is one of a company of scholars dedicated to this search. That under a system of government which itself depends for its very existence on the freedom of opinion he should be penalized for the opinions he holds in his own field by men who have themselves no scholarly pretensions is contrary not only to the spirit of democracy but also to the elementary decencies of civilized life.

The offense is not merely one against the scholar but against the company of scholars of which he is a member, against the institution of learning. It is no less so if its own board is the offender. To oust a scholar for his views, not for any legal crime or serious moral obliquity, is a betrayal of the ideals of the university. If it is charged that the scholar is dishonest in the expression of doctrine or corrupt or disloyal to the principles of the scholar, then surely the tribunal alone qualified to take cognizance of the charge must be composed of men who are themselves scholars and know from much experience the obligation of scholarship. It is very important to observe that the violations of academic freedom with which we have been primarily concerned in this volume are violations of the integrity and honor of the academy itself. In this connection it is noteworthy that these violations are more frequent and much more flagrant in regions where the prestige of the academy is low, that institutions whose status is inferior are subjected to the heaviest assaults, and that the most hostile pressure groups show little respect generally for the intellectual life or for the academies in which it is cultivated.

When we speak of the value of academic freedom, we must speak first and foremost of the high service rendered to society by the free institution of learning. Other organs exist to promote the freedom of opinion or, more frequently, the freedom of particular opinions. The university defends and advances something of which the freedom of opinion is merely a precondition. It seeks to turn opinion into knowledge, concerning all matters of enduring importance throughout the vast domain where evidence can be found through observation and experiment and the study of the record of the past. It is an endless quest, this search for the one kind of relative certitude that is the same for all men, this open and ever-advancing knowledge of the world, of the cosmos, of man, that is won through the patient application of the cooperative ingenuity of the world-wide brotherhood of learning.

This open knowledge is also a humbling knowledge. However deep it searches, it knows that it is still working in the shallows of an immeasurable ocean. It is always susceptible to further questioning; its conclusions are always partial and incomplete, concealing much ignorance beneath them. Its spirit is undogmatic, for it knows how little it knows. It keeps horizons forever open, though always bringing new gains.

This is the spirit of the genuine university. Individual members of it are "all too human," subject to egoistic impulses that lead them to stray from the mark of their high calling. Some of them have an inadequate conception of its demands; a very few may even betray it. But the spirit of the institution lives in the collectivity of scholarship, in the "public opinion" of the institution. The faculty taken as a whole has one unifying objective, the pursuit of knowledge and its dissemination; one faith in common, the belief in the worthwhileness of the pursuit. Therefore it is merely ridiculous when a body of political investigators claims that when it turns its attention to the colleges it has the grand aim of defending academic freedom. Such statements convey uneasy reminiscences of the inverted use of words indulged in by the communists. The faculty is quite able and alone qualified to defend the institution from any such danger from within. It is for the law and the guardians of the law to defend it from dangers from without.

The spirit of the free institution of learning is well suggested by Judge Learned Hand, speaking of his own college experience at Harvard, as follows:

You came to know that you could hold no certain title to beliefs that you had not won; and indeed you did not win many. But that did not so much matter, for you had come into possession of a touchstone; you had learned how to judge a good title; and although tomorrow might turn up a flaw in it, you believed that you could detect the flaw.

And chiefly, and best of all, you were in a company of those who thought that the noblest of man's works was the pursuit of truth; who valued the goal so highly that they were never quite content that the goal they had reached was the goal they were after; who believed that man's highest courage was to bet his all on what was no more than the best guess he could make; who asked no warranties and distrusted all such; who faced the puzzle of life without any kit of ready-made answers, yet trusting that, if they persevered long enough they would find—in the words of John Dewey—that they might safely "lean back on things." [3]

Salutary as the spirit of the institution of learning always is, combating as it does the intolerances and dogmatisms to which we are prone, it renders a special service under the conditions of modern society. The majority of our workaday pursuits are not conducive to the disinterested regard for unbiased knowledge. On the contrary, they put a premium on bias. Information is itself a competitive device, so long as one can make it out as favoring our side, our cause, our business. There are thus

[3] "The Present Is Our Own," *Harvard Alumni Bulletin*, LIV (February 23, 1952), 426.

the strongest temptations to suppress some aspects of the situation and to exaggerate others. When competitive information becomes a major instrument of salesmanship, whether the goods offered be cosmetics or a political party ticket, beverages or an economic system; when a multitude of organizations employ batteries of experts to persuade the public that what they respectively prescribe or believe is also the world's need; when convenience or ignorance or personal advantage induces large numbers to accept handed-out beliefs like ready-made garments; then the presence of an organization dedicated to straight intrinsic knowledge becomes a primary safeguard of civilization itself—a ground of stability and a means of liberation.

The university puts its trust in reason. This trust has been marvelously vindicated by its fruits. But the resources and powers thus won are apt to breed new enemies of the spirit of reason that evoked them. For power, when uncurbed, grows intolerant, and wealth creates vested interests that in their near-sightedness would bound the future by the past. We have in our times witnessed a resurgence of anti-intellectualist reaction, supported by powerful influences controlling important organs of communication and making appeal to popular prejudices. A superficial symptom of this attitude is that the scholar becomes the "egghead," just as in days gone by the word "academic" came to signify the impractical thinking of a mind remote from a sense of the realities.

We call it a reaction, but it is no more than an accentuation, stimulated by a variety of favoring conditions, of a distrust of the thinker, the "theorist," that seems to be almost indigenous in this country.[4] It is characterized by a pragmatic contempt for the free play of ideas and of those who devote themselves to this pursuit. To this mentality the free enterprise in ideas is the one kind of free enterprise that does not bring tangible returns. Therefore it is not admitted to the code.

Again, this shows the need for popular expositions of the meaning of the university. The attack on academic freedom weakens at the core the security of other freedoms, freedoms that men dare not openly assail. If the conclusions of the scholar are curbed, how can the opinions of the layman, when he is not a member of some dominant group, be safeguarded? If textbooks are rigorously censored, how can the books the public read be protected? What has been happening al-

[4] Richard Hofstadter, "Democracy and Anti-Intellectualism in America," *Michigan Alumnus Quarterly Review*, LIX (August, 1953), 281–95.

ready shows how inseparable academic freedom is from other freedoms. Other books than textbooks are being thrown out of libraries. Private censorial committees are doing business and asking for new laws and new police activities. It is not only the academy that is being "investigated" but every other kind of organization from the purging of which the inquisitors are not deterred by the fear of losing votes. They called off the assault on the churches, only because the magnitude of the outcry stopped them. They touched the hem of the freedom of the press and went no further, probably because the press is too powerful a guardian of its own freedom.[5] It is the freedom of opinion everywhere they would curb. And if they curb it enough, they will destroy democracy. For democracy not only guarantees the freedom of opinion: it needs the free diversity of opposing opinions in order to exist.

The lesson to be drawn is that these enemies of freedom will go to any lengths, will seek thereby more notoriety and more power, up to the point where they apprehend it will lose them votes. They bank on the inertness and the unenlightenment of the people. If the people could only realize that their own liberties are more and more endangered with every new encroachment on the liberties of particular groups, that their own liberties are attacked, directly and indirectly, when libraries are censored and educators intimidated, that the fundamental liberty of opinion is closely bound up with the liberty of the scholar, the dominance of these noisemakers would speedily cease.

What we need to appreciate and, so far as possible to make clear to the people, is the good and the glory of the free search for knowledge, and therefore the worth of the institution preeminently dedicated to its advancement. Even among scholars themselves there are those who lack a vital perception of the significance of this mission. Some seem to be under the influence of the prevalent attitude that prizes knowledge al-

[5] The reference is to the questioning of James A. Wechsler, Editor of the *New York Post*, before a subcommittee of the Committee on Government Operations (Hearings, State Department Information Program—Information Center, April 24 and May 5, 1953) to ascertain his political views—ostensibly on the ground that he was one of the authors whose works appeared in the State Department's Overseas Libraries. The subcommittee chairman, Senator Joseph McCarthy, was unable to say which of Wechsler's books was in use in the Overseas Program, and it seems likely, as charged by Wechsler, that McCarthy was using his senatorial prerogative to harass the editor of an independent newspaper in retaliation for its anti-McCarthy stand. A committee of the American Society of Newspaper Editors weighed this charge but did not arrive at a decision. Wechsler's account of the whole affair can be found in his book, *The Age of Suspicion* (New York, 1953), Chapters 12–15.

most exclusively for its utilitarian services. They come to think of it primarily as a means to "practical" discoveries. They do not think of it as an ever-expanding realm of illumination within which the mind of man, reaching ever closer to the reality of which it is a part, can find inexhaustible opportunities for contemplation and wonder, for guidance and for richer living. For them knowledge becomes mainly "research," where research is understood as the manipulation of techniques for the sake of findings that may be the basis for new manipulations. This is indeed an aspect of knowledge and has its own place and importance, but the ground of vindication of the scholar's freedom lies elsewhere.

To understand what the integrity of the institution of learning means and what significance it has for the free society, we must consider not only the high value of knowledge but also the great additional value that inheres in the spirit animating the search for knowledge. Knowledge is good in itself but the freedom to seek it is, for the well-being of society, a good of another and perhaps even more important kind. Knowledge removes our false conceptions of the nature of things and thus cuts down many baneful prejudices and superstitions. But the spirit that searches out knowledge, which finds its best institutional embodiment in the liberal college or university, goes to the very roots of these evils.

For knowledge, unless it is also free, loses its virtue. As J. S. Mill put it, however true a doctrine may be, "if it is not fully, frequently and fearlessly discussed, it will be held as a dead dogma, not a living truth." The truth will not make us free, will not even enlighten us, unless the truth itself is free. To quote Mill again, it will be "held in the manner of a prejudice," a "dogma becoming a mere formal profession, inefficacious for good but cumbering the ground, and preventing the growth of any real and heartfelt conviction." [6]

The modern university is not understood as merely or even mainly the purveyor of accepted knowledge. One of its greatest functions is to prevent doctrine from becoming dogma and truth, however understood, from degenerating into prejudice. In this way it is rendering a vital service to society. In any closed system, theocratic, class-authoritarian, or dictatorial, the university has a wholly different function. It becomes simply one of the numerous agencies for the propagation of orthodoxy—outside of that its work is purely technological. The critical mind, the spirit

[6] *On Liberty,* Chapter 3.

of independent inquiry, is killed, and with the death of that independence human dignity, the very basis of the sense of values, is maimed.

It is hardly possible to exaggerate the service to society of the free inquiring mind of which the modern university is the primary exponent. The central issue between democracy and dictatorship is not a question of what is true and what is false. They have different doctrines, certainly, but that alone never causes the conflicts that rend mankind. It is only when on one side, or on both, the spirit of free inquiry is banned, when either side's "truth" arms itself with arrogance and power, that the more disastrous forms of conflict occur. Such conflicts have constantly plagued mankind and a peculiarly ominous one threatens us again today. The only hope lies in the freedom of the mind. To advance this hope is also the mission of the university.[7] But if our democracy lacks sympathy for this mission, then our hope is vain, and democracy itself flounders in confusion. It forsakes its own morality, and its cause is lost.

There are those who genuinely fear the open search for knowledge because they think of it as a threat to values they cherish. This ambivalent attitude toward knowledge springs from another misconception. Knowledge is often thought of as an influence making only for change, always of necessity disturbing. Curiously enough, this charge can most effectively be brought against technological knowledge, the kind that is least subject to these resistances, the kind that is, at least in Western society, nearly always welcomed. But knowledge in its wider ambit is a ground of stability as well as a source of change. A very considerable portion of the teaching and the inquiry within every liberal institution of learning falls in the field of the humanities, including the literature, the lore, the philosophies, the creative arts, the historical developments of mankind. Here are recounted the enduring achievements of mankind, and here are again thought through the legacy of time-defeating thoughts concerning the good, the beautiful, and the true. So the university conserves and transmits the great traditions of all the ages. It interprets them anew and makes them intelligible to new generations. Not only in the humanities, however, but in every major area of inquiry the goal of learning is the discovery of the permanent realities. The natural sciences seek the laws and relationships that abide through all change,

[7] A fine discussion of this subject is contributed by Kurt P. Tauber, "The Free University in an Open Society," *Harvard Educational Review*, XXIII (Winter, 1953), 3–16.

that merely exemplify themselves in change. The knowledge itself changes only as it abandons more partial and less adequate conceptions of the nature of things. Knowledge changes only as it approximates nearer to a knowledge of the unchanging. If there is any place where men devotedly seek and teach what is beyond the changes of things, the established, the universal—*quod semper, quod ubique*—it is the university.

Therefore it is a gross confusion to regard the university as consisting mainly of irreverent scholars, of sceptics who throw doubt on the values men hold dear, of "radicals" who are working to undermine the social heritage. The university is engaged in perpetuating that heritage—and also in keeping it vital. For unless it is reinterpreted for the changing times, it hardens, loses its virtue, becomes obstructive, and dies. While some scholars are mainly concerned in rediscovering this heritage, others are also engaged in reinterpreting it. Both tasks are necessary. Scholarship must be creative, must help in reshaping traditions to new times for new needs. Thereby the scholar may be the more loyal to these traditions themselves, whereas the mere traditionalist, contented with the formula, denies the dynamism it once contained.

Conservatism is at least as congenial to scholarship as is liberalism—so far as the two are not really one. There is room within the university for many men of many minds. One belief to which all genuine scholars must subscribe is the belief in the free enterprise of ideas, and this belief is as compatible with intelligent conservatism as it is with any form of liberalism.

The search for knowledge cannot, without injury and distortion, be confined, divided, or regulated by any boundaries of faith, race, party, or nationality. It is universal by its very nature. It has no nationality. Most of their other affiliations set men in different camps. This affiliation makes them one. If the scholars of different countries make somewhat different contributions, they are alike contributions to the same goal. Knowledge serves the same good in China as in the United States—so long as it is free—in the Argentine as in France. Not only so, but the curbing of it in China or in the Argentine is a loss to us as well. For the advance of knowledge everywhere has greatly depended on the free exchange of ideas and of research findings across frontiers and on the interstimulation derived from the various modes of approach developed in different countries. Where academic freedom prevails, there is no kind of free exchange on earth that compares with the unlimited and untariffed freedom of the exchange of scholarly knowledge. Even the kind of knowledge that governments try to keep secret finds its way, sooner or later, to other lands. Scholarship is inherently international, and there is good evidence that scholars, belonging as they do to a world-wide brotherhood, have generally a wider perspective on international affairs—not to the detriment of their national loyalties—than is found among most other occupational groups.[8]

The search for knowledge, honestly undertaken, is a moral discipline. With the pursuit of this discipline goes the liberation from intolerance, wishful thinking, and complacency. But so strong are the influences bearing upon us that a man may be a competent scholar and within his own field remain true to its discipline while without he gives his interests or emotions the rein over his judgment. Nevertheless there is at least some carry-over, and various sociopsychological studies show that the scholar, including the student in training at the college, is distinctly freer than the average man from the acceptance of the "idols of the tribe" and particularly from group prejudice and group discrimination.

Thus the intellectual mission of the university becomes also a moral one. Men sensitive to experience may learn the lesson in other ways, but the institution of learning is a major training ground. Here is provided the great opportunity for the broadening of horizons, for the opening of the mind to the free contemplation of the works of man and the infinitely greater works of nature, for the gaining of perspectives, for liberation from the rigidity of outlook that cannot adjust itself to inevitable change, for the enlarged understanding that seeks to comprehend, without partiality, the ways of other men and other peoples and makes for the widening of effective communications and thus for the greater amplitude of living.

The attitudes generated in the open search for knowledge would be of immense benefit to society if only they were extended over into the conduct of affairs, and in the first place if they permeated the system of education, school as well as college. All worthy standards either depend on a knowledge of the relations of things or at least are purified in the light of knowledge. Through it false fears and vain hopes, with all their potencies for harm, may be controlled. Not knowledge itself but

[8] Cf. Quincy Wright, "The Citizen's Stake in Academic Freedom," *Journal of Higher Education,* XX (October, 1949), 339–45.

the free search for and the free communication of knowledge distinguishes the open mind from the closed mind, the open society from the closed society. Where the search for knowledge is controlled, the whole society is imprisoned. Where its freedom is suppressed, the loss of integrity it entails undermines all other human values; the whole civilization descends to a lower level.

This consequence is clearly seen wherever any form of totalitarianism is set up. When, for example, the Nazis came to power in Germany and turned the universities into servile instruments of their policies, all freeminded people within that country felt that there no longer was a firmament. Justice had become the will of the stronger. The moral bonds of community were broken. There was no basis for honor, for loyalty, for truth. Nothing was any longer determined by considerations of its intrinsic quality or worth. There were no standards save the standards of service and subservience to power. There was no right or wrong save utility or disutility for Party ends. All evidences were skewed to gratify the wishes of the dictator.

Unless men have faith in standards that are not relative and changeable as policy and interest dictate, unless they maintain these standards by fair appraisal of the evidences as to whether or not they have been met, then indeed the firmament of society is dissolved, leaving only might and cunning to rule the affairs of men. When these standards go under, then propagandist doctrine becomes ultimate truth, and knowledge becomes merely its servant. Human dignity is buried in the same grave with integrity and freedom.

The attack on academic freedom is an attack on all these values. Foremost among the conditions that sustain them is the open road to knowledge, where no authority and no power can decree what men must believe, concerning anything great or small, concerning the nature of the state, concerning the nature of the universe, concerning the policies of the nation, concerning the events of yesterday; where no sanctity and no censorship can preclude the appeal to evidences or silence the voice of the questioner; where no instrument of government, armed with subpoenas and citations for contempt, can harass or bully the unorthodox, simply because of the faith, political, religious, or social, that these men hold, with no evidence that they have committed any criminal acts. The standard of truth-seeking, so understood, is the one standard that the reason of man can universally accept.

The preservation of this standard is the only alternative to the dominance of force and deceit in the governing of man. Democracy provides the clearest opportunity for its realization. Democracy may be brought into being—historically to a great extent it has been—through other forces than the demand for this freedom, through socioeconomic changes and consequent changes in the effective distribution of power. But democracy is endangered where this freedom is in any way fettered by political or economic controls. Always, from the first, the champions of democracy have realized the necessity for it. Only in countries where the light of knowledge was made free, where some standard of cultural integrity was upheld against the encroachments of power—in ancient Greece, in Republican Rome, in the later medieval cities, in England and in the lands that successively took up the tradition thus developed—has democracy revealed its form and substance.

Democracy, once in being, has frequently been threatened and sometimes destroyed by insurgent dogmatisms and power-hungry groups. Among ourselves this threat has developed again, cloaked in a new disguise, ostensibly as a safeguard against communist infiltration. But the times have changed, and now the attack is centered on the institution of learning. Here also should be the center of the defense against it. Today it is not some particular faith that is being assailed by the power-armed dogmatism of another. It is directly the primary freedom, the freedom of the mind. To cultivate this freedom, to reap its rewards for the benefit of mankind, is the greater mission of the university.

This mission is inherent in its being. Like other agencies of great causes, the institution of learning works imperfectly. It fails to live up to its ideal. Its vision of it is sometimes dim. But it always has some vision and always brings some illumination—unless it is made wholly the servant of power. Unhappily, large numbers of our people do not understand the vast importance of this freedom for the nation as a whole, nor do they see through the cloak that disguises the attack upon it. Without more enlightenment the cause may well be lost.

XV: ACADEMIC FREEDOM AND AUTHORITY

To secure these rights, governments are instituted among men.

THROUGHOUT THIS WORK we have been meeting particular questions involving the relation of academic freedom to authority. It has been before us when we discussed the character of academic government in its various aspects, when we dealt with the operations of congressional committees, when we presented a variety of cases in which academic freedom was violated, when we considered the rights and obligations of the scholar. As we approach the end of the work, it is therefore meet that we look on this central issue in perspective.

Any group freedom, any individual or group right, always presumes an attitude and an activity on the part of some authority. Every freedom man in society enjoys requires in the first place an abstention by authority from any interference with it and in the second place a guardianship of it.

The business of education has its own authority structure. To begin with, there are the overall political rule-makers, federal, state, and municipal. They lay down general regulations, apportion funds, provide facilities and tax exemptions, and possess a broad supervisory power. Under the regulations they make and the charters they grant the next level of authority operates—the boards of education, the governing boards of institutions of higher learning, and so forth. These in turn appoint principals of schools and presidents of colleges and universities, besides ratifying the administrative and executive officials who carry on the day-to-day management of educational institutions. As a great background of all this authority there is the public, which elects not only the government as a whole but also, according to the area, the members of school boards and certain specific educational officers, and there are groups of the public which, as parents, as alumni, as fund raisers, or otherwise, exercise influence if not authority within the educational system.

Indeed, were we to include under the rubric of authority all those groups whose pronouncements or requests carry some weight in the determination of educational policies—religious groups, business groups, and numerous others—we would have a kind of inventory of the vast ramifying organizational activity of the whole country.

If we confine our attention to constituted authority, it is obvious that every part of the structure has its particular functions and that unless these functions are clearly delimited, nothing but confusion will result. Furthermore, it can easily be shown that the gravest dangers to academic freedom arise when any authority steps beyond its bounds and usurps functions of educational control that in accordance with well-established principles are or should be assigned elsewhere.[1]

The limitations we have in mind should not be thought of as merely legal limitations. Authority within any field must have a range of discretion, within which it is obligated by its own sense of responsibility. Thus the governing boards of our institutions of learning have the legal right to do various things we have spoken of as not falling within their province. What should in the first instance restrain them from doing these things is their direct concern for the integrity of education. Their moral duty is to uphold and advance the standards of the institutions over which they preside. Their legal right assigns them a very large discretion in the pursuit of this objective.

The delimitations we have just indicated are essential, as we have sought to show at appropriate places throughout this volume, for the safeguarding of the integrity of education against intrusive forces that would make it subservient to their own interests. When these delimitations are maintained, academic freedom is assured against its most serious dangers, and moreover authority itself thereby takes on as its own first obligation the defense of that freedom. Furthermore, when

---

[1] As an extreme example of the violation of this principle we cite the behavior of Governor Theodore Bilbo of Mississippi, who was once able to boast that he had fired three college presidents and hired three new ones in the space of two hours. By law the governor headed the state board of education which had jurisdiction over the three state-controlled educational institutions. He also had the power to appoint a majority of the board's members. Apparently trying to reward his political friends and punish his enemies, the governor fired 179 instructors in a few weeks' time. John B. Hudson, "The Spoils System Enters College," *New Republic*, LXIV (1930), 123–25. For further details see "Politics and the University of Mississippi," *School and Society*, XXXII (July 19, 1930), 86–88, and "Protests Against the Academic Dismissals in Mississippi," *School and Society*, XXXII (September 27, 1930), 420.

political government and academic government alike observe these limits to their authority, another authority is by that very process introduced into the educational structure—that of the body of educators, the faculty, the makers and inheritors of the academic tradition. The proper range of this last authority has already been indicated in Chapter 7 and Chapter 13.

Authority in our time is seriously overstepping these limits. In fact, it is hardly an exaggeration to say that the weight of authority in the United States is now adverse to the principle of intellectual freedom. By the weight of authority we mean that the forces unfavorable to it are more effective than its defenders in making their will prevail. Many of our legislators probably do not approve of recent book-banning episodes, but if certain legislators want *Middletown* or *The Loyalty of Free Men* ejected from the libraries of the Overseas Information Service, these books will disappear. Many faculties, we are convinced, disapprove of the Jenner doctrine that any one of their number who before a congressional committee pleads the Fifth Amendment should be *ipso facto* dismissed, but a number of states have made regulations to that effect, and the boards of more than a few colleges and universities have followed suit. The doctrine is carried even further, one exhibit being the case of a professor of classics who received a Fulbright award to study in Italy but had it canceled by the State Department because his wife had resorted to the Fifth Amendment. It made no difference that the professor himself had sworn that he was not and had never been a communist.[2] Another type of evidence is the extraordinary extension and perversion of the guilt-by-association principle. A distinguished bishop of the Methodist Church, falsely accused on this ground, is needled when he defends his record before the House Committee, and in consequence a hall in Los Angeles where he was booked to speak is closed against him because he is "controversial."[3] The very fact that being, or being thought, controversial has become an acceptable reason why one should not be heard and why one's books should be excluded from certain libraries is an ominous development. But we need not reiterate the evidence. It is sufficiently spread on the record.

We have pointed out that in any well-ordered educational system each

[2] "State Department Student-Teacher Exchange Program," Hearing Before the Permanent Subcommittee on Investigations of the Committee on Government Operations (United States Senate, 83d Congress, First Session, June 10 and 19), pp. 1–3.

[3] *New York Times*, November 23, 1953.

type of authority has its own area of control. When any type, whether political or directly educational, oversteps its mark and intrudes into the area of another, what then is the duty of that other? Let us take some illustrative situations.

1. When the offense is committed by a political authority, whether state or federal, its primary claim on our obedience precludes various forms of resistance that may be permissible elsewhere. But this emphatically does not mean that the encroachments of this higher authority should be meekly accepted. There are those who say: congressional committees have a perfect right to investigate wherever and whatever they think proper; this mode of investigation is one of the oldest devices of our system of government; therefore it is the duty of the citizen to cooperate with them, to give them any assistance in his power; and when they come to the gates of the university, that institution should bid them welcome.

We have been distressed that so many educational institutions have officially taken this line—and stopped there. They have impressed on their faculties that it is everyone's civic obligation to answer without reservation all questions put to him—and stopped there, as though that particular obligation summed up the whole duty of the scholar in this matter and the enunciation of it the whole duty of the administrator. Happily there are leading administrators who have shown more wisdom—we might cite as examples President Deane W. Malott of Cornell, President Nathan Pusey of Harvard, and President Grayson Kirk of Columbia—but the weakness of our educational system is demonstrated by the fact that so many others have failed to follow that lead.

We have not questioned the *right* of congressional committees to carry on whatsoever investigations are officially entrusted to their charge. We have not questioned their legal and constitutional authority to hunt for subversives—so long as they give a rational definition to the term—in our colleges and universities. We have questioned their judgment, their discretion, their methods, their assumptions, their announced objectives —and notably their claim to be defending academic freedom. We believe that in all these respects they have been misguided and in consequence have done serious damage alike to our civil liberties and to the prestige of our country. We should obey the law, but we should still refuse to go beyond our legal duty in "cooperating" with those who are bringing about these untoward results.

To take this position is not only our right but also our obligation, our obligation not only as members of colleges and universities but also as citizens. It is our civic as well as our moral obligation to protest and to criticize. No one questions the right of the citizen in a democracy to disagree and to protest when his own private interests are threatened by a legislative or executive act. It is preposterous that when instead our fundamental values are being threatened by governmental procedures, we should be bidden meekly to accept it. Such supine behavior imperils democracy itself. The defense of our liberties requires more robust convictions.

2. These direct intrusions of political authority are on the whole a recent, if particularly ominous, development, whereas throughout the modern history of education in North America the ever-recurring source of academic disturbance has been the failure of governing boards to recognize and to respect the area of authority properly belonging to the faculty. The same considerations that should limit the role of political authority apply equally to the authority of governing boards and, in relevant respects, to that of the administrative staff. Indeed, in any well-ordered system, it is a primary task of the higher ranges of authority to protect and sustain the educational role of the faculty. And, as was suggested above, the governing board can maintain its own area of control only if it does its part in warding off from the faculty the unwarranted encroachments of the state.

3. We have spoken of the public as the background of the structure of authority, or perhaps we might say the ground on which the whole structure rests. Any metaphor can mislead, but the implication here is that the public itself does not issue instructions or conduct the affairs of the educational system. In this area, as in most others, its function is to confer authority and to express its approval or disapproval by renewing or withdrawing it. The public exercises this function through the election of its political representatives, through the election of the members of school boards, and, directly or indirectly, in the appointment of members to the boards of state institutions. It does not, of course, possess these powers with respect to voluntary or nonstate academies, but public opinion, wherever it runs strongly in favor of or against any procedure, is always a potent influence.

Moreover, the university, whether it be state-controlled or a private endowment, can still be thought of as a public trust. Even the private university receives important rights and privileges from the state, and the continuance of these favors depends on the will of the people. Besides, although its students and alumni are only a limited group, the private university makes in many ways its own contribution to the welfare of the whole society. It may certainly be said therefore to exist for the good of society as a whole. And certainly the state institution must depend for its existence on the same claim.

Here, then, the question of authority arises again. Since our institutions of learning exist for the benefit of the people, should they not give the people the services the people require from it, the kind of education the people want? Those who state the issue in this way are likely to add that this kind of responsiveness is incumbent on the university in a democratic society.

True, the university is a public trust. It is encharged with one of the greatest of all public services. It is a service that, to be well fulfilled, must not be confused with any other. It must be assured of the conditions appropriate to its own nature. As with any professional or expert service, the people may reasonably demand that they receive the fullest benefit it can offer them and that it be so conducted that no professional interest or private privilege interfere with its quality or efficiency.

Suppose they demand something else instead, suppose they demand that the faculty teach certain doctrines, economic, political, theological, moral, or any other? Suppose they demand that any educators who do not adhere to the popularly accepted doctrines be dismissed? Is it not within their democratic rights to do so?

In the first place, no intelligent theory of democracy assigns such a right either to the people or to a government that presumably speaks for them. It is contrary to the first principle of democracy—the equal liberty of minorities and majorities, the protection of minorities from any oppression or compulsion to believe or think or speak according to any majority prescription. And direct or indirect assault on this principle sets democracy on the road to dictatorship.

In the second place, the demand is contrary to the law of all good organization, within which the man of special training, the expert, the craftsman, the professional, may be subject to instruction as to what he should do but not as to how he should do it. The limiting point comes where such instruction interferes with the quality or efficiency of the product, where it turns good craftsmanship into inferior craftsmanship, good art into meretricious art, good therapy into ineffective therapy, good engineering into faulty engineering, good education into poor education. The only judgment to which we can here appeal is the consensus of the men of skill or knowledge. When the product is a material one, commercial considerations may lead to violations of this law, in order to favor quantity as against quality. But where the product is an immaterial benefit, where it concerns the intellectual or spiritual or moral benefit of the people, no such considerations have any application. And the evils of enforced conformity are not offset by any gain that is not utterly unworthy or negligible against the loss.

We have been pointing out that the free institution of learning has a great mission beyond its immediate objective of imparting knowledge and extending the frontiers thereof. This mission its practitioners themselves need much more adequately to recognize. The free institution of learning is an integral element in the structure of every democratic society. Its freedom is not freedom from all authority, it is freedom sustained through and through by authority. The freedom it needs is freedom from irrelevant and antidemocratic abuses of authority. Only the higher civilizations possess this freedom, whereby authority is responsible and thus redeemed from the follies and brutalities of mere power. In turn, this freedom sustains the higher civilizations, feeds and informs its spirit, and in the process gives it ever-increasing strength and resources, fruits of the ever-growing tree of knowledge.

XVI: WHAT WE CAN DO ABOUT IT

Our problem is not merely to work out an adequate definition of academic freedom, but to induce the people to care about it. This is an undertaking of the first magnitude.

OUR TIME of educational trouble, if we face it resolutely, is one from which an advance may be made that not only relieves the trouble but remedies the situation out of which the trouble has arisen. Recent attacks on academic freedom have revealed serious weaknesses in our institutions of learning and indeed in our whole educational structure. These attacks have been so flagrant that they call for a resistance and counterattack which, to be effective, would give new vigor and direction to the whole educational process.

We should not think of the defense of academic freedom as merely the responsibility of scholars. It is indeed that, but it is no less the responsibility of the academy as a whole, including its board, its administration, its alumni, and its students. Moreover, alike because of its intrinsic worth and because it is closely interwoven with the primary freedoms of the whole people, it should be the concern of all who care for the democracy we inherit.

In the first place a high responsibility rests with the governing board. It stands for and acts for the institution. It should be sensitive to any attack upon the integrity of the institution. The saddest commentary on the present situation is that so many boards have aided and abetted, sometimes even led, the attack, while only a relatively few have taken a strong stand for the defense. This failure on the part of governing boards has weakened all the other defenses of academic freedom, and not least those made by the faculties of their institutions. The service rendered by those boards that are loyal to freedom has been most notable. Anything that could strengthen in other boards the conscious-

The quotation at the head of this chapter is from the University of Chicago Faculty *News Bulletin*, I (Winter Quarter, 1941), 2.

ness of their obligation would be a decisive gain. Possibly the loyal boards could help to enlighten some of the others. As a far-sighted university administrator has said, "The time has come for the trustees of these great public trusts to enter the debate. Their appearance on the side of the educational officers would render the defense impregnable." [1]

In the first place it is for the board to assert the proper autonomy of the educational institution, to protest publicly against any unwarranted infringements of that autonomy, and to use all lawful means to discourage such infringements. The vast majority of boards are, or certainly should be, aware that congressional investigations to uncover "subversives" among their faculty members constitute a wasteful, disturbing, and needless process. It would be well if more boards went on record to that effect, not letting political or other extraneous considerations influence their judgment and always remembering that they are the legal custodians of the long-established and vitally important tradition that assigns a genuine educational autonomy to the institution of higher learning.

In this context we respectfully call to the attention of governing boards a famous statement made on a crucial occasion by the Trustees of the Board of Trinity College, now Duke University, North Carolina. A professor of that college, John S. Bassett, had written an article in the *South Atlantic Quarterly* for October, 1903. It deprecated racial inequality and prognosticated a future state of equality for the Negro. He was at once assailed by newspapers and organizations throughout the state. From all over the state came loud cries for his expulsion from the college. Professor Bassett submitted his resignation. The Board met on December 1, 1903, refused to accept his resignation, and issued a declaration of principle. We quote from this declaration:

We are particularly unwilling to lend ourselves to any tendency to destroy or limit academic liberty, a tendency which has, within recent years, manifested itself in some conspicuous instances, and which has created a feeling of uneasiness for the welfare of American Colleges. Whatever encourages such a tendency endangers the growth of higher education by intimidating intellectual activity and causing highminded men to look with suspicion upon this noble profession. We cannot lend countenance to the degrading notion that professors in American Colleges have not an equal liberty of thought and speech with all other Americans. . . .

Neither, on the other hand, is it the business of governing boards like ours

[1] Samuel P. Capen, *The Management of Universities* (Buffalo, New York, 1953), p. 32.

to prescribe opinions for professors. The same broad principle holds both in the college and the state. While it is idle to deny that the free expression of wrong opinions sometimes works harm, our country and our race stand for the view that the evils of intolerance and suppression are infinitely worse than those of folly.[2]

The next line of defense is the administration. What it says and does receives wide public recognition. Its first spokesman is the president. One of the major calls on him is for public speeches. Whatever else he makes his theme—the state of the nation, the achievements of his institution, its financial straits, or anything else—he has an excellent opportunity to explain to the public what higher education means, what values it has beyond its utilitarian service, and why scholars must be free in its pursuit.

The situation requires action as well as exhortation. In the first place, the administration can in these times of pressure and of apprehension do much to sustain the morale of the faculty. It should emphatically not stand aside and leave the faculty to carry on the fight alone. When pressure groups clamor that this or that professor should be dismissed because of his dangerous opinions, the administration should make it perfectly clear that it stands inexorably for the intellectual liberty of the teacher. When a political group casts public suspicion on a faculty member because of his one-time affiliations, the administration should give him every encouragement to defend his cause. And if because of such suspicion the attitude of the governing board toward the faculty member is dubious or unfavorable, the administration, having first assured itself of the member's integrity, should clearly convey to the board its own position. It should repel all proposals from outside, whether coming from political or from private quarters, that are inimical to the educational autonomy of the faculty. It should extend no invitation to those investigatory bodies that show little respect for or understanding of the principles of a university. Nor should it accept offers from such bodies of the kind of "cooperation" that means the appointment of contact men for the exchange of information respecting "subversive" influences in the institution.

The temptation besetting university administrations is that of yielding to pressures or of making concessions for the sake of some immediate

---

[2] The full statement of the Trinity College Board is quoted in Paul Neff Garber, *John Carlisle Kilgo* (Duke University Press, 1937), pp. 276–78.

institutional advantage. If it is a state institution, it wants to keep on good terms with the legislature and not to offend any important members of it lest the institutional budget suffer. If it is a private institution, there may be alumni groups or substantial donors making demands prejudicial to academic freedom. Indeed the constant need to raise money is a constant danger to independence, and too many institutions lack the assurance as well as the spirit that is exemplified in Harvard's refusal to sacrifice principle for the sake of financial contributions.[3]

Often enough the administration has to face restrictive attitudes not only in outside groups but also in members of its own board. Indeed, the latter pressure is likely to be more insidious. Anticipating objections from the board, a dean may decide that a certain promotion or nomination to office should not be made, or a president may refuse to put forward such proposals for final approval. Perfectly good reasons can always be found. The line of least resistance is safe.

Instead, the president and his near associates are most true to their obligations when in matters of this kind they stand by their cause and endeavor to convince their board of its intrinsic importance and of its relation to the best interests of the institution. The administration is occupationally much closer to an understanding of these things. It should seek to convey that understanding to the board, where there is reason to believe that there is need to do so. With courage and tact it may achieve a signal success. We referred above to the pronouncement on academic freedom made in 1903 by the Board of Trinity College, North Carolina. It is unlikely that this board would have responded so finely to the situation, had it not been for the splendid plea made to the board by the president of the college, John C. Kilgo.[4]

The need for greater courage is clear. What has to be reinforced everywhere is the sense of the mission of the university. Primary considerations are subordinated to secondary ones. The scales are falsified. The integrity of the institution should weigh more than a new building or a new playing field or even a new department. The well-being, the achievement, the longer-run prestige of an institution of learning cannot be assessed by its acreage or the size of its population or even the volume of its researches.

[3] See Chapter 11, pp. 196–97.
[4] Garber, *John Carlisle Kilgo*, pp. 268–75.

It is not enough to utter some shining phrases about the glory of the university and the value of the free mind, shunning all direct reference to the immediate realities. He who extols the free mind must, if he is no timeserver, show its application to the teacher who is under fire because he has spoken his mind freely.

By this test the record of many administrations is not good. While some college and university presidents and other educational authorities have shown an excellent clarity and courage, too many have been subservient and timorous. There have been some sad exhibits along this line. Nor has there been any adequate pronouncement from the organizations that represent the administrators. The statements we have seen have been lacking in any leadership, in any inspiration, in any call to action, even in any specific recognition of the dangers that threaten the intellectual independence of the academies.

When we come next to the alumni, we reach a large and very important group the measure of whose potential influence on behalf of academic freedom is often underrated. Sometimes, indeed, the alumni are thought of as a body against whose demands the universities must defend their freedom. It is true that here and there a prominent alumnus or some group of alumni protests against the harboring of unorthodox or free-spoken professors, but in this as in other situations the voice of the complainant is heard while there is no reckoning of those who reject the complaint. It would indeed be strange if the majority of men and women who have passed through our institutions of learning were so regardless of their integrity. We have no reason to believe that it is so. Alumni represent all points of view, but they are attached to the institutions that trained them. It would be well worthwhile to bring more meaningfully to their attention the intellectual problems of these institutions, just as they now learn of their financial needs.

We have already pointed out the importance of the alumni journals in this respect. Perhaps some of these journals feel that they should not take sides on issues on which their readers may be divided. But the prior claim is the welfare of the institution. How effective a resolute stand can be, even in what might seem a rather adverse situation, is shown in the fine service rendered by the *Ohio State University Monthly,* the organ of the alumni association of that much-agitated university. Skillfully directed and entirely fearless, it not only held aloft the standard in the face of grave failure to do so on the part of both board and president but also, in spite of opposition, it rallied to the cause a considerable muster of alumni.

It is an encouraging thought that the students of today are the new alumni of tomorrow. For the evidence suggests that a strong majority of students are on the side of intellectual liberty. Sometimes they feel there is little they can do about it, that their occasional demonstrations carry little weight. This is not the case. Since the ground advanced for the silencing of nonconformist teachers is the protection of the students against dangerous or subversive influences, the rejection of this intrusive paternalism by the students themselves is salutary. Moreover, when they stand by a teacher—or a whole institution—subjected to attack, their attitude strengthens the morale of the teacher and of the institution. They are at the same time defending their own liberty.

They have, besides, another testimony to bear. Knowing their college or university at first hand, they have learned something of the way that knowledge is found, of the need for intellectual enterprise. Being nearer to this learning than their home folks usually are, they can do something to influence the judgment of members of their families, perhaps to remove some of the misconceptions and misvaluations that are so commonly accepted.

We turn now to the faculty, the main objective of the assault. There is much that the faculty member can do, and his efforts should begin at home. Too many scholars are inadequately aware of what is at stake. Too many do not realize sufficiently that they, and no other group, are the primary custodians as well as the expositors of this freedom, so that its jealous protection is their duty to society, to the nation and to mankind. With these deficiencies we have already dealt at length. Yet there is still another respect in which American scholarship is not wholly blameless for its present plight. It has in various areas been infected by the anti-intellectual bias of the times, which makes of knowledge a merely instrumental good. A contributory condition has been the pressure put upon colleges and universities to introduce all kinds of purely technical and utilitarian courses, many of which have little or no relation to "higher learning." The infection has weakened its defenses and impaired its morale. Since the twenties there have been increased manifestations of a tendency in the universities to adopt the same predominantly utilitarian attitude toward knowledge that pervades the country as a whole. The fault lies not in the demonstration that knowledge is the first and greatest of all the means at the command of man for the achievement of whatever ends he seeks. It lies in the disregard and sometimes even the disrepute attaching to the intrinsic worth of knowledge. Knowledge for what? If you cannot do something with it, if it is not a tool to get for you something you otherwise want, then it is "merely" theoretical. It may be all right for dilettantes, for dreamers in ivory towers, but good honest men have no use for it. The idea that knowledge may be also its own reward, that, in the language of the marketplace, it may be a consumers' good as well as a producers' good, that there may be light and liberation and the ground of wisdom in the contemplation of it, that there may be moral and spiritual values inherent in the genuine search for it—this idea is too often remote even from some faculty groups.

The infection has been especially prevalent in those areas of knowledge where it can do most harm, in the social sciences and in educational studies. For such scholars knowledge is practically equivalent to research. Research becomes the operation and discovery of techniques; theory, the schematism of techniques. Knowledge is emptied of meaning—unless you apply it to some practical problem. In fact, "meaning" means "application." Otherwise it is "verbalism," a "laryngial sound," a noise in the throat. Knowledge is "know-how," and everything else is "abstraction." This is the more extreme form of the tendency, but there are many approximations to it. How far-reaching it is, how deadly it can become, is illustrated by the 1948 *Report* of the President's Commission on Higher Education, which deprecates "the present orientation toward verbal skills and intellectual interest" in favor of more pragmatic courses.[5] Here we have the spectacle of a body, itself largely composed of educators, entrusted with an educational survey of national importance, recommending for the advancement of higher education that its vital principle, the cultivation of the mind, be still further diminished to make way for other things.

Much of our education, elementary and more advanced, already discourages the taking of thought. The native curiosity to know about things, the growing up "whys" of the older child, are too often blunted by the mechanism of the school. In one area learning is reduced to the drudgery

[5] For an excellent commentary see Richard Hofstadter, "Democracy and Anti-Intellectualism in America," *Michigan Alumnus Quarterly Review,* LIX (August, 1953), 292–95.

of memory tests, in another to the acquisition of techniques. You can do something with the latter, and you can play with them, but there's no fun in the business of memorizing and forgetting. So the intellectual side of the pupil's nature is denied evocation. So long as reading and writing are construed as merely "verbal skills," like the art of the advertiser, so long as any interest in the rich heritage of the world's great literature is regarded as only a "capacity for grasping abstractions," so long will the teaching of these subjects be as dismal and perfunctory as it now so frequently is.

If such teachers and such scholars kept away from the world of ideas altogether, the situation would not be as serious as it is. But some of them disparage the realm of values—after all, they are only "abstractions." When they deal with idea-systems, it is always as critics. Criticism is an important part of scholarship, but if criticism is solely destructive and never constructive, if we seek to pull down the old residences of human values without building new ones or at least proposing better residences instead, then we become the unwitting agents of social chaos. Only a few scholars go this far, but they receive disproportionate attention and falsely convey the suggestion that scholarship itself is a negative or destructive thing. This false suggestion is extremely useful to the enemies of academic freedom and in the prevailing climate of opinion is readily believed by many people.

We have dealt at some length with the mission of the university. We have not implied that its members fully live up to the call it makes on them. In this respect the university is no different from any other of our major institutions—the church, for example. Nevertheless, the mission we impute is not merely an ideal. There is in every significant institution of learning a body of scholars who are, in their various ways, continuously engaged in advancing it. What is needed, however, is a wider consciousness of the mission, a stronger perception of its meaning for our society, a greater determination to resist internal defections from it and external assaults upon it. The scholar cannot fulfill his obligation in the defense of academic freedom unless he is also devoted to the intrinsic values of scholarship.

Thus far we have been concerned with the spirit, the morale, that must animate the body of scholars and the whole institution of learning in the unending campaign for the liberty of the mind. We face next some questions of the strategy and tactics requisite for the immediate occasion.

Our institutional weakness is evidenced in the weakness of our strategy when the educational integrity of our institutions is assailed. With greater awareness of the issues' we would exhibit more unity and more courage. The defense has not been conspicuous for either of those qualities. We do not sufficiently recognize that if one member is unfairly attacked, all of us are implicated; or that if another institution is under fire, it is our concern as well. There is testimony both from administrators and teachers that colleges and universities, particularly the smaller colleges, feel insulated when they are struggling to protect themselves. One reason is that the academic profession is not nearly so well organized as are the other major professions, such as medicine and law. And there is the further disability that its own institutional guardians have in so many cases either stood aside from the battle or even sided with the enemy.

The only reasonably inclusive organization representing the body of scholars is the American Association of University Professors. By its constitution it enrolls only the educators and some students, and not the administrators, in institutions of higher learning. It has done fine work in various respects, through the reports of its standing committees, through its *Bulletin,* and through its continuous and thorough investigation of cases involving academic freedom. It has taken a firm and uncompromising stand on major issues. But it does not in any way knit together the profession. It does not inspire any collective responsiveness. It does not maintain regular communication with its constituent chapters. These chapters are often inert, except when some serious problem affects their respective institutions. There is a great lack of communication between headquarters and local groups. In times such as the present, when cases requiring its attention occur so frequently, it is unable to come to grips with them in time to give effective aid. It is insufficiently staffed for the magnitude of its task. It would be highly desirable that the chapters get together with the central office in order to work out a plan that would ensure more adequte financing and above all more effective interaction between the chapters and more effective communication from headquarters to the chapters and vice versa.

With greater awareness and greater professional coherence would come an improvement in strategy where action is needed. Too frequently in recent years a faculty has been confronted suddenly with a grave violation of its freedom. It is unprepared, has no policy in advance, has no clear leadership, and is likely to suffer from divided counsels. In this area the strategy of defense is more difficult than the strategy of attack, and the battle may be lost before it begins. Sometimes the faculty does get together, where the offense is very flagrant (as it was at Ohio State University), and aided by outside forces puts up a stout resistance. Under such conditions it may win concessions, but then again there is likely to be division of counsel, and in the end a too general acceptance of a very partial "victory" that restores only part of what was taken away.

Scholars need to be aware not only of the greatness of their cause but also of the community forces that are on their side and still more of those that would be if the case were clearly presented to them. One virtue of a firm stand is that it helps to evoke this potential aid. Here as elsewhere, timidity loses allies and defeats itself. Occasions are constantly arising nowadays where resolution and courage are called for and unhappily are not always forthcoming. Take, for example, the case of the scholar who, conscious of his integrity, nevertheless allows himself to be browbeaten when he has to answer before an investigating committee. Most scholars have of course had no previous experience of being in a situation of this kind. So they lose assurance and make an ineffective appearance, being unready to meet the loaded questions, the insinuations, the false inferences, and the appeals to prejudice to which they are at times exposed. The habits of the classroom no longer serve them.

Yet even without experience, courage could find a way. Any true scholar who is a witness in such a situation should realize that it is not he who is being brought into question but one of the greatest of all human liberties, which at that moment he has the honor to uphold. He should remember that he is still living in a democracy and that he is defending a prime condition of its very existence. Nor should he forget that he belongs to a great brotherhood of scholars, and that, so long as he testifies in honesty, his words are spoken in their behalf and in their name as well as in his own. He should respond not defiantly but with firmness and conviction. If the interrogators ask loaded questions, he should insist on analyzing them. If he is presented with false alternatives, he should decline to accept them. If they refuse to make distinctions he regards as essential, he should take his stand on his own position. If they bring against him movements he joined in earlier days, he should not be abashed or apologetic. He must maintain his integrity, and not betray the integrity of others.

Given more of this spirit, large achievements are possible. It would clear the way for the major task of strategy, which is also the intrinsic task of the scholar, that of educating the people. With all our educating we have not educated the people in the meaning of education. Instead, they have been miseducated about it. One consequence is that the tradition of academic freedom is not nearly so well-established in this country as it is in most other democratic countries.

This task of education is indeed one that should enlist the institution as a whole, its trustees and its administrators as well as its faculty. The need for this task can be put in the broadest terms. The complex world in which we live requires more for its well-being, even for its maintenance, than the specialized arts and crafts and skills by which the various parts of its intricate machinery are operated. It must have the consciousness of its own unity, the sense of the obligation of interdependent part to interdependent part, some conception at least of the "idea forces" that move in our age, some understanding of the basic conditions on which the promise of "life, liberty, and the pursuit of happiness" is predicated. This is a challenge to the university, perhaps a test of the worthwhileness of the learning it fosters.

What we are proposing is therefore something more than a series of pronouncements on the meaning of the university. Without something more, such pronouncements might fail of their effect. The university should directly and indirectly provide enlightenment not only for its enrolled students but also, in a measure, for a wider public. To begin with, it should give its own students, aside from the specialized knowledge appropriate to their various fields, an awareness, and not merely condensed information, concerning their own times. And it should employ what means are available to it so that "man's right to knowledge" is its genuine concern.

Nor should the scholar regard the endeavor to fulfil this service as an irksome chore, an interruption of his proper work, a kind of condescension. This may be the attitude of the narrow specialist, whose cultural horizon is sometimes as circumscribed and void of perspective as that of the lowliest mechanic. But it is not, or should not be, the attitude of the true scholar, who is engaged in seeing things in their relationships and has found by experience that the wider communication of knowledge can be, in its due place, as rewarding and as difficult an enterprise as his more intensive work in his own field. There, too, he can learn as he teaches, and the stimulus of this kind of learning may at times even redeem his own specialization from the scientific as well as the moral penalties of narrowness.

Some institutions are active in this field, though often peripherally and in a very limited way, and some scholars do fine work in it, but the need is vastly greater than the provision.

The more direct instruction of the citizen concerning the meaning and service of the university can be conducted on a broader scale, utilizing all the major agencies of communication. The subject should be approached along lines that carry it home to him. For example, he has a high respect for science—the relation between the growth of science and the struggle for intellectual liberty is clear. He believes in "fair play"—how this applies to the scholar, and to those who traduce him, can be shown with chapter and verse. He believes in democracy—how it depends on the liberty of the mind can well be demonstrated. He believes in America—what the spirit of repression does to its greater traditions, to its well-being, and to its standing among the nations can be given simple and effective illustration.

In the course of such instruction it will be necessary, at times, to deal with the assailants of academic freedom, and here outspokenness and some degree of courage is called for. A fair-minded probe of our unfair-minded probers is in order. In this connection we may cite the admirable words of President George N. Shuster: "I would remind you that the university has always been a forum in the presence of which the lords of the passing hour are subject to scrutiny. No doubt the time has come to ask on what meat this our Caesar has fed"—he is referring to the junior senator from Wisconson—"and to review his activities with the utmost objectivity, calm and chilly resolution, so that an authoritative report can be made to the people." [6]

But what is most important is that the people should come to appreciate the university, should learn how much of great and lasting worth it contributes to society and how essential it is that its freedom be sustained and its standards advanced, should recognize how devoted and how disinterested the work of the true scholar is, and should look upon the institution of learning, not with suspicion from a distance, but from near at hand with affection, so that they, too, will become the guardians of its integrity.

[6] Address delivered at the annual conference of the National Civil Liberties Clearing House in Washington, D.C., March 19–20, 1953.

APPENDICES

BIBLIOGRAPHY

INDEX

Appendix A: ACADEMIC FREEDOM AND THE DENOMINATIONAL UNIVERSITY

WE HAVE at one or two places in the text pointed out that some requirements of the structure of academic freedom then under review did not apply at all or at least in the main to denominational institutions and could not and should not be required of them. We cannot, for example, expect them to make the appointment and retention of their scholars depend simply on their professional competence and on their personal integrity, since it is a presumption that their teachers will be in harmony with the faith to which they adhere.

It is not possible, however, to make any general statement, concerning the extent or the degree of restriction on academic freedom, that will hold for all academic institutions regulated by or affiliated with an ecclesiastical system. Obviously it must vary according to the nature of the creed, the kind of prescriptions, if any, that it makes concerning the cosmic or the biophysical order, the form of the ecclesiastical hierarchy that officially interprets the creed, the authoritative import of the pronouncements this hierarchy delivers, and the character of the administration.

These factors determine how far and with what bindingness on its members the faith invades the area of actual or potential scientific investigation. Obviously the more it does so, the more severe the limitations it imposes on academic freedom and the more likely the administration is to regard scientific knowledge as an inferior kind of knowledge, compared with the body of "truth" it espouses. For example, sects that accept the literal inspiration of the Bible reject the doctrine of evolution and discredit the evidences on which it is based.

In the course of many centuries, with the growth of science and the decline of the control of religious authorities over it, the major fields of chemicophysical knowledge became no longer subject to any of the dogmatic preconceptions that once restricted investigation. Their study can be pursued with as much freedom in the denominational institution as in any other. To this extent there is no longer any conflict between science and theology. In this respect the modern denominational university allows its educators practically the same academic freedom that the best nondenominational universities enjoy—with one indirect reservation presently to be mentioned.

There are, however, other areas of study in which the range of academic freedom in these institutions is less assured. Here, again, there is no general rule. In some a more liberal spirit prevails; in others the ecclesiastical discipline holds jealous guard. But the major factor determining what limits may be set to academic freedom is the degree to which the particular faith, as interpreted by ecclesiastical authority, makes pronouncements concerning the moral and social relationships of men, concerning the social consequences of behavior contrary to the rules thus laid down, and the forces that in the longer run guide or determine human behavior and the course of history. It is in the area of social and historical science that we are likely to find in denominational institutions implicit or explicit formulas of prescription that do not apply in other academic institutions.

To give one illustration, let us suppose a scholar undertakes the task of investigating the conditions underlying the poverty of certain thickly populated areas, say in Puerto Rico or in one of the Asiatic countries, and of making recommendations for improvement on the basis of his study. Let us suppose he finds that the population is increasing too fast for the resources of the area and concludes that measures of amelioration, such as the introduction of new methods of agriculture, would not avail without some check to the rate of reproduction. Now, if the scholar were identified with a denominational college the theological doctrine of which condemned the resort to contraceptive devices as sinful, he might in the first place be less likely to interpret the facts as evidences of overpopulation and in the second place he would certainly be barred from recommending the introduction of birth-control clinics. In other words, to the scholar who is under theological discipline *one possible conclusion from the facts is ruled out* in advance while to the scholar not so obligated it remains open. The former might of course follow the line of Thomas Malthus and prescribe continence instead of contraceptives, but he would be remarkably ignorant of human nature if he believed that under the given conditions this prescription could be of much effect.

Given any set of theological premises, it is an entirely reasonable position for anyone who accepts them to acknowledge that they may or do require that certain limits be set to the full range of academic freedom. It is entirely consistent for them to assert further that thereby no injury is done to the search for knowledge, since nothing can be true that is in contradiction with the higher truth or divine revelation or the pronouncements of those who are directly guided by it.

Were the admission generally made that denominational universities have a double function; that one of these functions is common to all institutions of higher learning whereas the other is particular to themselves and at the same time paramount for them; and that in consequence they must, and in fact do, so far as they fulfill the second function, set some limits to the range of academic freedom—then we might for our present purpose let the subject rest here. But there are those who claim that this limitation is no limitation, that on the contrary the true denominational university is intrinsically freer than those which do not postulate any prior system of revealed truth. Thus Archbishop Karl J. Alter, in a graduation address at Xavier University (June 6, 1951), declared that a Roman Catholic institution such as the university in question enjoys a greater intellectual freedom than nondenominational academies because "it possesses a coherent philosophy which excludes inconsistencies and contradictions but places no inhibitions on the sum total of truth."

Every other body that accepts a clearly articulated and authoritatively interpreted faith, no matter what the faith may be, could with equal logic make the same claim for itself. No one who does not adhere to that faith can possibly concur. Each faith would thus arrogate to itself an absolute freedom claimed by every other faith. There is no way out of the relativity of such conflicting absolutes. For the realm of scientific knowledge and the realm of authoritative theological truth are separate.

When we speak here of academic freedom, we must not limit ourselves to the viewpoint of any one faith, for we must think of the university as such, the university as first and foremost an association of scholars for the advancement and the spread of knowledge, with no doctrinal commitments other than a loyalty to the course of knowledge. Any theological commitments postulated by an academy of learning must from this viewpoint constitute a limitation of academic freedom.

It is necessary to observe that we are referring to systems of *theological* concepts and not to systems of value concepts that may be inculcated by religion. The scholar can have, indeed must have, value commitments that are not derived from knowledge and that need constitute no limitation whatever on the most free and unlimited inquiry. It is important also to notice that we are speaking here of *institutional* commitments and not of the theological faith of the individual scholar. Moreover, nothing we say concerning the character of the limitation on the range of academic freedom implied in a theological foundation should be understood to constitute any argument against any theology. Finally, we do not mean that those who are loyal believers in a theology feel any less free in their own search for knowledge than those who do not accept it. A truth that is "given" need not be sought, and if any scholar begins to question it within an institution that proclaims it, he should in honesty seek a different kind of academic home.

With these provisos we return to the question whether or not any limitation on academic freedom is implied in a genuinely denominational university, one that accepts as a postulate an authoritatively defined theology. Any such institution differs in certain relevant respects from the nondenominational kind.

Let us detach our argument from any particular denomination. Let us take denomination X, which has a distinctive theology and which controls university Y. And let us ask the reader to think of denomination X as any such denomination to which he does not himself belong. From this point of view let us consider whether the control of university Y by denomination X may not involve the following limitations on the full usage of academic freedom.

In the first place, university Y recruits most or all of its faculty from scholars who subscribe to its creed, and most of its students are likely to belong to the same faith. It frequently sets this prerequisite ahead of other qualifications in making appointments to important positions, whereas nondenominational universities can choose more freely and more widely and would not be restricted from appointing the most eminent scientist available because his views on theology were "heretical." In the nondenominational universities the student is exposed to a wider range of viewpoints.

In the second place, in the nondenominational university there is no authoritative prescription of any body of truth, whereas in university Y this given body of truth is regarded as providing an architectonic frame within which all other knowledge falls. It has, to quote the words of one high-placed exponent of a denominational system, a "principle of organization," which acts "as the pivot and center of the entire program of studies." The place of authority in the whole scheme of knowledge is thereby elevated. This tends to develop in the student a corresponding habit of mind. It may be questioned whether this attitude is favorable to the free search for knowledge, especially in such fields as history and the social sciences. As one of the greatest scholars within that area said: "fundamental doubt is the father of knowledge." This doubt, this readiness to question accepted things, is a heuristic principle and not a goal. By doubting and questioning, within any area of study in which we have some competence, we may arrive at tested and retested knowledge, and in view of the endless evidence history affords us of the errors to which human beings are prone when they make proclamations of eternal truths, the caution to "prove all things" has particular significance for the scholar.

University Y may render high services to the cause of learning. But the considerations we have advanced, for which there is good support in the modern history of academic institutions, strongly suggest that the nondenominational university is likely to give freer scope to its scholars in certain fields and to set generally a higher value on the entire principle of academic freedom.

Our broad conclusion should be accompanied by the recognition that denominational institutions have played an important part in preparing the way for academic freedom. In the first place they kept the light of learning aloft through long ages in which the cloister was the only avenue to scholarship. In the second place, when political intolerance oppressed a particular denomination, its scholars were prominent in the assertion of the civic rights of conscience and of free inquiry. The struggle for the freedom of religion had to be won before other freedoms, including academic freedom, could be attained.

APPENDIX B: THE UNIVERSITY OF COLORADO INVESTIGATES

NOTE: *The following account of one university's attempt to head off a political investigation through a confidential "self-investigation" is given at some length because it is believed to be the first experiment of this kind and scope ever undertaken by an American institution of higher learning. As such, it may be interesting and instructive to educators, administrators, and others who have faced and are facing the same problems that have beset the University of Colorado. The statement here presented has been prepared by Leo Koutouzos, research member of the Project staff, after an investigation conducted by him in Colorado.*

When in December of 1950, David Hawkins, a Professor of Philosophy at the University of Colorado, admitted in testimony before the House Committee on Un-American Activities that he had been a member of the Communist Party from 1938 until 1943, the stage was set for a series of fateful events, including the release or resignation of a number of faculty members, the revival of a state loyalty oath for teachers, and an investigation of the University of Colorado faculty by the Regents to determine whether it harbored any subversive elements.

Prior to his appearance before the Committee, Hawkins had conferred with certain University officials, telling them substantially what he later told the Committee. At this time he signified his intention of testifying fully and honestly—which he apparently did as far as his own record was concerned. But he declined to confirm or deny the Communist Party membership of other persons, except for individuals who had already publicly admitted to past or present membership or who were under accusation of crime, and he respectfully suggested to the Committee that such persons be subpoenaed to testify for themselves.[1] He declared that

---

[1] Report of the Special Committee on Un-American Activities, December, 1950. *Hearings Regarding Communist Infiltration of Radiation Laboratory and Atomic Bomb Project at the University of California, Berkeley, California,* Vol. III.

he felt it would be morally wrong for him to implicate other persons through his testimony. His refusal to answer was based on the constitutional provisions of the First and Fourth Amendments.

Within the next weeks, various groups and individuals began to clamor for an investigation of communism at the University of Colorado. The *Denver Post* in an editorial, "How a Great University May Fail," [2] sounded a call for action. Hawkins, it said, may have honestly broken with the Marxist faith, but the fact that he was once a Communist shows that he is unstable and perhaps still disloyal. Moreover, he concealed his Party membership at the time he joined the University staff, thus exposing the University to attack through his silence. The editorial went on to say that the Hawkins case would probably create a public demand for some kind of loyalty oath and, in the light of what happened at the University of California, it was hoped that this measure could be avoided. Therefore, the editorial proceeded, it behooved the University's president, Robert L. Stearns, to take strong action, and if he was unwilling to do so, the Regents ought to get a new president.

Three days later the *Post* returned to its theme, this time emphasizing the responsibility of the University to quiet the fears of the public and calling for an investigation of the faculty—not, however, by the legislature. The title of this editorial was, appropriately enough, "Not Everyone's Suspect."

In rapid succession these developments followed:

1. A loyalty oath law for teachers, enacted in 1921 during an earlier "red peril" but virtually unenforced since 1935, was revived. There was some question as to whether this law could be made to apply to the state university, with its tradition of semi-autonomy, but the state's Attorney General ruled that it did, and the Regents accepted the verdict without resistance. This oath involved a simple affirmation of loyalty to the constitution, flag, and laws of the State of Colorado and of the United States.

2. President Stearns declared that the University would not knowingly hire a communist but stated that neither Hawkins nor any other faculty member would be fired without a full hearing.

3. At the direction of the Regents, President Stearns drew up a number of allegations concerning Hawkins as the basis for an investigation by the University's Senate Committee on Faculty Privilege and Tenure. The charges, he explained, should not be construed as prejudgment of the case.

[2] January 29, 1951.

He enjoined the University and the townspeople to maintain an attitude of "judicial calm" while the confidential inquiry was under way.

4. The Regents ordered a confidential probe of the University faculty to determine whether subversive influences existed among them, and Stearns was authorized to hire as expert investigators two local attorneys who had seen service with the FBI. Governor Thornton announced that since the administration appeared to have the situation well in hand, he would propose no further steps for the time being.

Within the next few months, the contracts of two nontenured faculty members who ran afoul of the investigation in different ways were not renewed. These teachers and their supporters subsequently claimed that they were victims of political discrimination.

Periodically, during the following two years, members of the State Legislature referred to the University's "self-investigation" as a "white-wash." Three of the University's most prominent educators were attacked as members of communist "fronts" or enemies of the "American system."

These developments will be considered in greater detail subsequently but first a word should be said about the governing structure of the University of Colorado and its relation to the state. The University is of the "constitutional corporation" type; the Regents, six in number and elected for six-year terms by popular vote, are accorded "general supervision of the University" and exclusive direction of its funds.[3] One of the Regents' main tasks is to select the President, who serves as an *ex officio* member of the Board, voting only in case of a tie. Since the autonomy of the University has traditionally been respected by the Governor and the Legislature, it is sometimes referred to as the "fourth branch of government." The greater part of its income comes from legislative appropriations; the remainder, from the proceeds of a special mill tax, from student fees and supplementary legislative appropriations, and to a minor extent from private gifts and federal grants for special research.

Early in 1951, when the Hawkins case erupted, a Republican governor was in office, and the Republican Party dominated the State Legislature as well. The University's President was himself prominent in that party's affairs, as were three members of the bipartisan Board of Regents. As it turned out, this political congeniality had some bearing on the handling of the faculty investigation.

[3] The Constitution of Colorado, Art. IX, § 10 (12), (14).

On February 2, 1951, the Board of Regents met in special session to take action on the case of David Hawkins and voted unanimously to refer the matter to the Faculty Committee on Academic Privilege and Tenure. President Stearns was directed to prepare a memorandum suggesting the scope of the investigation. The formal grounds for such a hearing are found in the Rules of the Regents,[4] which provide that a staff member may be ousted for cause when "the good of the University so requires"— but only after consultation with appropriate faculty committees at the option of the instructor.

The issues to be weighed as President Stearns formulated them were that Hawkins had admitted former membership in the Communist Party; that he did not disclose that fact when applying for a position at the Los Alamos Atomic Project and at the University of Colorado; that he refused to answer some questions and gave evasive answers to others at the Congressional committee hearing in Washington; that a campus Marxist Study Group which he advised became a political action committee, and that his separation from the American Communist Party was never clearly defined and was more nominal than real.

Our evidence shows that during this period the sentiments of the faculty were sharply divided. There were those who, fearing a legislative investigation and a possible cut in appropriations, hoped that the University would "clear itself" by ousting Hawkins. On the other hand, there was a highly articulate group of able professors who looked upon the very idea of a hearing as a complete capitulation to pressure groups. Some members of the faculty and some students participated in the raising of funds for Hawkins, but for the most part the academic community awaited the verdict of the faculty committee in silence.

For approximately two months this committee questioned Hawkins about his political attitudes, heard numerous witnesses for and against him, and deliberated on the evidence. We have seen a transcript of this hearing and can attest that the entire investigation was of a model kind, thorough and judicious. The questions asked of Hawkins revealed that the members had a highly competent knowledge of communist doctrines and the communist movement. At the end of its exhaustive labors the committee concluded unanimously that there was no evidence of subversiveness or disloyalty on the part of Hawkins, that he had never ex-

[4] *Ibid.*, Art. IX, § 6 (5).

ploited his classroom position to slant his teaching in favor of communism, and that he was otherwise fully qualified to hold his position on the faculty.

The Regents deliberated for two weeks in secret on this report and then arranged an open meeting to which were invited all those who had further testimony to offer against Hawkins. Nothing of significance was added to the record, and the Regents voted four to one to uphold the committee's report and retain Hawkins.

It is significant that not a single one of the charges or allegations against Hawkins originated in the University community. The charge that he allowed the Marxist Study Group to become an "action group" is one which the University was in the best position to assess, but this charge was originally made at a Congressional Committee meeting in Washington. As for his refusal to answer certain questions, the House Committee had taken no steps to cite him for contempt, a fact that the University seemed to ignore. Moreover, there was at that time no law or regulation that required faculty members to confess past or even present membership in the Communist Party as a condition of employment.

We look upon the trial of Hawkins as an effort by the University to protect itself and maintain favorable community relations at a time when it was under siege. Since Hawkins's name was cleared, the critics were not appeased, but it is an open question whether they would have been fully satisfied even had he been dismissed. On the other hand, if the administration and the Regents had stood firm at the beginning, much of what happened later might perhaps have been avoided.

In the wake of the Hawkins affair demands were made in the legislature and elsewhere for new measures to investigate and combat subversion in the educational institutions of the state. Late in January, Representative Hewett introduced a bill into the legislature prohibiting the payment of state funds to any communist, and shortly afterwards he asserted that "there were all shades of reds and pinks at the University."

Soon it was discovered that there existed on the statute books a loyalty oath law that applied to all teachers in the state and imposed a punishment of up to one hundred dollars fine or six months in jail, or both, for those in charge of any school who permitted a teacher to assume his duties before he had taken and signed the oath.[5] The law had been allowed to

[5] *Colorado Statutes Annotated 1935,* Chapter 146, § 237.

lapse, however, and one president of a Colorado college frankly admitted he had never heard of it.

President Stearns characterized the revived loyalty oath as "discriminatory," since it applied to only one profession. But the Regents voted to apply it, and within eight days some seven hundred members of the staff signed without protest. By custom if not by law, visiting professors from foreign countries were exempt, and though one British instructor did leave the University at this time, his opposition was directed more against the faculty investigation than against the oath.

However, at nearby Denver University all did not go so smoothly. The chaplain of this university took exception to that part of the oath which required him to ". . . teach . . . undivided allegiance to the government of one country, the United States of America." After asserting, in effect, that if political loyalty conflicted with religious belief he would be compelled to choose the latter, he resigned his position.

For the most part, those who signed the oath regarded it as harmless or as a simple affirmation of loyalty to which no citizen could reasonably object. It was on this ground that President Stearns later defended it.[6] But on June 29, 1951, the Board of Regents changed the nature of the oath by declaring that the University would employ no person belonging to any organization intent on changing the form of government of the United States or the State of Colorado by illegal means.[7] It further added that membership in such groups would be deemed a violation of the oath previously taken and would subject the offender to dismissal in accordance with established procedures.[8]

Next came the Judd case. Morris Judd, a young philosophy instructor at the University, who had taught under two one-year appointments without tenure, was among those questioned by the two investigators about his political beliefs and affiliations. He refused to answer any questions of this nature, except to state that he was not at that time a member of the Communist Party, and he further declared to President Stearns that he was opposed on principle to the setting up of any political tests for teachers.

[6] *Denver Post,* April 11, 1951.
[7] Minutes of the Regents, June 29, 1951.
[8] A committee appointed early in 1953, which included some faculty members, was charged with recommending a possible revision or rewording of this oath "implementation," but it had not yet reported when this study was made.

Following this incident Judd received a one-year contract for 1951–52 "for two semesters only." Since this phrase customarily appeared in all limited contracts, he was not aware until some months later that he had been given a *terminal* contract.[9] He knew that he enjoyed the confidence of his colleagues in the Department of Philosophy, because they had unanimously recommended him for promotion. Therefore he felt that his academic freedom had been violated, and that he was being judged not on scholarly competence but on his attitude toward the investigation. He appealed to the Faculty Committee on Academic Privilege and Tenure for an investigation, and that body voted to accept jurisdiction.

When called upon to testify before this committee, President Stearns refused to give any reasons for the nonrenewal of Judd's contract beyond June, 1952, although in private conversations with various individuals he had mentioned such things as dullness as a teacher, failure to make progress in attaining his Ph.D. degree, and intellectual dishonesty—i.e., refusal to answer candidly the questions put to him by the investigators and by the President. Stearns, while testifying officially before the faculty committee, would neither confirm nor deny what he said privately, on the principle that no administrator can exercise discretion in preserving the quality of the faculty if he is required to defend himself every time he does not renew the contract of a nontenure instructor. Stearns also denied that the Faculty Committee on Privilege and Tenure had any jurisdiction in a case of this kind, but since hearings had already started he was willing to await the findings.

The Department of Philosophy played a prominent role not only in the defense of Judd as an individual, but in defense of what they regarded as the two major principles involved in his case; namely, that departmental recommendations ought not to be overruled by the administration without adequate reason and full consultation with the department, and that nontenured faculty members as well as those enjoying tenure were entitled to due process in cases involving academic freedom.

It may be interjected here that one consequence of the Judd affair was a protracted faculty discussion on the rights and privileges of nontenured instructors that eventually produced changes in the University's rules. A Grievance Committee of the Academic Senate is now empowered to receive all complaints of faculty members, including those in which an in-

---

[9] New regulations now in force at the university clearly distinguish terminal contracts from limited tenure contracts renewable at the discretion of the university.

structor on limited tenure feels that nonrenewal of his contract is unjusti-
fied.[10] However, in such instances the burden of proof is on the aggrieved
faculty member, and the committee may not intercede unless he initially
establishes at least a *prima facie* case.

Some incidents in Judd's background may be regarded as having a
bearing on the action taken against him. Some of the townspeople associated his name with "left-wing" causes, and he had been fairly vocal in
opposing the ban on the campus American Youth for Democracy chapter in 1947. He belonged to an organization "loosely affiliated with the
Progressive Citizens of America," and rumor had it that a bookstore he
owned in Boulder prior to joining the faculty was "a hangout for the
AYD crowd."

Faculty opinion was again sharply divided. Some regarded Judd as an
embarrassment to the University and favored eliminating him as quickly
as possible. Others asserted that Judd was selected as the perfect scape-
goat for appeasing the wrath of the University's critics who were still disgruntled over the outcome of the Hawkins case.

In his appearance before the faculty committee Judd was at a serious
disadvantage, for he had to defend himself against charges that everyone
had heard (they were even reported in the press) but which would not be
brought forward officially. Consequently, he had first to show that these
were the actual grounds for his removal and then refute them. The committee majority of four placed the entire burden of proof on Judd and
concluded that there was no evidence that his academic freedom had been
infringed (though they did not altogether endorse the administration's
conduct in the case). Two members dissented. The minority statement was
concurred in officially by the Denver Chapter of the American Civil Liberties Union. Of interest also is the statement of a member of the Board
of Regents, Vance Austin, which was made public at that time. If Judd
can be shown to be incompetent, he said, he should be dropped immediately—not retained for another year. If he is guilty of anything, charges
should be preferred and aired. The "suspicions and innuendos" emanating from anonymous accusers are not sufficient, and Judd must be considered innocent until proven guilty.[11]

Judd was accorded the right to counsel in the hearings before the faculty
committee; his case and the related issues received wide attention and de-

[10] Laws of the Regents, Art. X (B), (1), as revised 1953.
[11] Minutes of the Regents, August 10, 1951.

bate within official bodies and elsewhere. Yet, in view of certain factors in his personal background, and because of the tense situation that then existed, there were those who insisted that "the victim in the Hawkins case was Judd."

A second case involved Irving Goodman, a young and promising assistant professor of chemistry who joined the University of Colorado faculty in the fall of 1943, after having been a student as well as a graduate assistant there. In the summer of 1947 he received a promotion to assistant professor, followed in 1948 by a three-year contract in the same rank.

Back in 1947, as the result of information given him by an officer from the Office of Naval Research, President Stearns called Goodman to his office to ask him whether he was or ever had been a member of the Communist Party. Goodman was surprised to see notes being taken and other persons present. According to Stearns, Goodman admitted at this conference that he had been a member of the Communist Party until 1945, when he resigned. It was only after this assurance had been given, said Stearns, that Goodman's three-year contract was approved.

In the fall of 1949 Goodman went abroad for study under a Guggenheim award, and the University granted him a leave of absence, an arrangement that continued through 1950–51, when his award was renewed. On February 6, 1951, Goodman received a letter from a member of his department advising him that the University was upset over the "serious business of the Hawkins case" and implying that Goodman's contract might not be renewed. Further correspondence elicited the "friendly suggestion" that it might be to his advantage to seek employment elsewhere.

In April, 1951, while still in Europe, he received official notification that his contract would not be renewed. He protested this action to the head of his department, from whom he claims to have received no answer. However, his letter eventually reached President Stearns, who rejected the protest. Goodman then wrote to the Faculty Committee on Academic Privilege and Tenure and requested an investigation on the ground that action in his case had been inspired by political reasons; but this body, we are informed, would not act on his case. In May he protested directly to the Board of Regents after receiving a second notice of nonrenewal from them. His protest was rejected on the grounds that (a) his case had been disposed of on the basis of administrative action; (b) he had not been recommended by his department for reappointment; (c) information supplied by the President had disclosed that he had been untruthful about the date of his disaffiliation with the Communist Party and had been a member of it since that time.[12] In a separate statement President Stearns emphasized that there was no imputation that Goodman was still a communist—only the date of his resignation from the Party was under dispute.

Late in July Goodman bitterly assailed the Regents' statement, claiming that he was being pilloried on the basis of a conversation held four years before. He denied that he had ever lied about his political affiliations. As for the allegation that he had been fired on the basis of information gathered by the two investigators, he argued that the first hint of the nonrenewal of his contract came a day before the investigators began work. He also maintained that the action in February indicated that a decision had been made about him prior to departmental discussions which, he said, took place in April.

The Regents' action in publicly branding as a liar a faculty member who was out of the country and had no opportunity to defend himself, indeed, did not even know of the charge until he had seen it in the public press, was criticized by the Faculty Committee for the Study of Academic Freedom, an unofficial group of professors at the University.

A particular feature of the Colorado situation was the mode of investigation into university "subversives" adopted by the Regents at the beginning of the Hawkins case. Four possible types of investigation were considered: by the Regents; by an agency or a counsel selected by the Regents; by the Faculty Committee on Privilege and Tenure; by a committee of the State Legislature. After a long discussion the second method was unanimously adopted, and President Stearns hired for the purpose two local attorneys who had once been with the FBI.[13]

These men were given no special instructions, no criteria of loyalty to guide them, and it may be assumed that they followed standard FBI techniques in accordance with their previous training. President Stearns expressed the hope that the faculty would cooperate with them, but he made no demands that they do so.

For those who favored the plan of "self-investigation," its main virtues were that it would preserve at least a semblance of institutional autonomy, show the community that the University was responsive to its demands, protect innocent persons from being "smeared" in the press, and head off

[12] Minutes of the Regents, June 29, 1951.
[13] *Ibid.*, February 2, 1951.

what was much more threatening—a legislative investigation. Self-investigation seemed the least objectionable of several unpleasant alternatives. No one at the University, as far as we know, expected that a serious "red menace" would be uncovered.

There were those who hoped the Regents would oppose every type of investigation into the beliefs and affiliations of faculty members. They did not concede that a legislative investigation was the inevitable alternative if the self-investigation were voted down, and some were inclined to believe that if a legislative investigation should come there was every likelihood that it would soon be discredited by its own excesses.

The investigators completed their work in about a month. The investigation was declared closed, but it must be remembered that the dossiers that had been assembled were still "open" in the sense that new and pertinent material might be added. In this connection, President Stearns told our staff investigator that he felt obliged to look into all reports concerning subversive ties among members of the faculty, even those submitted anonymously. The report itself, however, has not been published, nor have any announcements been made concerning action taken against anyone named in it. To the best of our knowledge no one except the President, the Regents, and the two investigators themselves knew anything of its contents until early in 1953.

The policy of secrecy was by no means easy to maintain, for as early as the spring of 1951 Representative Hewett and others of the Colorado Legislature demanded the outright release of the report. At that time they appeared mollified when the Regents issued their policy declaration of June 29, 1951, with respect to the exclusion of faculty members belonging to subversive organizations. The following year Hewett modified his demands somewhat, now insisting only that the text of the report be read to the State Legislature meeting in executive session, a demand that the *Denver Post* characterized as out of line with proper legislative authority. The popularly elected Regents are directly answerable to their own constituents, said the *Post,* and while it is true that the Legislature appropriates money for the University, infringement on the rightful domain of the Regents cannot be countenanced on that score.[14]

In the spring of 1953 Senator Wyatt was the leading spirit in the campaign for disclosure of at least a portion of the report. An open battle between the Republican Regents and a Republican President and Gov-

[14] Editorial, January 14, 1952.

ernor on one hand, and Republican legislators on the other, was obviously not in the interests of the party. Accordingly, a caucus meeting of the Republican Regents and nine Republican legislators from both houses was called and met in the governor's office.

There are conflicting accounts as to what happened at the meeting. According to one participant, portions of the report were actually read; another testified that it was summarized in a general way but that no names were mentioned. Another person also present stated that names definitely were given.[15]

The press reported various figures about the number of instructors who had been investigated, the number cleared, and the number still subject to examination. According to the *Rocky Mountain News,* eight persons had been investigated and were "no longer in the employ of the university." This newspaper carried banner headlines, "Regents Report: 8 CU Teachers Leave Posts After Inquiry," implying that some or all of the eight had left as a consequence of the investigation.[16] The administration explained that faculty members were constantly leaving the University for other positions or for further study and that it should not be assumed that all or any of the eight had been dismissed. Senator Wyatt then insisted that the names of those who had been compelled to leave as subversives be released in order to protect those who had left for other reasons. This the President and the Regents absolutely refused to do. Two days later the President countered with the announcement that all present members in the employ of the University had been "cleared completely" and that he knew that "un-American elements do not exist at the University." [17] He categorically denied that five or six instructors were still under suspicion, as claimed by Wyatt, and again refused to issue a list of those who for any reason had left the employ of the University since the investigation.

On the following day Senator Wyatt, under the protection of senatorial immunity, attacked three professors of the University's faculty, charging that one had been fired from another university, that another was a member of three communist "fronts," and that a third (on the evidence of Representative Hewett's son) had stated that "we ought to change our form of government and try another one." The professor who was al-

---

[15] *Colorado Daily,* March 13, 1953.
[16] March 11, 1953.
[17] *Denver Post,* March 13, 1953.

leged to belong to fronts had previously been accused on the same ground by Representative Hewett. He had resigned from the groups named—all of which, he said, were devoted to exploring peaceful alternatives to war —solely in order to protect the University and not because he believed them to be subversive.

Some time before this latest clash, President Stearns had announced that he was resigning his post at the University to assume a new position. Senator Wyatt now seized upon this event and suggested—or so he was understood by several reporters present—that the resignation was a forced one and was due to the President's "soft policy" toward communism. Governor Thornton was also castigated for having hampered a "real" investigation into communism.

Senator Wyatt's insinuation met with considerable protest. The Governor expressed his confidence in Stearns and the Regents and his satisfaction with the way they had dealt with the problem of subversives. He declined to "dignify with an answer" the charges made against him personally. An informal meeting of faculty members and others was held at the University of Colorado, and a resolution denouncing Wyatt's attack on the three faculty members was unanimously carried by an audience of about three hundred. The *Rocky Mountain News* carried an editorial with the piquant heading, "Now Shut Up!" giving its view that the University had met the issue of subversion squarely and that the Senator was using "this dead issue as a platform for his own illogical oratory." [18] A group of sixteen senators from both parties signed a resolution reaffirming their faith in the University of Colorado administration and governing board. These strong rebuffs from so many highly placed individuals and important agencies seemed to have the effect, at least temporarily, of quelling Wyatt.

In our own view, the University of Colorado's "self-investigation" was at best a compromise in which the institution surrendered a part of its autonomy vis à vis the state in order to preserve the remainder. This policy was not freely entered into, for it was not entertained until the threat of investigation by outside forces became imminent.

Even so, many state universities in the land could not have fended off a legislative inquiry by such means. The special conditions at the University of Colorado that enabled the University to adopt and carry through this

[18] March 15, 1953.

policy are believed to be the following: the fact that this institution is a constitutional corporation protected by law; the general tradition of non-interference in university affairs by the Governor and the Legislature and the consistent support given to this viewpoint by the influential *Denver Post;* a president widely respected by the academic community and by virtually all segments of the population of the state; a Board of Regents considerably better than average in its understanding of educational needs.

Any kind of "self-investigation," ferreting out the attitudes and doctrines of the faculty members, is inherently undesirable and can be justified, if at all, only as a protection against more insidious forms of inquisition. Aside from this consideration it has some particular evils. It tends to go on endlessly perpetuating itself, and there is always the danger that information will "leak out" or that a change of administration will mean a change in policy with regard to publication.

Confidential reports, precisely because they are expected to be held in confidence, usually contain more inaccuracies and unproved statements than those designed to see the light of day. This is not to imply that any administrative action that may have been taken on the basis of this particular report was not itself responsible and considered. However, the publication of the report as such may do as much harm to innocent persons two years from now or even five years from now as it would today.

The poor academic practices observed in the Judd and Goodman cases represent a departure from the generally excellent record of the University in matters of academic freedom.

Resistance to the imposition of the loyalty oath in its original, innocuous form on the faculty of the State University might have been tactically unwise on the part of the Regents. Yet experience shows that once this swearing business begins, the tendency is to make the oaths more and more elaborate and at the same time more restrictive. In this case it was the Regents who arbitrarily converted a simple oath of affirmation into something of a quite different order. Manifestly, loyalty to any government implies at the very least that one will not seek to overthrow it by illegal means, but when a person is required to demonstrate his loyalty through nonmembership in groups which are neither named nor adequately defined, and when this provision is considered binding on him at the time he took an oath of allegiance though it was not then part of the oath, then there is sufficient ground for strong protest.

In general, it should be said that the University administration proclaimed its policies openly, weighed them thoughtfully, and made no effort to suppress criticism, including some very unfavorable comment on the handling of the Goodman and Judd cases and on the faculty investigation—criticism that continued for a long time in the student newspaper and elsewhere. It was President Stearns who invited a representative of the American Academic Freedom Project to visit the campus and made available to him all pertinent records and facilities (with the sole exception of the investigators' report).

Our knowledge of the University of Colorado community suggests that, by any reasonable standards, the facts brought to light by the "self-investigation" were scarcely of sufficient value to compensate for the expense, the turmoil, and the major dislocations it engendered. We have also the testimony of a significant number of professors who felt humiliated and degraded by the whole proceeding and who believe that it produced a widespread fear and suspicion which has generally done damage to the scholarly mission of the University.

The tremendous confidence the faculty had in Stearns's judgment and what impressed our observer as a deep affection for him was undoubtedly a tribute to his great administrative skill and his personal qualities. He had to make some very difficult decisions, and when at some points he yielded to pressures, it was because he was endeavoring to save the institution from worse dangers. Perhaps, on the other hand, the high regard in which they held their president made it easier for large portions of the faculty to refrain from taking part in the making of the monumental decisions before them. All too often teachers were uninformed, indifferent, or frightened, burying themselves in their special fields and hoping above all for peace and quiet—in spite of their responsibilities as citizens of an academic community. The slogans so often heard during the first half of 1951—"Let Bob [Stearns] do it!" or "Don't rock the boat!" (by talking to reporters or organizing protests against the faculty probe or the oath implementation)—left the burden of participation to a relatively small group.

SELECT BIBLIOGRAPHY

NOTE: *The bibliography here presented has no pretensions to be exhaustive but seeks to cover relevant available materials pertaining to the various issues dealt with in the text. For the most part it does not include the bibliographical references given in the footnotes, unless the works thus cited are significant for other aspects of the subject as well.*

GENERAL

"Academic Freedom and Academic Responsibility." Pamphlet of the American Civil Liberties Union. New York, 1952.

Barth, Alan. The Loyalty of Free Men. New York, 1952.

Beale, Howard K. Are American Teachers Free? New York, 1936.

—————— History of Freedom of Teaching in American Schools. New York, 1941.

Bowman, Claude C. The College Professor in America. Philadelphia, 1938.

Bunting, David E. Liberty and Learning. Washington, D.C.: American Council on Public Affairs, 1942.

Capen, Samuel P. The Management of Universities. Buffalo, 1953.

Cole, K. C. "Academic Freedom as a Civil Right," *Western Political Quarterly,* II (September, 1949), 402–11.

De Kiewiet, C. W. "Academic Freedom Today," *Educational Record,* XXIX (October, 1948), 400–409.

Dewey, John. "Academic Freedom," in Paul Monroe, ed., Cyclopedia of Education, II, 700–705. New York, 1919. Bibliography.

Emerson, T. I., and David Haber. Political and Civil Rights in the United States. Buffalo, 1952. Pages 795–912 and Bibliography.

Essex, M. W. "What Does Academic Freedom Mean for Elementary and Secondary Teachers?" *Educational Leadership,* IX (January, 1952), 237–42.

Fine, Benjamin. "Survey on Academic Freedom," *New York Times,* May 29–30, 1949.

Fraenkel, Osmond K. The Supreme Court and Civil Liberties. Rev. ed. New York: American Civil Liberties Union, 1952.

Highet, Gilbert. Man's Unconquerable Mind. Columbia University Press, 1954.

Hook, Sidney. Heresy, Yes—Conspiracy, No. New York, 1953.

Hullfish, H. Gordon. "Keeping Our Schools Free." Public Affairs Pamphlet No. 199 (September, 1953).

Hullfish, H. Gordon, ed. Educational Freedom in an Age of Anxiety. New York, 1953. Twelfth Yearbook of the John Dewey Society.

Johnsen, Julia E., ed. Academic Freedom. New York: H. W. Wilson Co., 1925. The Reference Shelf, Vol. III, No. 6. Bibliography.

———— Freedom of Speech. New York: H. W. Wilson Co., 1936. The Reference Shelf, Vol. X, No. 8. Bibliography.

Johnson, Alvin. "Academic Freedom," in Ruth Ashen, ed., Freedom: Its Meaning. New York. 1940.

Johnson, E. N., ed. Freedom and the University. Cornell University Press, 1950.

Johnson, F. Ernest. "This Freedom of Ours," Social Action, XX (November, 1953), 2–32.

Jones, Howard Mumford, ed. Primer of Intellectual Freedom. Harvard University Press, 1949.

Karelsen, F. E. "A Layman Looks at Academic Freedom," School and Society, LXIX (April 2, 1949), 241–44.

Lovejoy, Arthur O. "Academic Freedom," in Encyclopedia of the Social Sciences, I (New York, 1930), 384–88. Bibliography.

Meiklejohn, Alexander. Freedom and the College. New York, 1923.

Melby, Ernest O., and Morton Puner. Freedom and Public Education. New York, 1953.

Newman, John Henry. The Idea of a University. New York, 1919.

Rockwell, L. L. "Academic Freedom: German Origin and American Development," Bulletin of the American Association of University Professors, XXXVI (June, 1950), 225–36.

Spalding, W. B. "Academic Freedom," Progressive Education, XXVIII (February, 1951), 111–17.

Stewart, George R. The Year of the Oath. New York, 1950.

Stokes, Anson Phelps. Church and State in the United States. Vol. I. New York, 1950.

Tauber, K. P. "The Free University in an Open Society," Harvard Educational Review, XXIII (Winter, 1953), 3–16.

Wilcox, Clair, ed. Civil Liberties Under Attack. University of Pennsylvania Press, 1951.

Wilson, Logan. The Academic Man. New York, 1942.

THE CLIMATE OF OPINION

Ahrens, Maurice. "Freedom to Learn," Social Education, XVII (April, 1953), 165–70.

Alsop, Joseph. "What is Academic Freedom?" Atlantic Monthly, CXCI (June, 1953), 41–43.

Amen, J. H. "Toward a Definition of Loyalty," *New York Times Magazine,* December 13, 1953.

Ashby, L. W. "Is the Greatest Thing in Science in Danger?" *Science Teacher,* XX (October, 1953), 221–24ff.

"Attack on Books in Libraries," Report of a Library Public Relations Council Meeting on Censorship, *Wilson Library Bulletin,* XXVII (June, 1953), 807–12.

Bainbridge, John. "Danger's Ahead in the Public Schools," *McCall's,* LXXX (October, 1952), 56ff.

——— "Save Our Schools!" *McCall's,* LXXX (September, 1952), 44–47ff.

Bendiner, R. "Has Anti-Communism Wrecked our Liberties?" *Commentary,* XII (July, 1951), 10–16.

Berninghausen, David K. "A Policy to Preserve Free Public Education," *Harvard Educational Review,* XXI (Summer, 1951), 137–54. Bibliography.

Biddle, F. The Fear of Freedom. New York, 1951.

Brinckman, W. W. "Attack and Counterattack in American Education," *School and Society,* LXXIV (October 27, 1951), 262–79. Bibliography.

Can We Afford Academic Freedom? A Discussion Sponsored by the Harvard Law School Forum. Robert Braucher, moderator; Carey McWilliams, Allen A. Zoll, and McGeorge Bundy, speakers. Beacon Press, 1952.

"Control of Subversives Under Internal Security Act of 1950," *Temple Law Quarterly,* XXIV (April, 1951), 462–70.

"Creeping Censorship," *Time,* LIX (May 5, 1952), 72–74.

Cushman, R. E. "Repercussions of Foreign Affairs on the American Tradition of Civil Liberty: The Loyalty Tests," *Proceedings of the American Philosophical Society,* XCII, No. 4 (1948), 257–63.

"Danger Signals, The," *Time,* LXI (April 13, 1953), 85–87.

De Voto, Bernard. "Easy Chair: Case of the Censorious Congressmen," *Harper,* CCVI (April, 1953), 42–45.

Emerson, T. I. "An Essay on Freedom of Political Expression Today," *Lawyers Guild Review,* XI (Winter, 1951), 1–7.

Fine, Benjamin. "The Truth About School Book Censorship," *Parents Magazine,* XXVII (December, 1952), 46ff.

Freedom of Information: A Revised Supplementary Survey of Recent Writings. The Library of Congress European Affairs Division, October, 1952.

Hoyt, Palmer. "The Causes of Public Unrest in Education," *Colorado Quarterly,* II (Winter, 1954), 269–76.

Hulburd, David. This Happened in Pasadena. New York, 1951.

"If in Doubt Don't Join," *United States News and World Report,* XXIX (September 22, 1950), 20–21.

Jones, Howard Mumford. "How Much Academic Freedom?" *Atlantic Monthly,* CXCI (June, 1953), 36–40.

Knapp, R. H. "Social Education and Citizens' Organization," *Social Education,* XIV (April, 1950), 166–67ff.

Kuhn, Irene Corbally. "Your Child Is Their Target," *American Legion Magazine,* LII (June, 1952), 18–19ff.

Levenstein, A. "The Demagogue and the Intellectual," *Antioch Review,* XIII (September, 1953), 259–74.

Lipset, S. M. "Opinion Formation in a Crisis Situation," *Public Opinion Quarterly,* XVII (Spring, 1953), 20–46.

McClenaghan, W. G. "An Author Looks at Textbooks," *Saturday Review of Literature,* XXXV (April 19, 1952), 17–18.

Maverick, Maury, Jr. "Texas Brand in the Library," *Nation,* CLXXVI (June 20, 1953), 525.

"Meeting the Attacks on Education," *Progressive Education,* Vol. XXIX, entire number of January, 1952.

Moe, H. A. "The Power of Freedom," *Pacific Spectator,* V (Autumn, 1951), 435–48.

"New Crisis for Education," *Platform, Newsweek Club and Educational Bureaus,* January, 1952.

Ogden, A. R. The Dies Committee. The Catholic University of America Press, 1945.

Pearson, R. M. "Can Textbooks Be Subversive?" *Phi Delta Kappan,* XXXIII (January, 1952), 248–50.

Rice, Elmer. "New Fashions in Censorship by Special Interest Groups," *Survey,* LXXXVIII (March–April, 1952), 112–15.

"School Boards, School Books and the Freedom to Learn," *Yale Law Journal,* LIX (April, 1950), 928–54.

Serviss, T. K. "Freedom to Learn," *Social Education,* XVII (February, 1953), 65–70.

Shafer, Paul W. "Is There a 'Subversive' Movement in the Public Schools?" Speech of the Honorable Paul Shafer of Michigan in the House of Representatives, March 21, 1952. U.S. Government Printing Office, 1952. Bibliography.

Skaife, Robert A. "Groups Affecting Education," in William Van Til, ed., Forces Affecting American Education, pp. 63–86. Yearbook, Association for Supervision and Curriculum Development, National Education Association. Washington, D.C., 1953.

Spaulding, W. E. "Can Textbooks Be Subversive?" *Educational Record,* XXXIV (October, 1953), 297–304.

Stocker, Joseph. "The Corporal and the Textbook," *Progressive,* XVI (March, 1952), 24–26.

Truman, David. The Governmental Process. New York, 1951.

Williams, D. C. "The Cold War in America," *Political Quarterly,* XXI (July, 1950), 280–87.

Wisconsin Citizens Committee on McCarthy's Record. The McCarthy Record. Madison, 1952.

ACADEMIC GOVERNMENT AND ACADEMIC FREEDOM

Alexander, R. J. "Should the Faculty Run the Board of Trustees?" *American Teacher,* XXXVIII (December, 1953), 14–15.

Baker, J. E. "Liberty and the Pursuit of Truth," *Bulletin of the American Association of University Professors,* XXXVIII (Autumn, 1952), 402–12.

Brumbaugh, A. J. "Freedom to Teach and Freedom to Learn," *Educational Record,* XXXI (October, 1950), 418–28.

Butts, Freeman R. "Faculty and Lay Participation in Policy Formulation," in John Guy Fowlkes, ed., Higher Education for American Society. University of Wisconsin Press, 1949.

Cappon, A. P. "Democratically Administered University," *Journal of Higher Education,* XVIII (October, 1947), 351–56.

Carr, Robert K. The House Committee on Un-American Activities, 1945–50. Cornell University Press, 1952. Cornell Studies in Civil Liberty.

Caughey, John Walton. "Trustees of Academic Freedom," *Bulletin of the American Association of University Professors,* XXXVII (Autumn, 1951), 427–41.

Chambers, M. M. "The Tenure of State University Trustees," *Educational Record,* XVIII (January, 1937), 125–36.

Chase, Lucius P. "Faculty and Lay Participation in Policy Formulation," in John Guy Fowlkes, ed., Higher Education for American Society. University of Wisconsin Press, 1949.

Countryman, Vern. Un-American Activities in the State of Washington. Cornell University Press, 1951. Cornell Studies in Civil Liberty.

Cumings, Edgar C. "Some Observations on the Trustees," *School and Society,* LXXVII (January 3, 1953), 1–3.

"Curtailment of the AEC Fellowship Program, The," *Bulletin of the Atomic Scientists,* VI (February, 1950), 34ff.

Danton, J. P. "The Appointment and Election of Boards of Control in Institutions of Higher Education in America," *Journal of Educational Research,* XXX (April, 1937), 583–91.

Deutsch, Monroe. "Choosing College Presidents," *Bulletin of the American Association of University Professors,* XXXIII (Autumn, 1947), 520–24.

Drever, James. "Academic Freedom in British Universities," *Journal of Social Issues,* IX (November 3, 1953), 17–24.

Eckelberry, R. H. "Academic Freedom at Ohio State University," *Journal of Higher Education,* XXII (December, 1951), 493–98.

Fullman, C. E. "God and Man and Mr. Buckley," *Catholic World,* CLXXV (May, 1952), 104–8.

Graham, E. K. "National Security and Freedom in Higher Education: The Viewpoint of the College Administrator," *College and University,* XXVI (October, 1950), 20–26.

Himstead, Ralph E. "Academic Freedom and Tenure at the University of Texas, an Interim Report," *Bulletin of the American Association of University Professors,* XXX (Winter, 1944), 627–34.

Hudson, N. P. "Freedom in Research in a University," *American Journal of Physics,* XX (May, 1952), 270.

Hughes, R. M. "College and University Trustees and Their Responsibilities," *Educational Record,* XXVI (January, 1945), 27–32.

Hutchins, R. M. "Freedom of the University," *Ethics,* LXI (January, 1951), 95–104.

Johnshoy, Howard G. "The Government and Administration of Institutions of Higher Education." Unpublished dissertation, Teachers College, Columbia University, New York, 1951.

Kandel, I. L. "Relations between Government and Higher Education," *School and Society,* LXV (March 1, 1947), 158–59.

Kunkel, B. W. "The College President as He Is Today," *Bulletin of the American Association of University Professors,* XXXIV (Summer, 1948), 344–49.

Levitan, S. A. "Professional Organization of Teachers in Higher Education," *Journal of Higher Education,* XXII (March, 1941), 123–28.

Long, Henry J. "Why College Presidents?" *Bulletin of the Association of American Colleges,* XXXVII (October, 1951), 379–82.

McCallister, Charles E. Inside the Campus. New York, 1948.

McGregor, Douglas. "Strengthening the Foundations of Democracy," in Addresses on Current Issues in Higher Education. Washington, D.C.: Department of Higher Education, National Education Association, 1951.

McVey, Frank L. A University Is a Place . . . a Spirit. University of Kentucky Press, 1944.

Marvin, Cloyd H. "The National Commission on Accrediting," *Bulletin of the Association of American Colleges,* XXXVI (March, 1950), 53–64.

Moore, W. "Ethical Argument for Democratic University Administration," *Bulletin of the American Association of University Professors,* XXXIII (Summer, 1947), 286–89.

Munford, J. K. "Functions of Faculty Committees," *College and University.* XXVII (October, 1951), 79–84.

Murray, Irving B. "How to Kill a University. II," *Christian Register,* CXXXI (July, 1952), 11–13.

Newburn, H. K. "Organization and Administration of Universities in France, Italy and Great Britain," *Educational Record,* XXXIV (July, 1953), 245–74.

Pendergast, W. B. "State Legislatures and Communism: The Current Scene," *American Political Science Review,* XLIV (September, 1950), 556–74.

Quattlebaum, C. A. "Review of Federal Educational Activities," *Educational Record,* XXXII (October, 1951), 393–408, Tables.

Reisner, Edward H. "The Origin of Lay University Boards of Control in the

United States," *Columbia University Quarterly*, XXIII (March, 1931), 63–69.

Rodell, Fred. "That Book About Yale," *Progressive*, XVI (February, 1952), 14–16.

Rosebury, Theodor, and Melba Phillips. "Two Aspects of the Loyalty Problem; with Comment by Scientists' Committee on Loyalty Problems," *Science*, CX (July 29, 1949), 123–24.

Russell, James E. Federal Activities in Higher Education after the Second World War. New York, 1951.

Silwell, H. "Civil War in Texas," *Colliers*, CXV (January 6, 1945), 18–19ff.

Strom, C. W. "College Education: Free or Regimented," *American Foreign Service Journal*, XXIV (January, 1947), 11–13.

Thompson, Alan R. "The Professor and the Governing Board," *Bulletin of the American Association of University Professors*, XXXV (Winter, 1949), 678–87.

"Threat to Intellectual Freedom, The," *AAC News*, XX (May–June, 1953), 3–8.

Ward, L. R. "Buckley's Attack on Yale," *Commonweal*, LV (February 15, 1952), 473–74.

Wecter, Dixon. "Prowling for Campus Presidents," *Bulletin of the American Association of University Professors*, XXXIV (Autumn, 1948), 493–504.

Wilkins, E. H. "The Professor Administrant," *Bulletin of the American Association of University Professors*, XXVII (February, 1941), 18–28.

Wildermuth, Ora L. "A University Trustee Views the Academic Profession," *Bulletin of the American Association of University Professors*, XXXV (Summer, 1949), 233–39.

Wilson, Logan. The Academic Man. New York, 1942.

THE LINES OF ATTACK ON ACADEMIC FREEDOM

THE ESTABLISHED WAYS

Burns, R. W. (pseudonym). "No Hearts Bleed for Conservative Teachers' Rights," *Saturday Evening Post*, CCXXIII (September 30, 1950), 10.

"By Their Own Petrad: The Universities Troubles Are Partly of Their Own Making," *Barron's*, XXXII (December 1, 1952), 1.

Cogley, J. "Rutgers Affair, Concerning 'Cumberland Street,'" *Commonweal*, LIII (January 5, 1951), 329–30.

De Voto, Bernard. "Why Professors Are Suspicious of Business," *Fortune*, XLIII (April, 1951), 114–15ff.

Johnson, Alvin W., and Frank H. Yost. Separation of Church and State in the United States. University of Minnesota Press, 1948.

Mayer, Milton. "The Christian College," *Progressive*, XIII (February, 1949), 23–24.

Moulton, H. G., and C. W. Makee. "How Good Is 'Economic Education'?" *Fortune,* XLIV (July, 1951), 84–86ff.

Shils, Edward A. "Limitations on the Freedom of Teaching and Research in the Social Sciences," in Edward P. Cheyney, ed., Freedom of Inquiry and Expression. *Annals of the American Academy of Political and Social Science,* CC (November, 1938), 144–64.

Sontag, Frederick H. "Communism, Campus and Church," *The Living Church,* CXXIV (April 6, 1952), 7–9.

"Test and Tragedy at Olivet," *The Christian Century,* LXVI (January 26, 1949), 102–3.

COMMUNISM AND THE CAMPUS

"Academic Freedom; Symposium," *Journal of Higher Education,* CCI (October and November, 1949), 346–54ff., 422–28ff. Contributors: John K. Ryan, Harold W. Stoke, Constance Warren; Peter A. Carmichael, Raymond B. Allen, Sidney Hook.

Allen, R. B. "Communists Should Not Teach in the Schools," *Educational Forum,* XIII (May, 1949), 433–40.

"American Scholar Forum; Communism and Academic Freedom Symposium," *American Scholar,* XVIII (July, 1949), 323–54. Contributors: Max Lerner, T. V. Smith, Arthur O. Lovejoy, Helen Lynd, Raymond B. Allen, Joseph Butterworth, Ralph H. Gundlach, Herbert J. Phillips.

Axtelle, G. E. "Should Communists Teach in American Universities?" *Educational Forum,* XIII (May, 1949), 425–32.

Ayres, C. E. "What Should Teachers Swear," *Southwest Review,* XXXV (Autumn, 1950), 240–48.

Bendiner, Robert. "Civil Liberties and the Communists," *Commentary,* V (May, 1948), 423–31.

Brickman, W. W. "Communism and American Education," *School and Society,* LXXI (March 25, 1950), 180–88. Bibliography.

Brubacher, J. S. "Loyalty to Freedom," *School and Society,* LXX (December 10, 1949), 369–73.

"Can We Curb Subversives without Sacrificing Our Freedoms?" *Platform, Newsweek Club and Educational Bureaus,* September, 1950.

Chambers, Whittaker. "Is Academic Freedom in Danger?" *Life,* XXXIV (June 22, 1953), 90–92ff.

Commager, Henry Steele. "Guilt—and Innocence—by Association," *New York Times Magazine,* November 3, 1953.

"Communism and Academic Freedom: A Problem for Educators," *Platform, Newsweek Club and Educational Bureaus,* November, 1949.

Communism and Academic Freedom: The Record of the Tenure Cases of the University of Washington. University of Washington Press, 1949.

Cushman, Robert E. "Academic Freedom Goes on Trial," *Cornell Alumni News* (April 1, 1953), pp. 367–69.

Dowling, Noel T. "I Stand on the Fifth Amendment," *New York Times Magazine*, May 17, 1953.

Frank, Richard. "The Schools and the People's Front," *Communist*, XVI (May, 1937), 432–45.

Frantz, Laurent B., and Norman Redlich. "Does Silence Mean Guilt?" *Nation*, CLXXVI (June 6, 1953), 471–77.

Fuchs, Ralph H., and Robert M. Hunter. "Communists and the Colleges: Two Views," *Antioch Review*, IX (June, 1949), 199–209.

Gallup, George C. "Barring of Communist Teachers Is Favored by Big Vote in Survey," *Public Opinion News Service*, September 21, 1949.

Gideonse, H. D. "Changing Issues in Academic Freedom in the United States Today," *Proceedings of the American Philosophical Society*, XCIV (1950), 91–104.

"Guilt by Association—Three Words in Search of a Meaning," *University of Chicago Law Review*, XVII (Autumn, 1949), 148–62.

Hammond, Harold E. "Academic Freedom in the State of New York," *Educational Forum*, XV (May, 1951), 463–69.

Havighurst, R. J., and R. F. Peck. "Communism and American Education," *School Review*, LVII (November, 1949), 453–58.

Heston, H. N. " 'Investigate-the-Colleges' Proposals," with editorial comment, *School and Society*, LXXVII (March 14, 1953), 161–64, 171.

Hook, Sidney. "The Fifth Amendment—a Moral Issue," *New York Times Magazine*, November 1, 1953.

———— "Should Communists Be Permitted to Teach?" *New York Times Magazine*, February 27, 1949.

Hultzen, Lee S. "Communists on the University Faculty," *Journal of Higher Education*, XXI (November, 1950), 423–29.

Irish, Marian D. "You'll Never Make Them Loyal That Way!" *Saturday Evening Post*, CCXXII (February 4, 1950), 25ff.

"It Also Happened at Harvard," *Educational Record*, XXXIV (October, 1953), 359–70.

"It Did Happen at Rutgers: Basic Documents Concerning the Case of Two Professors Who Refused to Answer Questions Asked by the Internal Security Subcommittee of the United States Senate," *Educational Record*, XXXIV (April, 1953), 154–78.

Johnson, Bruce, and Jean Lomenick. "Oklahoma's Loyalty Oath," *Nation*, CLXXIII (August 11, 1951), 106–8.

Jones, Howard Mumford. "Do You Know the Nature of an Oath?" *American Scholar*, XX (October, 1951), 457–67.

Journal of Philosophy, XLIX, 85–122 (entire issue of February 14, 1952). Contributors: Victor Lowe, Arthur O. Lovejoy, Sidney Hook, Herbert W. Schneider.

Kerwin, J. G. "Fear and Freedom," *Commonweal*, LVIII (July 3, 1953), 315–17.

Kirkland, E. C. "Do Anti-Subversive Efforts Threaten Academic Freedom?"

Annals of the American Academy of Political and Social Science, CCLXXV (May, 1951), 132–39.

Konvitz, Milton R. "Justice and the Communist Teacher," *New Leader,* XXXVI (April 20, 1953), 16–19.

Kristol, Irving. "Civil Liberties, 1952—A Study in Confusion," *Commentary,* XIII (March, 1952), 228–36.

"Loyalty Oaths in Colleges: Summary of the Arguments," in University Debaters Annual, 1950–51, pp. 122–54. Bibliography.

McWilliams, Carey. "Test of a Teacher," *Nation,* CLXVIII (March 5, 1949), 270–73.

Marshall, James. "The Defense of Public Education from Subversion," *Columbia Law Review,* LI (May, 1951), 587–604.

Matthews, J. B. "Communism and the Colleges," *American Mercury,* LXXVI (May, 1953), 111–44.

Meiklejohn, Alexander. "Should Communists Be Allowed to Teach?" *New York Times Magazine,* March 27, 1949.

Meltzer, Bernard D., and Harry Kalven, Jr. "Invoking the Fifth Amendment —Two Lawyers' Views," *Bulletin of the Atomic Scientists,* IX (June, 1953), 176–86.

Morgan, E. M. "The Privilege Against Self-Incrimination," *Minnesota Law Review,* XXXIV (December, 1949), 1–45.

Morse, W. L. "Academic Freedom Versus Communistic Indoctrination," *Vital Speeches of the Day,* XV (April 15, 1949), 400–403.

Pates, Gordon. "California: The Oath Epidemic," *Reporter,* III (December 26, 1950), 29–31.

Perry, R. B. "Academic Freedom," *Harvard Educational Review,* XXIII (Spring, 1953), 71–76.

Reutter, Edmund E., Jr. The School Administrator and Subversive Activities. New York: Bureau of Publications, Teachers College, Columbia University, 1951.

Russell, W. E. "American Versus European Policies Regarding Communism and Education," *Teachers College Record,* LIV (January, 1953), 175–83.

Sanford, Nevitt. "Individual and Social Change in a Community under Pressure: The Oath Controversy," *Journal of Social Issues,* IX (November 3, 1953), 25–42.

Schlesinger, Arthur M., Jr. "What Is Loyalty? A Difficult Question," *New York Times Magazine,* November 2, 1947.

"Should Communists Be Allowed to Teach in Our Colleges?" *America's Town Meeting of the Air,* March, 1949.

Smith, Bradford. "The Making of a Communist," *American Scholar,* XXII (Summer, 1953), 337–45.

Smith, Henry Nash. "Legislatures, Communists and State Universities," *Pacific Spectator,* III (Summer, 1949), 329–37.

"Some Aspects of Waiver of the Privilege Against Self-Incrimination," *Brooklyn Law Review,* XVIII (April, 1952), 287–99.

Sorensen, T. C. "Legislative Control of Loyalty in the School System," *Nebraska Law Review,* XXIX (1950), 485–505.

"States and Subversion, The." Pamphlet of the American Civil Liberties Union. New York, 1952.

"Subversive Influence in the Educational Process." Report of the Subcommittee to Investigate the Internal Security Act and other Internal Security Laws to the Committee on the Judiciary, United States Senate, 83d Congress, 1st Session, July 17, 1953.

Sumski, J. M. "Oregon Rejects Negative Loyalty Oaths," *Journal of the American Association of University Women,* XLVI (May, 1953), 245–46.

Thayer, V. T. "Should Communists and Fascists Teach in the Schools?" *Harvard Educational Review,* XII (January, 1942), 7–19.

Wahlke, John C., ed. Loyalty in a Democratic State. Boston, 1952. Problems in American Civilization, Department of American Studies, Amherst College.

Wecter, Dixon. "Commissars of Loyalty," *Saturday Review of Literature,* XXXIII (May 13, 1950), 8–10ff.

Westin, Alan F. "Do Silent Witnesses Defend Civil Liberties?" *Commentary,* XV (June, 1953), 537–46.

Wilner, Daniel M., and Franklin Fearing. "The Structure of Opinion: A Loyalty Oath Poll," *Public Opinion Quarterly,* XIV (Winter, 1950–51), 729–43.

Wittenberg, Philip. "How to Say No to the Demagogues," *Nation,* CLXXVI (May 9, 1953), 390–92.

Woody, Thomas. "Why Raise an Oath-Umbrella?" *School and Society,* LXXIV (July 21, 1951), 33–38.

Worden, W. L. "UCLA's Red Cell: Case History of College Communism," *Saturday Evening Post,* CCXXIII (October 21, 1950), 42–43ff.

Wormuth, Francis D. "On Bills of Attainder: A Non-Communist Manifesto," *Western Political Quarterly,* III (March, 1950), 52–65.

Wright, B. F. "Should Teachers Testify?" *Saturday Review of Literature,* XXXVI (September 26, 1953), 22–23.

Wriston, Henry M. "A Fire Bell in the Night," *Vital Speeches of the Day,* XV (December 15, 1948), 137–41.

THE STUDENT AND THE TEACHER

"Academic Freedom and Academic Responsibilities." Pamphlet of the American Civil Liberties Union. New York, 1952.

Allison, S. K. "The Responsibilities of a University Professor," *Bulletin of the Atomic Scientists,* VII (December, 1951), 367–70.

Boas, Franz. "Administrators, Faculties and Students Should Co-operate in University Control," *Wilberforce University Quarterly,* II (July, 1941), 69–72.

Chambers, George G. "Codes of Ethics for the Teaching Profession," *Annals of the American Academy of Political and Social Sciences,* CI (May, 1922), 121–26.

Chase, E. P. "Professional Ethics for College Teachers," *Bulletin of the American Association of University Professors,* XXVI (October, 1940), 441–51.

Close, Kathryn. "Students in Action, Hopefully: Today's Collegians Organize," *Survey Graphic,* XXXVII (December, 1948), 505–7ff.

"Comes the Revolution," *Mademoiselle* (August, 1949), pp. 193, 324–27.

Crambs, J. D. "Teachers as a Minority Group," *Journal of Educational Sociology,* XXII (February, 1949), 400–405.

Douglas, Paul H., *et al.* "How Can Schools and Colleges Teach Controversial Issues?" *America's Town Meeting of the Air,* Vol. XIV, No. 22 (September 21, 1948).

Eckelberry, R. H. "Our Duty in Difficult Times," *Journal of Higher Education,* XXIII (January, 1952), 51–52ff.

———— "Test Case in Campus Government," *Journal of Higher Education,* XXIV (March, 1953), 159–60.

Evans, Bergen. "How to Liberate the Colleges," *American Mercury,* LXVI (June, 1948), 659–64.

Falvey, Frances E. Student Participation in College Administration. New York: Bureau of Publications, Teachers College, Columbia University, 1952.

Fitch, Robert E. "Needed: An Ethical Code for Teachers," *Christian Century,* LXVIII (February 28, 1951), 269–70.

Fitzpatrick, E. A. "Administration Looks at the Students," *School and Society,* LXVI (November 22, 1947), 385–89.

Glicksberg, C. I. "Communist Students in the Classroom," *School and Society,* LXXI (March 25, 1950), 177–80.

Hazelton, B. A. "Communism on the Campus," *Freedom and Union,* III (September, 1948), 6–8.

Himstead, R. E., H. F. Cabell, and R. L. Stearns. "Academic Tenure," *Proceedings of the Association of Governing Boards of State Universities and Allied Institutions,* 30th Annual Meeting, 1952.

Houseman, William. "Are U.S. Teenagers Rejecting Freedom?" *Look,* XVI (February 26, 1952), 29–31.

Kelley, Janet A. College Life and the Mores. New York: Bureau of Publications, Teachers College, Columbia University, 1949.

Kirkland, Edward C. "Recipe for Responsibility," *Bulletin of the American Association of University Professors,* XXXIV (Spring, 1948), 15–26.

Knapp, A. Blair. "Student Organization and Student Activities," in Current Trends in Higher Education, pp. 55–63. Washington, D.C.: Department of Higher Education, National Education Association, 1948.

Lieberman, J. B. "Should the School Press Be Free?" *California Journal of Secondary Education,* XXIV (October, 1949), 340–46.

Lipset, S. M. "Opinion Formation in a Crisis Situation," *Public Opinion Quarterly,* XVII (1953), 20–46.

Ludlum, R. P. "Academic Freedom and Tenure: A History," *Antioch Review,* X (March, 1950), 3–34.

Martin, T. D. "Codes of Ethics for Teachers," in W. S. Monroe, ed., Encyclopedia of Educational Research, pp. 216–18. Rev. ed. New York, 1950.

Murad, Anatol. "Democracy in European Universities," *Educational Forum,* XIV (May, 1950), 457–61.

Narmore, Philip B. "Student Activities," in *Current Trends in Higher Education,* pp. 26–30. Washington, D.C.: Department of Higher Education, National Education Association, 1949.

Nock, S. A. "Ideas and Inquisitors," *School and Society,* LXXVII (June 6, 1953), 353–56.

Redfield, R. "Difficult Duty of Speech," *Quarterly Journal of Speech,* XXXIX (February, 1953), 6–14.

Richard, Otis H. "Appraising and Rewarding Teaching Effectiveness," in Addresses on Current Issues in Higher Education, Department of Higher Education, pp. 194–98. Washington, D.C.: National Education Association, 1951.

Scott, Dr. "Due Process in Higher Education," *Bulletin of the American Association of University Professors,* XXXII (Summer, 1946), 367–73.

Smith, P. M. "Teacher Loyalty and Academic Freedom," *Journal of Educational Sociology,* XXIII (January, 1950), 251–57.

Strang, Ruth. Group Activities in Colleges and Secondary Schools. Rev. ed. New York, 1946.

Strozier, R. M. "Authority, Responsibility and the Individual," *Journal of the National Association of Deans of Women,* XV (June, 1952), 161–65.

Troxell, Louise. "Is It Self-Government?" *Journal of the National Association of Deans of Women,* XI (March, 1948), 132–35.

Williamson, E. G. "The Need for Consultation Between Students and Administration," *College and University,* XXVI (April, 1951), 323–29.

——— "Responsible Academic Freedom for Students," *School and Society,* LXXI (May 13, 1950), 289–91.

Winetrout, K. "Academic Freedom for the Student, Too," *Progressive Education,* XXIX (March, 1952), 164–66.

Withers, A. M. "Academic Tenure Investigations," *Educational Forum,* XI (November, 1946), 89–92.

Woodward, D. K. "Academic Freedom, Privileges and Responsibilities," *Vital Speeches of the Day,* XVI (December 15, 1949), 137–40.

Wright, Louis B. "Freedom and Responsibility," *Proceedings of the Western College Association, 1946–47* (March 29, 1947), pp. 19–21.

THE UNIVERSITY AND THE SOCIAL ORDER

THE GREATER MISSION OF THE UNIVERSITY

Boyd, J. P. "Subversive of What?" *Atlantic Monthly,* CLXXXII (August, 1948), 19–23.

Capen, S. P. "Reflections on Freedom in Education," *Philosophy and Phenomenological Research,* VIII (June, 1948), 494–507.

Cole, K. C. "Academic Freedom as a Civil Right," *Western Political Quarterly,* II (September, 1949), 402–11.

Donnelly, T. C., and J. E. Holmes. "Newspaper Editors, Politicians and Political Scientists," *Western Political Quarterly,* III (June, 1950), 225–32.

Kandel, I. L. "Purpose of a University: Challenge or Repression," *School and Society,* LXXIV (October 27, 1951), 269–70.

Kerr, Clark. "The University in a Progressive Society," *Pacific Spectator,* VII (Summer, 1953), 268–77.

Kirkland, Edward C. "Academic Freedom and the Community," *Bulletin of the American Association of University Professors,* XXXVI (Autumn, 1950), 417–27.

Mason, J. B. "Academic Freedom Under Nazism," *Social Science,* XV (October, 1940), 388–94.

Munger, W. L. "Academic Freedom Under Peron," *Antioch Review,* VII (June, 1947), 275–90.

Root, E. M. "Our Left-Handed Colleges," *Freeman,* III (October 20, 1952), 350–52.

"Scientific Truth and Freedom in Our Time," *Bulletin of the Atomic Scientists,* Vol. V, entire number of June–July, 1949.

Scott, D. R. "Rationale of Academic Freedom," *Bulletin of the American Association of University Professors,* XXXVI (Winter, 1950), 629–45.

Spalding, W. B. "Academic Freedom," *Progressive Education,* XXVIII (February, 1951), 111–17.

"What Is a Free Press and What Are Its Perils? Ten Views," *Newsweek,* XXXVII (April 30, 1951), 50–51.

ACADEMIC FREEDOM AND AUTHORITY

Barth, Alan. "Universities and Political Authority," *Bulletin of the American Association of University Professors,* XXXIX (Spring, 1953), 5–15.

Cushman, Robert E. "American Civil Liberties in Mid-Twentieth Century," *Annals of the American Academy of Political and Social Science,* CCLXXV (May, 1951), 1–8.

Ernst, M. L. "Some Affirmative Suggestions for a Loyalty Program," *American Scholar,* XIX (Autumn, 1950), 452–60.

Fraenkel, O. K. "Law and Loyalty," *Iowa Law Review,* XXXVII (Winter, 1952), 153–74.

Hudson, N. P. "Freedom in Research in a University," *American Journal of Physics,* XX (May, 1952), 270.

Jones, Lewis Webster. "Academic Freedom and Civic Responsibility." Pamphlet. Rutgers University, 1953.

Joughin, Louis. "The Current Questionings of Teachers: Notes for a Social Pathology," *Social Problems,* I (October, 1953), 61–65.

Nock, S. A. "Ideas and Inquisitors," *School and Society,* LXXVII (June 6, 1953), 353–56.

WHAT WE CAN DO ABOUT IT

Caughy, John W. "The Practical Defense of Academic Freedom," *Bulletin of the American Association of University Professors,* XXXVIII (Summer, 1952), 244–60.

Eckelberry, R. H. "Academic Freedom Versus Intellectual Freedom," *Journal of Higher Education,* XXIV (November, 1953), 442–43ff.

———— "Our Duty in Difficult Times," *Journal of Higher Education,* XXIII (January, 1952), 51–52ff.

Eurich, A. C. "Freedom to Learn and Teach," *Junior College Journal,* XXIII (May, 1953), 490–96.

Duryea, E. D., Jr. "Academic Freedom: A Long View," *Journal of Higher Education,* XXIV (October, 1953), 345–48ff. Bibliography.

Fisher, W. H. "Democracy and Academic Freedom," *Social Education,* XII (November, 1948), 307–8.

Harper, L. A. "Shall the Professor Sign?" *Pacific Spectator,* I (January, 1950), 21–9.

Levitan, S. A. "Professional Organization of Teachers in Higher Education," *Journal of Higher Education,* XXII (March, 1951), 123–28.

McGowan, W. N. "Time's Up! School People Must Battle Thought Control!" *Clearing House,* XXV (April, 1951), 491–93.

Melbo, Irving R. "What Can School Board Members Do to Answer Criticism of Public Education?" *American School Board Journal,* CXXII (May, 1951), 127–28ff.

Meyer, Agnes E. "Freedom of the Mind," reprint from *NEA News,* Vol. VII (February 27, 1953).

Newman, R. G. "Educator's Function in a Democracy," *Education,* LXXII (January, 1952), 337–40.

Redfield, R. "Difficulty Duty of Speech," *Quarterly Journal of Speech,* XXXIX (February, 1953), 6–14.

Smith, P. M. "Teacher Loyalty and Academic Freedom," *Journal of Educational Sociology,* XXIII (January, 1950), 251–57.

ACADEMIC FREEDOM AND THE DENOMINATIONAL UNIVERSITY

Barbour, I. G. "Faculty Christian Fellowship," *The Christian Century,* LXX (March 25, 1953), 348–50.

Butts, R. Freeman. The American Tradition in Religion and Education. Boston, 1950.

Coe, George A. "Academic Liberty in Denominational Colleges," *School and Society,* XXX (November 16, 1929), 678–80.

Groves, Walter A. "The Christian College Today: Vital Role of Independent Colleges," *Vital Speeches of the Day,* XV (January 1, 1949), 166–68.

Hardon, J. A. "Prophets of Error: Non-Sectarian Universities," *Catholic World,* CLXIII (September, 1946), 527–31.

Heimann, Eduard, "On Academic Liberty," *Christianity and Crisis,* XII (July 7, 1952), 90–94.

Kildahl, P. A. "Freedom and Authority in Christian Education," *Christian Education,* XXXIV (June, 1951), 157–65.

Lankard, F. G. "Church-Related College in a Disordered World," *Vital Speeches of the Days,* XVIII (January 15, 1952), 214–21.

Lynch, J. "Academic Babel," *Catholic Educational Review,* XLII (December, 1944), 607–13.

McMahon, P. B. "State Aid to Education and the Doctrine of Separation of Church and State," *Georgetown Law Journal,* XXXVI (May, 1948), 631–47.

Mayer, Milton. "The Christian College," *Progressive,* XIII (February, 1949), 23–24.

Pieper, M. B. "Catholic Educators and Science," *America,* XC (October 3, 1953), 14–16.

Pullias, E. V. "Democracy and the Small Liberal Arts College," *School and Society,* LXXII (December 23, 1950), 413–15.

Shuster, George N. "Academic Freedom," *Commonweal,* LVIII (April 10, 1953), 11–13.

Soper, Edmund D. "Academic Freedom in a Christian College," *School and Society,* XXX (October 19, 1929), 521–33.

"Threat to Academic Freedom: We Have an American Philosophy," *America,* LXXXI (June 11, 1949), 330.

Williams, Daniel D. "Christian Freedom and Academic Freedom," *Christian Scholar,* XXXVI (March, 1953), 11–22.

INDEX

AAC News, 106

AAUP, *see* American Association of University Professors

Academic administration: and academic freedom, 8, 273-75; functions of, 85; attitude toward campus press, 222; *see also* President

Academic freedom: meaning of the word, 3, 6; book banning and, 39; Buckley's views on, 107-8; religion and, 134-35; Western acceptance of the principle of, 253; defense of, 279-82; faith and, 287-88

Academic Freedom and Tenure, 1940 Statement of Principles on (AAUP), 225

Academic government, 67-120; authority and, 264, 266; *see also* Academic administration; Faculty; Governing board; Political controls; President

Accrediting agencies, 112, 236

Agriculture, Department of, 116

Akeley, T. Barton, 148-49

Alabama, 40

Allen, Raymond B., 158, 182

Alter, Karl J., 287

Alumni, 104-11; attacks against academic freedom by, 8; representation of, on governing boards, 69, 99, 104-5; councils, 104; influence on and services to universities, 105-6; journals, 106, 275-76; responsibilities in defense of academic freedom, 275-76

American Alumni Council, 106

American Association of University Professors: cases of violation of academic freedom before, 21; quoted on academic government, 69; attacks by Regents of University of Texas, 73*n*; blacklisting of institutions by, 82; in Hartmann case, 144; in Marshall College case, 151–52; principles on fight against communism accepted by, 199; statement on civic limitations of teachers, 231; Declaration of Prin-

ciples (1915), 231-32, (1940), 225, 245; tenure policies of universities approved by, 242; policy on dismissals, 246*n*; role in defense of academic freedom, 279

American Bar Association, quoted, 195-96

American Business Consultants, 59

American Civil Liberties Union, 51, 221; report on Olivet College case, 148; constitutionality of Smith Act and, 168; research on tenure policies, 245; and Judd case, 297

American Coalition of Patriotic Societies, 53

American Communist Party, *see* Communist Party, American

American Council on Education, 116

American Education Association, 59

American Federation of Labor, 199

American Flag Committee, The, 43*n*

American Government (Magruder), 38, 39, 57

"Americanism," 30, 42-43

American Legion, 35, 54-55

American Legion Magazine, 54

American Library Association, 36

American Medical Association, 130

American Patriots, 60

American Philosophical Society, 252

American Scholar, The, quoted, 83

American Society of Newspaper Editors, 257*n*

American Sunbathers Association, 153

American Youth for Democracy, 213, 297

Amherst College, 97, 104

Andrews, Benjamin E., 56

Antioch College, 98

Anti-Semitism, 60

Arkansas, University of, 115

Arnold, Thurman, 40

Ashby, Aubrey, 148

Association for Education in Journalism, 214